Colonial America from Settlement to the Revolution

D0164618

Other titles in ABC-CLIO's

TURNING POINTS—ACTUAL AND ALTERNATE HISTORIES

series

Books in the Turning Points—Actual and Alternate Histories series ask the question, What would have happened if . . .? In a unique editorial format, each book examines a specific period in American history, presents the real, or actual, history, and then offers an alternate history—speculations from historical experts on what might have happened had the course of history turned.

If a particular event had turned out differently, history from that turning point forward could be affected. Important outcomes frequently hinge on an individual decision, an accidental encounter, a turn in the weather, the spread of a disease, or a missed piece of information. Such events stimulate our imagination, accentuating the role of luck, chance, and individual decision or character at particular moments in time. The examination of such key turning points is one of the reasons that the study of history is so fascinating.

For the student, examining alternate histories springing from turning points and exploring, What would have happened if . . .? gives insight into many of the questions at the heart of our civilization today.

TURNING POINTS—
ACTUAL AND ALTERNATE HISTORIES

Colonial America
from Settlement to the Revolution

Rodney P. Carlisle and J. Geoffrey Golson, *Editors*

A B C · C L I O

Santa Barbara, California
Denver, Colorado
Oxford, England

Copyright 2007 by ABC-CLIO, Inc.

Library of Congress Cataloging-in-Publication Data
Colonial America from settlement to the Revolution / Rodney P. Carlisle
and J. Geoffrey Golson, editors.
    p. cm.—(Turning points—actual and alternate histories)
    Includes bibliographical references and index.
    ISBN 1-85109-827-5 (hard cover: alk. paper)—ISBN 1-85109-828-3 (eBook)
    1. United States—History—Colonial period, ca. 1600-1775.   I. Carlisle,
Rodney P.   II. Golson, J. Geoffrey.
    E188.C6973 2006
    973.2—dc22   2006020294

11 10 09 08 07   10 9 8 7 6 5 4 3 2 1

ISBN 13: 978-1-85109-827-9   (ebook) 978-1-85109-828-6
ISBN 10: 1-85109-827-5   (ebook) 1-85109-828-3

Production Editor: Vicki Moran
Editorial Assistant: Alisha Martinez
Production Manager: Don Schmidt
Media Production Coordinator: Ellen Brenna Dougherty
Media Resources Manager: Caroline Price
File Manager: Paula Gerard
Text design: Devenish Design

This book is also available on the World Wide Web as an eBook. Visit
http://www.abc-clio.com for details.

ABC-CLIO, Inc.
130 Cremona Drive, P.O. Box 1911
Santa Barbara, California 93116-1911

This book is printed on acid-free paper ∞

Manufactured in the United States of America

Contents

4 New Hampshire 51

TURNING POINT

John Wheelwright established Exeter, New Hampshire, in 1638, after being banished from Massachusetts. What if Wheelwright had found more tolerance among the Puritans?

5 New York 71

TURNING POINT

The Dutch colony of New Amsterdam surrendered to the British in 1664. What if New York was never established and the colony remained under Dutch control?

6 Delaware 89

TURNING POINT

Sweden first claimed the Delaware area in 1638. What if the Swedish colonies prospered and were able to repel invasions from the Dutch and British?

7 New Jersey 107

TURNING POINT

James, Duke of York, granted the charter for New Jersey in 1664. What if James had died before establishing the colony, thus affecting the future course of the United States?

Contributors

Chapter 1 • Massachusetts
John H. Barnhill
Independent Scholar

Chapter 2 • Connecticut
Marcella Bush Trevino
Barry University

Chapter 3 • Rhode Island
Luca Prono
Independent Scholar

Chapter 4 • New Hampshire
Kelly Boyer Sagert
Independent Scholar

Chapter 5 • New York
William P. Toth
Heidelberg College

Chapter 6 • Delaware
John F. Murphy Jr.
American Military University

Chapter 7 • New Jersey
Margaret Sankey
Minnesota State University

Chapter 8 • Pennsylvania
Chapter 10 • Maryland
Alexis A. Antracoli
Brandeis University

Chapter 9 • *Virginia*
Mitchell McNaylor
Independent Scholar

Chapter 11 • North Carolina
Catherine Armstrong
University of Warwick, England

Chapter 12 • South Carolina
Virginia G. Jelatis
Western Illinois University

Chapter 13 • Georgia
Nathaniel Millet
College of Mount Saint Vincent

Chronology of Colonial America
Glossary
Mark Aaron Bond
Roanoke City Public Schools, Virginia

Introduction

I . . . regard the chief utility of all historical and sociological
investigations to be to admonish us of the alternative possibilities
of history.

—Oscar Jaszi, *The Dissolution of the Habsburg Monarchy*

There is nothing new about counterfactual inference. Historians
have been doing it for at least two thousand years.

—Philip Tetlock and Aaron Belkin, *Counterfactual*
Thought Experiments in World Politics

The question, What would have happened if . . . ? is asked all the time
as historians, students, and readers of history examine past events. If some
event had turned out differently, the whole course of history from that particular turning point forward could have been affected, we are often
reminded. Important outcomes frequently hinge on an individual decision,
an accidental encounter, a turn in the weather, the spread of a disease, or a
missed piece of information. Such events stimulate our imagination, accentuating the role of luck, chance, and individual decision or character at particular moments in time. The examination of such key hinge points is one
of the reasons that the study of history is so fascinating.

"Alternate history" has become a fictional genre, similar to science fic-
tion, in that it proposes other worlds, spun off from the one we live in,
derived from some key hinge point in the past. Harry Turtledove, among
others, has produced novels along these lines. Turtledove has written a
widely sold sequence of books that follow an alternate past from a "counterfactual" Confederate victory at the battle of Antietam, resulting in the
rise of the Confederate States of America as a separate nation, with consequences well into the twentieth century.

Alternate or counterfactual history is more than a form of imaginative
speculation or engaging entertainment, however. Historians are able to
highlight the significance of an event they examine by pointing to the
consequences of the event. When many significant consequences flow
from a single event, the alternate history question is implicit—the consequences would have been different, and a strange and different history
would have flowed from that time forward if the specific event in question had turned out differently. Those events that would have made the

most dramatic or drastic alternate set of consequences are clearly among the most important; thus key battles in wars are often studied in great detail, but not only for their own sake. The importance of such battles as Gettysburg and Antietam is not simply military. Instead, those battles and others are significant because such deep consequences flowed from their outcomes. The same could be said of General Erich Ludendorff's offensive in 1918—had it been successful, the Allies might have been defeated in World War I, and the map of Europe and the rest of the twentieth century would have been very different than the way they actually turned out. Similarly, if for some reason the nuclear weapons used at Hiroshima and Nagasaki in 1945 had failed, the outcome of World War II could have been very different, perhaps with a greater role for Russia in the dissolution of the Japanese Empire. Others have argued that had the bombs not been used, Japan would have been defeated quite promptly even without them.

Every key event raises similar issues. What might the world have been like if Christopher Columbus and his sailors had failed to return from their voyage in 1492? What if Hernán Cortés and Francisco Pizarro had been soundly defeated in their attempts to defeat the Aztecs and the Inca Empire? What if John Wilkes Booth had failed in his assassination attempt against Abraham Lincoln? What sort of world would we live in if any of the other famous victims of assassination had survived, such as John F. Kennedy, Martin Luther King, Jr., or Malcolm X?

For the student, examining alternate histories springing from multiple turning points and exploring what would have happened if . . . , gives insight into many of the questions at the heart of history. What was the role of specific individuals, and how did their exercise of free will and choice at a moment in time affect later events? On the other hand, to what extent are the actions of individuals irrelevant to the larger outcomes? That is, in any particular period of history, were certain underlying forces at work that would have led to the same result, no matter what the individual did? Do underlying structures and deeper causes, such as economic conditions, technological progress, climate, natural resources, and diseases, force events into a mold that individuals have always been powerless to alter? Do certain ideas have such importance that they would spread, even if particular advocates had never lived to voice them?

The classic contest of free will and determinism is constantly at work in history, and an examination of pivotal turning points is key to understanding the balance between deep determining forces and the role of individuals. Frequently, it seems, no matter what individuals tried to do to affect the course of events, the events flowed onward in their same course; in other cases, however, a single small mistake or different personal decision seems to have affected events and altered the course of history. Close study of specific events and how they might have otherwise turned out can illuminate this challenging and recurrent issue.

Of course, when reviewing what would have happened if . . . , it is important to realize exactly what in fact really did happen. So in every chapter presented in this series, we are careful to explain first what actually happened, before turning to a possible alternative set of events that could have happened, and the consequences through later history that might have flowed from an alternate development at a particular turning point. By looking at a wide variety of such alternatives, we see how much of history is contingent, and we gain greater insight into its specific events and developments.

Alternate histories would have flowed, had there been different outcomes of a great variety of events, many of them far less famous than the outstanding battles, and the lives and deaths of explorers, conquerors, statesmen, and political leaders. Seemingly obscure or little-recognized events in the past, such as legislative decisions, court cases, small military engagements, and even the lives of minor officials, preachers, writers, and private citizens, frequently played a crucial part in shaping the flow of events. It is clear that if any of the great leaders of the world had died as infants, the events in which they participated would have been altered; but we tend to forget that millions of minor players and less famous people take actions in their daily lives in events such as battles, elections, legislative and judicial decisions, sermons, speeches, and published statements that have sometimes altered the course of history.

Alternate histories are known as "counterfactuals," that is, events that did not in fact happen. Some counterfactuals are more plausible than others. A few historians have argued that all counterfactuals are absurd and should not be studied or considered. However, any historical work that goes beyond simply presenting a narrative or chronological list of what happened, and begins to explore causes through the use of such terms as "influenced," "precipitated," or "led to," is in fact implying some counterfactual sequences. A historian, in describing one event as having consequences, is by implication suggesting the counterfactual that if the event had not occurred, the consequences would have been different.

If history is to be more than a chronicle or simple listing of what happened and is to present "lessons" about statecraft, society, technology development, diplomacy, the flow of ideas, military affairs, and economic policy, it must explore how causes led to consequences. Only by the study of such relationships can future leaders, military officers, business people and bankers, legislators and judges, and, perhaps most important, voters in democratic nations, gain any knowledge of how to conduct their affairs. To derive the lessons of history, one has to ask what the important causes were, the important hinge events that made a difference. And once that question is asked, counterfactuals are implied. Thus the defenders of the approach suggest that counterfactual reasoning is a prerequisite to learning lessons from history. Even many historians who resolutely avoid talking about "what might have been" are implying that what in fact happened was important because the alternative, counterfactual event did *not* happen.

Two scholars who have studied counterfactuals in depth, Philip E. Tetlock and Aaron Belkin, in an edited collection of articles, *Counterfactual Thought Experiments in World Politics* (Princeton University Press, 1996), have concluded that counterfactual reasoning can serve several quite different purposes in the study of history. They define these types of counterfactual work:

1. Case-study counterfactuals that "highlight moments of indeterminacy" in history by showing how things might have turned out differently at

such hinge points because of individual free choices. These studies tend to focus on the uniqueness of specific events.

2. "Nomothetic" counterfactuals, that focus on underlying deterministic laws or processes, examining key events to show how likely or unlikely it was for events to have turned out differently. The purpose of this type of study is to test how powerful an underlying law or process is by imagining alternative situations or decisions.

3. A combination of types one and two above, blending the test of theory or underlying law approach with the unique event approach.

4. "Mental stimulation" counterfactuals that highlight underlying assumptions most people have by showing how causes that most people believe are inconsequential could have major effects, and other causes that most people believe are very important might have little or no effect in changing the course of history.

The reader will recognize aspects of each of these different models in the accounts that follow. Moreover, the reader can find the contrasts between actual history and alternate history quite puzzling and thought provoking, as they are intended to be. As readers study the cases, they may want to keep asking questions such as these:

What was the key hinge point on which the author focused?

Is the altered key event a plausible change—something that could easily have happened?

Was the change "minimal" in the sense that only one or a few turning point events had to turn out differently than they in fact did?

Did the alternate outcome seem to develop in a realistic way; that is, does the alternate sequence of events seem to be one that would be likely once the precipitating change took place?

How plausible is the alternate long-term outcome or consequence that the author suggested?

Was the changed key event a matter of an individual person's choice, an accident, or a change in some broader social or technological development?

Does the counterfactual story help us make judgments about the actual quality of leadership displayed in fact at the time? That is, did key actors in real history act more or less wisely than they did in the counterfactual account?

Does the outcome of the episode suggest that, despite the role of chance and individual choice, certain powerful forces shaped history in similar directions, in both the factual and counterfactual account?

Does the account make me think differently about what was important in history?

Does the counterfactual story challenge any assumptions I had before I read it?

Remember, however, that what really happened is the object of historical study. We examine the counterfactual, alternate histories to get a better understanding of the forces and people that were at work in what really did occur. These counterfactual stories will make you think about history in ways that you have never encountered before; but when you have explored them, you should be able to go back to the real events with fresh questions in mind.

Introduction to the Colonial America Volume

In this volume of the series, we see how counterfactual and alternative history can shed light on what really happened by looking closely at the history of the original 13 colonies that formed the United States of America during the American Revolution.

The colonies that united to join in the Revolution in the period 1776–1783 were British colonies, settled over the period beginning in 1620. This does not mean, however, that the colonies were simply smaller replicas of British society. Several factors shaped colonial life, giving a very different imprint to society on the North American continent than existed in England. First of all, the land had been occupied by a wide variety of Native American populations, many of whom died off from contact with European diseases, while others were driven from their lands at different rates and under different conditions by the colonists. In some regions, other Europeans preceded the British. The Dutch in New York and Swedes and Finns in southern New Jersey had well-established communities before the British took over. The Spanish held Florida through the colonial period, and they sought to extend their control northward. Furthermore, many of the British colonists who arrived were what we would now call political or religious refugees. Some sought to establish havens for their own denominations, and Massachusetts, in particular, sought to exclude those who did not conform to their own conception of the Christian faith. When William Penn led the settlement of Pennsylvania, he established Philadelphia as a planned city, anchored in the faith of the Society of Friends or Quakers, who soon dominated Philadelphia and southern New Jersey but who extended tolerance to members of other faiths.

Roger Williams and others who fled from the strict religious conformity of Massachusetts established Rhode Island, and began to develop the concept of religious toleration there. In Virginia, Maryland, the Carolinas, and Georgia, planters raised tobacco, rice, and indigo, employing African American slaves imported from the Caribbean and sometimes directly from Africa. By the mid- and late eighteenth century, on the eve of the American Revolution, the colonies had already developed a diverse set of societies that resembled Britain in language and to some extent in cultural heritage. However, the social, religious, and political nature of the colonies had already evolved in new directions that were quite different from Britain and varied greatly from colony to colony.

Instead of a single, established church, each colony had a different religious makeup. In some, a dissenting church was the established religion. In others, each community could establish its own church, and tax residents to support it. In still others, multiple religions existed side by side. Furthermore, some of the regions had large populations that were not British in ethnic ancestry, including regions still in Native American hands, plantation communities with large numbers of African Americans, and pockets that traced their ancestry to the Dutch, Swedes, and newly arriving German and French immigrants.

Out of these varied religious and ethnic groups and under the leadership of its wealthiest and most powerful merchants, landowners, and planters, the colonies were able to come together in the struggle for independence. In some regions, Loyalists who refused to support independence represented a significant factor and even formed military units to resist the Patriots in their fight. The American experience, from the beginning, was one of contests for power and influence among peoples of different backgrounds, who sometimes would find ways to compromise their differences and live side by side, and who at other times resorted to arms and violence to exert their dominance.

When viewed in the light of the diversity and complexity of the Colonial settlements, American history in the century and a half from 1620 to 1770 went through a vast number of Turning Points. At numerous specific moments in history, it would have been quite possible for history to have taken a different course, it seems. If a battle had been lost here, or a trial had gone differently there, or if an expedition had failed to reach its destination, a completely different pattern of settlement could have evolved. The emergence of certain characteristics that shaped much of later American history might have been so altered by a small event that the later history of the American nation would be completely different than it was in actual history. If the Dutch had held New York, or if the Swedes had succeeded in extending their control, the evolution of an English-speaking nation in North America would have been delayed or might not have happened at all. If the religious struggles in New England had turned out differently, the tradition of religious toleration and diversity might never have taken root in America. If the Spanish had succeeded in extending their control from Florida through Georgia and into other regions, the whole history of the United States, even if it had been formed out of a revolution against the British, would have been different. If Virginian planters had been unable to import African American slaves, they conceivably could have turned to other sources for forced labor to raise crops.

By thinking about these questions and the alternative histories that might have emerged, we find ourselves thinking more deeply about the key factors that made the colonies what they were and that shaped the destiny of North America and what became the United States of America. By examining what never happened and what might have been the alternate consequences, we can gain some insights into the factors that created the colonies, which in actual history, did unite to gain independence and form a new union.

The authors who developed the chapters for this volume grounded each study on a solid knowledge of the actual history of the colonies. Each has provided a list of solid historical reference works that give further information and, often, very recent research that has shed new light on the history of the period.

WARNING!

You are probably used to reading a book of history to find out what happened. We offer this book with a major warning. In this volume, the reader will see and be led to think deeply about what actually happened, and that part of history is always designated ACTUAL HISTORY. However, the last part of each chapter presents a history that never happened, and that is presented as the ALTERNATE HISTORY.

> To be sure that it is clear that the ALTERNATE HISTORY is an account of what would have happened differently if a TURNING POINT had turned out differently than it really did, the ALTERNATE HISTORY is always presented against a gray background, like these lines. The ALTERNATE HISTORY is what might have happened, what could have happened, and perhaps what would have happened, if the TURNING POINT had gone a little differently. Think about this ALTERNATE HISTORY, and why it would have been different. But don't think that it represents the way things actually happened!

Each chapter is also accompanied by informative sidebars and a few discussion questions that take off from the ACTUAL HISTORY and the ALTERNATE HISTORY that allow readers to think through and argue the different sides of the issues that are raised here.

We also want to warn readers that some may be surprised to discover that history, when viewed in this light, suddenly becomes so fascinating they may never want to stop learning about it!

Rodney Carlisle

TURNING POINT

In the early history of Massachusetts, Pilgrims from England first settled the coastal area in 1620. What if the Pilgrims were not successful and the area was instead settled by the French?

INTRODUCTION

On July 22, 1620, a group of English Separatists from Leiden, Holland, sailed to Southampton, England, on the 60-ton *Speedwell*. These men and women had left their homeland 12 years before because they felt that Anglican beliefs were incompatible with theirs. Now they were leaving Holland because they feared that the "alien" environment was further endangering the integrity of their small community. They were going to the New World to start fresh in Virginia.

From Southampton, the *Speedwell* and the 180-ton *Mayflower*, a 12-year veteran of the wine trade, carried 120 passengers to sea on August 15. The *Speedwell* was dangerously leaky, so the passengers consolidated on the *Mayflower*. On September 15, the *Mayflower* set sail with 102 passengers, only 37 of whom were Separatists. The others included hired help, such as the professional soldier Myles Standish and the cooper John Alden. Still others were there because the London financiers insisted they be taken along. Separatist leaders included William Bradford and William Brewster. During the 65-day voyage, two persons died and one, Oceanus Hopkins, was born. Peregrine White was born while the ship lay off Cape Cod, Massachusetts. On November 19, the ship came within sight of the cape, then sailed south toward the Hudson River before turning back to anchor at Provincetown on November 21.

The Separatists (Pilgrims) were a minority in a place not in their land grant, and they were concerned about whether the strangers would follow their rule, so the 41 men on board the *Mayflower* signed the Mayflower Compact, modeled on the standard Separatist church covenant. The signers established a temporary civil government that they swore to obey. The Pilgrims elected John Carver as governor, and the compact was the governing document of Plymouth Colony.

The *Mayflower* cruised the area as the Pilgrims sought a suitable place to settle. On December 26, they landed at Plymouth. The initial contact with Indians was alarming, with Standish and his men firing at what they took to be wolves or other wild beasts in the darkness. During a brief encounter the next day, Standish learned that they were Indians with arrows and that muskets had deterred them. The initial contact gave way to privation and hardship; a lucky find of just enough beans and other provisions got the party

KEY CONCEPT Separatism, Anglicanism, and Puritanism

The various European states competing for North America sponsored their own religions. France was Catholic, Spain was Catholic, and England was not. The settlement of North America and the subsequent competition among the various European states coincided with the Reformation and the Counter Reformation and the religious wars of Europe. Although religion was not the basis for war as it was in Europe, it was, nevertheless, a significant contributor to the friction and conflict. France and England had religious undertones to their political rivalries. Even the differences between Church of England, Puritan, and Separatist were significant to the development of the colonies. Thus, it is beneficial to clarify the differences.

Early in the 16th century there was one united European church, the Catholic Church headquartered in Rome and defended by all Europe's monarchs. After Martin Luther listed the problems with current church practice in 1517, the Reformation began, with kings and princes choosing sides between Rome and Reformation. Protestant–Catholic wars ensued, including an ongoing one between Spain and England after Henry VIII broke England from Catholicism in name if not in practice.

The Church of England was the result of Henry VIII's need for an heir and his desire for a divorce to help accomplish his goal of having a recognized heir. Henry declared the Church of England his church, and all English men and women would be Anglicans.

Pilgrims sign the Mayflower Compact, establishing a civil government in the New World. (The Foundation Press/Library of Congress)

through the winter. Rumor had it that they scavenged clothing from the Native graves so common to the area. The ship's captain and part owner, Christopher Jones, threatened to leave unless they found a place to land, but he kept the *Mayflower* at Plymouth through the winter of 1620–1621.

KEY CONCEPT *Separatism, Anglicanism, and Puritanism (Continued)*

Some members (Separatists) thought it was too much like the Catholic Church in structure and practice (which it was). The Separatists disapproved also of the lax public morals and Sabbath observances of the English. The Separatists thought they were God's elect and that contact with strangers would contaminate them. They wanted the church destroyed; absent that, they would walk away from it. The Pilgrims were Separatists, the radical fringe of English religion.

The Puritans were less extreme. They agreed that the church had problems, but they regarded themselves as Church of England and were willing to correct those problems within the system. They had legitimate concerns because of the way Henry had appropriated the church's property, turned out the monks and nuns, and sold the church's property to his nobles to collect money and breed loyalty.

The Church of England wasn't a Reformation project. It was a political act that had religious ramifications internally and internationally. Internally it did generate problems when Edward VI's state Calvinism gave way to Mary I's aggressive Catholicism (which created the refugees that became Puritans). After Mary, Elizabeth calmed the waters with her broad-based, doctrinally loose Church of England, then the Stuarts returned, bringing divine right and Catholic preference.

Internationally, Henry's Church of England was an affront to the divine right Catholic monarchs, defenders of the faith. And it was Puritans who executed Charles I of England. The conflict between Catholic and Protestant and the conflicts within English Protestantism were vigorous and significant in the affairs of the New World.

The Separatists, or Pilgrims, land at Plymouth Rock in the early winter of 1620. (National Archives)

That winter about half of the 102 settlers, including Oceanus, died. Ten of the 17 husbands and 14 of the 17 wives died. It was a rough winter but not atypical—European settlements struggled early on, and many failed. People died in the New World.

In the spring, Samoset walked into the settlement and welcomed the Englishmen. Samoset was a sachem of an Algonquian tribe in southeast Maine. He was visiting Massasoit, chief grand sachem of the Wampanoag. Samoset had acquired broken English from fishermen off Monhegan Island, off the coast of southeast Maine. About 30 years of age, Samoset impressed the Pilgrims with his good posture and direct speech. He was also tall. Generally, New England natives were taller than English Pilgrims.

Samoset introduced the Pilgrims to Massasoit and Tisquantum (Squanto, 1585?–1622), who also spoke English because he had escaped to England after being sold as a slave in Spain. He traveled with Thomas Dermer through the Narragansett lands in 1619. Although his native town of maybe 2,000 souls was eradicated by the English plague, Squanto remained friendly with the English and influenced Massasoit to seek a treaty with them, especially because they had muskets and Massasoit had enemies. Squanto, whose English was sometimes hard to understand, served as interpreter.

Massasoit (c. 1590–1661) was from Pokanoket (near modern Bristol, Rhode Island), one of many Wampanoag towns ravaged by the epi-

Massasoit and his warriors marching into the night, flanked by Pilgrims. (Library of Congress)

demics of the late 1610s. As he had with other Europeans, Massasoit offered friendship, and the Pilgrims and Indians signed a Treaty of Friendship and exchanged gifts.

About an hour after noon on March 22, 1621, Samoset and Squanto brought skins and fish to the village to trade. They said that Massasoit was nearby with his brother, Quadequina, and their men. The Pilgrims had trouble understanding what Squanto wanted. After an hour, Massasoit himself appeared atop the hill with about 60 of his men. The Pilgrims were loathe to send their governor up the hill, and the Indians were averse to entering the village, so Squanto went to Massasoit, and returned with the message for the Pilgrims that the sachem wanted trade and peace. Massasoit wanted a Pilgrim to parley with. Edward Winslow volunteered. The Pilgrims gave knives and chains and earrings, biscuit and butter —and "strong water." Winslow made the speech of friendship and alliance on behalf of King James. Massasoit ate and drank some, then gave the rest to his company. He offered to buy Winslow's armor and sword, but Winslow declined to sell.

William Brewster became the spiritual leader of the Plymouth Colony. (Library of Congress)

Leaving Winslow in the custody of Quadequina, Massasoit led 20 unarmed men to meet the Pilgrims. Standish and Brewster and half a dozen musketeers met Massasoit at the brook, and the two leaders exchanged salutes. The Pilgrims took six or seven hostages. Standish and Brewster escorted Massasoit to a house under construction. Then Governor Carver, accompanied by a drum and trumpet and more musketeers, greeted Massasoit. Carver kissed Massasoit's hand and Massasoit kissed Carver. Carver toasted Massasoit, who drank and sweated. Carver gave Massasoit and his followers meat. Some of the Indians attempted to play the trumpet. Carver and Massasoit established a treaty of mutual support.

Winslow felt confident that the Indians were sincere because they had had previous opportunities, had they wanted, to harm Pilgrims working or hunting in the woods. Nevertheless, one provision was that the Indians would come to Plymouth unarmed.

Governor Carver meeting with Native American leader Massasoit. (Library of Congress)

For his part, Massasoit needed an ally against the Narragansetts.

TURNING POINT

The Wampanoag–Pilgrim Treaty that allowed the Pilgrims to survive never happened. Because the slavers and their disease had destroyed his band to the point that he was subservient to another sachem, Massasoit should have spurned Squanto's approach and taken on the Pilgrims when he could. But Massasoit was not the sort to let his personal feelings interfere with his practical need—an ally to help his Wampanoags against the Narragansetts. Squanto, on the other hand, was not totally straightforward. And he should have felt at least a twinge of resentment toward the English who had enslaved him and caused the deaths of all of his band. When Squanto saw how pathetic the guns were in shooting birds, he determined that their 60 men could take the handful of Pilgrims, by sheer numbers if nothing else. Squanto recognized that Massasoit was going to make a deal because the Wampanoag sachem saw that, even though the Pilgrims were not particularly powerful allies, they did have armor and guns.

Squanto understood that Massasoit was not to be swayed. Quadequina on the other hand was weaker. But Quadequina had been with Massasoit in 1619 when Captain Thomas Dermer came through Wampanoag territory. Quadequina had an exaggerated respect for the Pilgrim's guns, so Squanto realized he had to create an alarm to overcome Quadequina's fear. When Massasoit went off with his two escorts and Quadequina took his hostage back to the band, Squanto and Quadequina waited and waited. Their unarmed chief was surrounded by musketeers and taken into a building where he was lost from sight. Squanto made sure Quadequina read the worst into it. And Squanto further fed Quadequina's uneasiness by pointing out that the governor had gone into the building with an escort of even more armed men. Then the dying loon sound of the Indians playing trumpet startled Quadequina. Squanto told Quadequina that Massasoit was in danger. Afraid and panicked, Quadequina jumped up and ordered his men to rescue Massasoit and the other hostages.

Leaving their hostage behind, the Wampanoag raced from the woods. Alarmed and not totally trusting of the painted savages that confronted them, the Pilgrims at first backed away, then began running away from the confrontation. In the unfinished house, the Wampanoag hostages were left untended in the excitement and quickly made their way into the woods, then onto the field of conflict. Massasoit sat calmly drinking with the governor as the musketeers raced outside to stabilize the situation. Standish began yelling orders, rallying the Pilgrims who had first run away, and his musketeers formed a skirmish line between the camp and the Indians. Seeing the muskets, Quadequina lost his nerve, but by then it was too late. Standish ordered his men to commence firing. Fortunately, the muskets were so inaccurate that the only loss was vision due to the smoke. Hidden by that smoke, Squanto entered and retrieved Massasoit. Then the Indians retreated into the woods, distrustful of the English ways and their guns. Standish's men began seriously debating the possibility of coming to an understanding with the Narragansett.

In the brief battle, the Pilgrim muskets and armor proved marginally sufficient to allow them to repel the onslaught. Afterward, they listened seriously to the strong arguments of Standish for holding their ground and taking on the Indians. As the debate progressed, the Pilgrims recognized that, without Native help their situation was tenuous. And, with hostile Indians surrounding them, even with friendly Indians they could not trust, the Separatists understood that this would not be a place where they could live in peace and harmony, left alone to worship as they chose. Besides, the Native warriors outnumbered their militia 60 to 20.

Because the treaty negotiations failed, the two sides eyed each other warily. Massasoit, feeling betrayed, began listening to Squanto and the anti-English contingent. The Pilgrims lacked the knowledge to plant successfully or to gather the rich resources of the ocean. Slowly they weakened. The woods seemed full of wild animals—wolves or worse. As an occasional Pilgrim fell to the dangers in the woods or to starvation in the camp, the Indians acquired arms and armor and confidence. When the *Mayflower* sailed in April, it took the surviving Pilgrims back to England and the Plymouth settlement was abandoned.

ACTUAL HISTORY

Samoset cleared the Separatist conscience by telling them that their village was on land that had no owner because the pestilence had taken the previous owners. Squanto taught the settlers where to find fish, how to plant corn, and other necessary skills. The fall harvest was abundant, and the Pilgrims and Wampanoag shared in thanksgiving feasting. Massasoit kept the Wampanoags neutral in the Pequot War, and he remained allied with the Pilgrims until he died.

On April 15 the *Mayflower* set sail for England, arriving on May 16. The Pilgrims were left in the colony on their own, depending for their very survival on the faithfulness of Massasoit and the helpfulness of Squanto.

Plymouth survived and its people were content to be left alone. Never prosperous, Plymouth established an economy based on furs and fish because agriculture on the sandy and rocky land was adequate for home consumption but not for commercial agriculture. Its leaders were the Indian fighter, Captain Myles Standish, and 30-time governor William Bradford. The Pilgrims were wary of outsiders who might corrupt their experiment.

When, in March 1622, the Pilgrims heard that the Algonquian Indians in Virginia had

Algonquian Samoset introduced the Pilgrims to other Native American leaders. (Library of Congress)

ANOTHER VIEW Pilgrims and Puritans

Assume for the moment that the Pilgrims turned back but the Puritans came anyway, effectively blocking the French from the area. How much of Massachusetts and U.S. history changes with the Puritans but without the Pilgrims? Probably not all that much.

After all, it wasn't the Pilgrims but the Puritans who made a go of New England, who expanded into Indian territory by the tens of thousands, who sparked the First Great Awakening, who established the settlement pattern that sent towns into the wilderness instead of families, who invaded and fought the Canadians, who settled the upper Midwest and Oregon. The Pilgrims were historically a novelty item, struggling in their small community, economically marginal, intellectually insignificant, until finally Puritan Massachusetts absorbed them.

The Puritans could have kept a toehold in New England without the Indians. Unlike the Pilgrims, they had decent financing and large numbers to replace those who inevitably died during the transition. They had no particular incentive to head

William Bradford, governor of the Plymouth Colony, is credited with proclaiming the first Thanksgiving. (Cyrus E. Dahlin/Library of Congress)

killed 347 people, the people of Plymouth fortified their town. They had reason to be wary: Squanto was not totally faithful.

In April 1622, the Pilgrims decided to visit the Massachuset people. Squanto said the Massachuset tribe had allied with the Narragansetts and were plotting to destroy Plymouth when it was unguarded. Squanto also said Massasoit was conniving with the Pilgrims' enemies. The Pilgrims sent a friendly Indian to check out the story before reestablishing their relationship with Massasoit.

Native Americans, only 7,000 in 1620 versus 30,000 in the 15th century, became a nuisance rather than a threat once European population growth accelerated. After the Pilgrims established a stable colony, other English settlers came into the area. Among them were the failed 1623 Dorchester Company colony at Gloucester on Cape Ann, then at Salem in 1626. John Endicott led Puritans to Salem under the New England Company in 1628. The New England Company reorganized as the Massachusetts Bay Company in 1629 with a more secure royal patent.

The Great Puritan Migration began in 1630, when John Winthrop led 11 ships with 900 passengers. Over 70,000 Puritans left England for the New World, and between 1630 and 1642, 11,000 Puritans arrived in New England. Boston became the colonial capital, and Winthrop became governor. For the next 2 decades, Winthrop and clergyman John Cotton dominated the colony. Under them the colony was a Puritan Bible commonwealth.

to Virginia, where the Anglicans were already ensconced in power. They had a sense of mission as strong as that of the Pilgrims, probably stronger. After all, the Pilgrims just wanted to be left alone while the Puritans wanted to be a model, almost confronting the Anglican establishment they left behind.

Had the Puritans kept coming in waves despite the absence of the Pilgrims, they would still have pushed the disease-ravaged Indians inexorably out of the area. With their superior numbers and technology, they probably would not even have tarried to negotiate. God had given them the land, even blessing it with smallpox and typhus and other plagues to purify it of the un-Christian Indians. The Puritans did become zealously ruthless in the Pequot and King Philip's War, unlike the Pilgrims who negotiated peace first. Presumably, as population pressures squeezed them, they would have recognized that Massachusetts agriculture was at best a marginal pastime. They would have taken up fishing and shifted to commerce with no difficulty. The Pilgrims, those marginal farmers who never could find economic success, were less adventuresome and entrepreneurial.

Until 1664, only church members were citizens. Within the religious framework, the colony established representative institutions. In 1632, freemen began electing the governor, and in 1634 they began sending deputies to the General Court. In practice, Winthrop was wealthy and upper class and committed to his religious mandate to establish a "city on a hill." Giving the vote to freemen (Congregational Church adult males or 40 percent of all males) disenfranchised 60 percent of the adult male population. In town meetings though, all male property owners had the right to speak and vote. Although clergy were barred from holding public office, they did have a strong influence over their congregations and publicly interrogated members to determine the adequacy of their conversion.

Dissenters such as Quakers and Roger Williams and Anne Hutchinson were fined, flogged, or banished. Roger Williams, a Salem Separatist, challenged governmental regulation of religion, forced conversion of the Indians, and taking of Native lands without compensation. Exiled to England, he fled to an unclaimed territory that became Rhode Island. Anne Hutchinson was banished there in 1638.

New immigrants continued to arrive. Settlement remained restricted to the coast or a short distance inland. The economy relied on fishing, lumbering, and agriculture. As the population grew and expanded, the Indians' resentment grew. Finally in 1637, the tension blew up in the Pequot War, which virtually cleared Massachusetts of Indians. The war led the four Puritan colonies to establish the New England Confederation.

On Massasoit's death in 1661, his son, Metacomet (1639?–1676) succeeded him. Metacomet was better known under his English name, King Philip. The confederation of Massachusetts Bay, Plymouth, Connecticut, and New Haven broke the Indians' power for good in King Philip's War (1675–1676), but the southern New England frontier remained treacherous. As late as the French and Indian wars of the first half of the 18th century, frontier settlements such as Deerfield were easy prey for warring Indians.

The New England Confederation frequently disagreed with the English government, particularly after the return of the Stuart monarchy in 1660.

IN CONTEXT   Mercantilism

The age of colonialism was also the age of what Adam Smith in retrospect would call mercantilism. The mercantilist countries defined wealth in terms of hard metal—gold and silver bullion. Even with the Spanish discoveries of large amounts of bullion in the New World, there was never enough bullion to go around. And the Asian countries that European mercantilists sought to trade with didn't really care for European goods. "Made in Europe" meant inferior. The Manila galleons of Spain carried bullion to trade for spices and other niceties.

The shortage of wealth in the form of bullion meant that each mercantilist sought to establish a closed system from which it could raid the others. That's why colonies mattered. England, for instance, preferred to unload its woolen goods on the colonies in return for timber, grain, and other raw materials for English manufacturers. That was definitely superior to buying French raw materials and giving up all that bullion Sir Francis Drake and other pirates had taken from Spanish ships for the English treasury. France had similar aspirations—and the resources to make a competition of it after Spain fell victim to inflation and underdevelopment and Holland fell by the wayside because it was just too small.

The crown revoked the colony's charter in 1684 and merged Massachusetts Bay and Plymouth in the Dominion of New England under Sir Edmund Andros in 1686. The dominion collapsed in 1689 after the colonials rose against Andros during the Glorious Revolution. In 1691, a royal charter included Maine and Plymouth within Massachusetts under a royal governor and ended the religious qualification for voting. The established religion remained Congregationalism. In 1692, anxiety induced the witchcraft panic in Salem that resulted in the crushing to death of one person and the hanging of 19 others.

Late in the 17th century, the colony became embroiled in the European competition between France and England and the related conflict for control of North America. In 1689, the English possessed most of the Atlantic coast while the French had a presence on the St. Lawrence River and around the Great Lakes, as well as a line of forts along the Mississippi River valley. Although both claimed vast territory, the Indians still controlled it. The four wars of the French and Indian War (1689–1763) began when Indians allied to the English raided Montreal. In 1690, in retaliation, the French and their native allies struck against New York and New England. The English took Port Royal but failed against Quebec. The next year, the French attacked New Hampshire, and the English again failed against Quebec while the French retook Port Royal. The war ended officially in 1697 with France and England reverting to the prewar territorial status quo. In the second war, Britain got Newfoundland and French territory around Hudson's Bay. The third war ended with a reversion to the territorial status quo in 1748. In 1753, the French began fortifying the Allegheny River, and the next year the Virginians demanded that the French withdraw to Canada. The final war went well for the British, and when it ended in 1763, France was virtually out of North America.

For Massachusetts, the early 18th century was a time of rapid growth as settlement moved into the interior and the Connecticut valley. The

IN CONTEXT   *Mercantilism (Continued)*

France and England had been fighting since at least 1066. For centuries England had continental territory, but slowly France pushed England back onto the island. Then the Reformation fueled the rivalry, with France coming down on the Catholic side while England took the Protestant. By the time France and England were maneuvering in North America, they were also making inroads in Asia, the fight for India was in its early stages, and European politics brought them to war four times between 1690 and 1763.

By the time the English had managed to push the French out of North America, the competition proved so costly that England decided to get the colonies to pay for it. The effort to impose taxes was a major contributor to the deteriorated relations that generated the American Revolution, which ended with England losing a good chunk of its American empire. The Anglo-French rivalry had benefits for the United States when France, looking for an excuse to get back at England, provided the edge that allowed the rebellion to succeed. By the time the United States and Britain figured out that they were still natural trading partners, mercantilism was giving way to free trade, and the bitterly contested pie was proving to be large enough that one country could occasionally take a slice without starving the others.

---

frontier settlers tamed the smaller rivers and streams with mills for sawing wood, grinding grain, forging iron, and processing wool. On the coast, seaport towns grew. New England ships traded timber and salt fish to the Caribbean for molasses and sugar. The molasses became rum in Newburyport and Medford, and it went to Africa with utensils and cloth to purchase slaves who went to the Caribbean and South America under the "triangular trade." Massachusetts shipowners and captains profited greatly, and the colony flourished.

All was not ideal though. The French wars were expensive, and the British government sought to recoup some of the costs by taxing the colonies, which it claimed had benefited from the wars. In 1761, James Otis protested a colonial court's issuance of writs of assistance, general search warrants, which the customs office had begun using when the colonials began smuggling to avoid paying duties on sugar (definitely a problem for the profitability of the triangular trade) the issue blew into a dispute between Governor Thomas Hutchinson and anti-British legislators Samuel Adams, John Adams, James Otis, and John Hancock. The British government persisted by issuing the Stamp Act (1765) and the Townshend Acts (1767). The Boston Massacre of 1770 added fuel to the fire. The Bostonians reacted to the Tea Act by staging the Boston Tea Party (1773). General Thomas Gage went to Massachusetts to control the rebels under the Intolerable Acts (1774.)

The rebels of Massachusetts established committees of correspondence to spread their antigovernment views to sympathetic Virginians, New Yorkers, and others. In 1774, the dissidents met at the First Continental Congress in Philadelphia, and in 1775, the American Revolution began with the battles of Lexington and Concord, Massachusetts. After the Battle of Bunker Hill in 1775, George Washington of Virginia took command of American forces. The British evacuated Boston in 1776. The fighting shifted away from Massachusetts.

After the war, the colonial economy was depressed, particularly in Massachusetts, which had relied heavily on the British trade prior to the

"A View of the City of Boston, Capital of New England" in 1775. (National Archives)

war and lacked alternate trading partners. Soon enough, the British trade resumed, and eastern Massachusetts was returning to its prosperous ways. The west of the state was discontented, culminating in the antitax farmers' revolt, Shays's Rebellion, in 1786–1787. Although the rebellion failed it alarmed conservatives, who began supporting a stronger federal government. Massachusetts ratified the Constitution in 1788.

Not wanting to be overly dependent on the English market, Massachusetts opened a valuable trade with China. The ports boomed, and the commercial class strongly supported the Federalists. The English and French went to war again early in the 19th century, benefiting New England shippers until both sides attacked Massachusetts ships to force them attack the other side. To avoid war, President Thomas Jefferson limited trade through the Embargo Act of 1807. The Massachusetts economy suffered as the United States moved nearer to war with England. Not wanting the War of 1812, New Englander Federalists talked of secession at the Hartford Convention of 1814–1815. Massachusetts largely sat out the war. When the United States claimed victory, the antiwar Federalists faded.

Prosperity resumed after the war. Farmers tilled marginal lands in the far Berkshires, a network of canals and toll roads and railroads tied the major cities, and the Lowell system in textiles made Massachusetts a leader in American industry.

The workers at Lowell's water-powered mills were initially young farm girls from the surrounding community, but the Irish, French Canadian, then other non-English immigrants began taking the jobs in the 1840s. Some mill cities doubled in size in a decade. Expansion made water power inadequate, so coal-fired steam engines powered the industrial growth. The workers, of course, protested their labor conditions—even the Lowell girls struck.

Early-19th-century Massachusetts was a hotbed of radical ideas. Ralph Waldo Emerson, Henry David Thoreau, and Nathaniel Hawthorne were among the Massachusetts intellectuals with national influence. Massachusetts was also home to other reformers, women's suffragists and abolitionists being the most prominent.

The Civil War was popular at first because Massachusetts was a center of abolitionism. As far back as 1764, James Otis asked how it could be permissible to enslave a person just for being black. Massachusetts abolished slavery after the American Revolution. In the 1830s, what had been a small minority movement in the early 19th century became a strong national movement, and Massachusetts was a major home to abolitionist sentiment. Eighty-five percent of the radical abolitionists lived in or grew up in the Northeast, 60 percent from New England. Massachusetts alone was home to 30 percent. Furthermore, because New Englanders settled upper Ohio and Indiana, midwestern abolitionists had strong New England backgrounds, some dating to the Pilgrims. Massachusetts abolitionists settled Lawrence, Kansas. The New England Anti-Slavery Society came into being in 1832 under William Lloyd Garrison. Arthur and Lewis Tappan (New Yorkers with Massachusetts roots) established the American Anti-Slavery Society in 1833. By 1837 Massachusetts had 145 antislavery societies. In New York there were 274, in Ohio, 214. So abolitionism made Massachusetts support the Civil War.

Also, during the Civil War industry boomed as Massachusetts provided guns, tents, blankets, shoes, and other products to the volunteer forces and the U.S. Army. And French Canadians migrated to the factories in large numbers.

After the war, the suffragists resumed their agitation for women's rights. Susan B. Anthony, Margaret Fuller, and Crystal Eastman were among the many suffragists of Massachusetts. Also, Massachusetts industry continued to flourish. Industrial prosperity peaked in the late 19th century, and immigrants came from Canada as well as southern and eastern Europe. Massachusetts led the country in production of textiles and shoes but, more significantly, machinery for making textiles and shoes. It was a major producer of silverware, machine tools, locomotives and fire engines, and many other products. World War I generated a new military-fed boom and brought wage increases to the workers. The Boston police didn't get the benefits. They struck and lost, and Calvin Coolidge got the notoriety that would land him in the White House as the third president from Massachusetts. The state garnered publicity for its mishandling of the Sacco-Vanzetti case, which outraged liberals. Labor unions got recognition in the 1930s.

The textile industry moved mills and headquarters to the southern states, where labor was cheaper. And Massachusetts was left with aged mill cities and tenements. Massachusetts switched to service industries—banking, insurance, retailing, and wholesaling. Industry revived during World War II, and the economy made the transition after the war. Agriculture and fishing declined in the 1950s, but Massachusetts industry switched to electronics and computer-oriented industries as well as higher education, health care, and insurance.

ALTERNATE HISTORY

If the English Pilgrims had sailed away, Massasoit's little band would have slowly recovered with the additional firepower. Using Squanto as go-between, Massasoit would have negotiated a treaty of friendship with the Narragansetts. The area would have been quiet, but the English still would have fished off the coast and traded with the coastal tribes. Occasional outbreaks of smallpox would have continued to reduce the combined Narragansett-Wampanoag band until they were gone, the few survivors absorbed by their neighbors who, more numerous, would have moved into the Wampanoag lands.

When the English from the south would have forced Champlain out of Quebec in 1629, he would have hesitated but went to Provincetown/Plymouth and would have occupied the abandoned Pilgrim site. He would have established a city named for the humpback whales whose song impressed him as he sailed. *Baleine a bosse ton* became Boston, a provincial outpost that would have been loosely tied to New France, and forgotten after Champlain's death. Massachusetts would have become a backwater with limited potential in the fur trade and agriculture.

The French settlers would have got along well with the local tribes, who would have been relieved that the French were not disease-bearing, land-grabbing, slave-taking English. The Indians would have been mostly friendly but cautious about letting Europeans take hostages. The French would have said they wanted no land, just trade. The Indians would be skeptical but also aware that the French were weak numerically and could be pushed into the Atlantic if they got out of line.

Like New France under Samuel de Champlain, Massachusetts would have encouraged its young men to become *coureurs de bois*, intermarry, and live with the tribes in order to adapt to North American life. That would have helped to increase trade and reduce friction with the numerically superior indigenous peoples.

Because the French would have been in Plymouth, the Great Puritan migration would have been diverted to the West Indies and to Virginia, which had had Puritans in its initial complement at Jamestown. In Virginia, the Puritans would have endured life in an Anglican crown colony for a decade then took control with the rise of Cromwell and the Commonwealth. They would have agitated for independence off and on for a century after the Restoration but slowly succumbed to the Virginia plantation way of life.

Early Massachusetts would have looked to New France but would not see much to admire. Still, as a royal colony, Massachusetts would have copied New France's limited franchise, royal governor, and state religion, Catholicism. The church would have provided education and tended to the poor in body and spirit, but mostly the church would have gone into the wilderness to Christianize the Indians and the *coureurs de bois* alike.

Population growth would have been slow, so the colony could not expand to the west or south. New Yorkers and Pennsylvanians would have settled the prime farmlands of the Connecticut valley, and every Massachusetts male from 16 to 60 would have been drafted in a *levee en masse* to garrison the area against the encroaching English.

Boston enjoyed a good harbor and access to the fur country to the north. The trade would have been inferior to that developed from Quebec up the St. Lawrence and into the west, but it would have supplemented the excellent fishing and the agriculture that was good but not adequate for export. Massachusetts would have become a nation of small farmers rather than *seigneurs* (lords). The colony's sailors would have joined the French fleets that fished and whaled the Atlantic. Their experience would have allowed them to be effective blockade runners and smugglers when times were tense.

Massachusetts would have prospered under the mercantilist policies of Jean Baptiste Colbert, who was Louis XIV's chief minister from 1661 through 1683. Although Colbert banned the export of money, forcing the colonials to use only scrip, and implemented high tariffs on foreign manufactures that would have forced Massachusetts to buy French goods rather than English or Dutch, he subsidized shipping. He encouraged settlement in French colonies andFrench manufacturers to buy colonial raw material. Massachusetts would have had the raw material and the ships and an eye on the Caribbean markets. .

But the political scene was getting ugly as France and England would have fought for the continent. In actual history, to get their share of the fur trade, the English established the Hudson's Bay Company north of New France in 1670. The French built forts along the Ohio and Mississippi rivers to the Gulf of Mexico. The French also established forts in the older but still unpopulated areas of New France, which would have included Massachusetts. Friction would have intensified as France's claims reached from Massachusetts (Maine and Quebec too) to New Orleans, hemming in the English. The result would have been war

The French and Indian wars would have been difficult times for Massachusetts, as for all frontier areas. An English invasion from New York and Rhode Island would have reached Boston, but Massachusetts Minutemen would have been able to repel the poorly trained and undisciplined English militias. After the initial English thrust, war would have continued intermittently for 70 years. Both sides would have used Native allies and, occasionally, guerrilla tactics. The wars would have been bloody and the warriors ruthless.

France would have ceded Massachusetts and New France to England in 1763, and the church still would have controlled education and social welfare, but the 50,000 residents of New France and the 30,000 residents of Massachusetts would have lived in uneasy union with a million English and half-a-million slaves. France would have sacrificed Massachusetts for the return of more profitable colonies in the Caribbean. The English would have accepted Massachusetts as a Catholic and French-speaking colony. Protected by the English mercantile system, Massachusetts would have flourished, although its population would have remained small because English Protestants would have been unwilling to migrate to a place of religious variety. French Canadians, limited in numbers, would have provided few emigrants.

Massachusetts would have begun exploring the joys of the triangular trade, having a competitive edge in the French Caribbean due to cultural similarities. There would have been Gallic joy in sneaking a cargo past inept British customs officials. The clamping down on the mercantile colonies through a series of oppressive acts would have alienated the sons of Massachusetts, but they could not have ignited the southern colonies, disinterested in war because the business of supplying raw material to the imperial world was going along nicely. With the colonies divided in alternate history, the rebellion would have died without action.

Massachusetts would have shared Quebec's grievances under the English: discrimination, pressure to acculturate, disestablishment of the Catholic Church, disenfranchisement, English domination of the economy. New Yorkers and Pennsylvanians would have held a decades-long grudge because of a Quebec/Massachusetts Act and other efforts by the English government that would have been enacted to keep the colony pacified. French Massachusetts would have begun to look sympathetically to Quebec, the other French orphan in British North America.

Massachusetts would have not wanted to merge with Quebec though. It would have had its own identity, and it would have been doing better than the backward northern province. Exploiting the resources of its territory of Maine, it would have built a strong economy, trading with both France and England in ships stores. Because Canada would have been primitive and southern English colonies would have been increasingly reliant on slavery, Massachusetts would have attracted immigrant French Canadians looking for better opportunity and English Quakers and Puritans alienated by slavery. The Puritans would have stayed only briefly in Catholic Massachusetts. As the English-speaking colonies of New England would have tightened controls over their slaves in the aftermath of Haiti's successful slave rising of 1791, Massachusetts would have become part of the "Underground Railroad" that helped slaves to freedom. A few proslavery Catholics would have emigrated from the unstable Caribbean, as would have newly independent blacks.

New England slaveholders fearful of democracy engendered by the Haitian Revolution of 1791 would have had problems with Napoleon's emancipation of French colonial slaves. Happily (for all but the slaves) Napoleon would have revoked emancipation. Slavery would have remained legal in France and in the New England colonies from Delaware to Georgia. Practical Massachusetts shippers would have ignored abolitionist complaints and maintained profitable trade relations with all communities.

Early in the 19th century, France and Britain would have renewed their age-old war. Both would have harassed Massachusetts merchantmen plying the West Indies and Southern trade. Provoked but unwilling to fight for the British or against the French, the merchants of Massachusetts would have sat out the war. When the French fell for good at Waterloo, Massachusetts would have been home to émigrés from the French troubles. With a strong economy and growing population, Massachusetts would have expanded north to Maine, tightening the link with Quebec, still under the English thumb.

Domestically in the 19th century, Massachusetts parochial schools would have produced brilliant minds freed by the frontier life from their stale European ways. Modeling themselves on English tinkerers but molding a new world outlook, they would have used Massachusetts' water power resources to develop a textile industry, specializing first in delicate fabrics for the elite trade in Paris and Boston, then expanding to provide cheaper cloth for the local Native and the West Indian slave trade. Dependency on New England cotton would have stifled the antislavery impulse. The mills would have attracted French Canadian laborers through the Maine road.

The British would have freed their slaves in 1834 and the French would have freed theirs in 1848, and Massachusetts would have suffered economic disruption when the Southern colonies attempted to confederate and secede. That effort would have failed because the secessionists would have been unable to bring along New York and Pennsylvania and would have lacked even a semblance of an industrial base without them. New England would have confederated with the British West Indies as an agricultural dependency of the British Empire during the 1860s.

Periodically, Massachusetts would have had the impulse to join with Quebec in some sort of Francophone state. If the French Canadians rose against the British in 1837, though, the Massachusetts militia would have remained at home. The rebellion would have reminded Massachusetts that it had more freedom and autonomy than either upper or lower Canada. Massachusetts would have watched with interest as the Durham Commission would have investigated the reasons for the risings of 1837, dismayed at the Durham report, which would have said that French culture in Canada had remained largely stagnant for 200 years while English culture progressed. Durham would have spoken of two warring nations in one state. Massachusetts would have had no interest in joining that state.

Thirty years later, Canada would have attained dominion status, and Canada's one million French speakers (of a total population of 3.5 million) would have received guarantees that French as well as English would be the language of government, that Quebec's French-based civil law would continue, and that public financing would be available for separate Catholic and Protestant schools. Massachusetts would have had all that already and would see no need to affiliate with a small and backward province that was already providing transient cheap labor.

Boston and Massachusetts would have used the wealth gained from the triangular trade to develop a highly respected university, museums, and culture. Emphasizing industrial development and banking services, Massachusetts would have enjoyed its own industrial revolution through the 19th century. Somewhat rigid class lines would have begun to form as society divided into the wealthy and the workers.

Boston would be by then a major cultural center, welcoming people of all kinds without serious discrimination. It would have brought in Irish Catholics from the 1840s when the English colonies would have persisted in their high to low Protestantism. Blacks from Francophone Africa and the Caribbean migrated to the city.

Massachusetts would have avoided the European conflict of 1914–1918, but when the postwar world economy would have collapsed,

Massachusetts' foreign trade would have shrunk and the economy would have gone into a 15-year tailspin. With prosperity shaky, Massachusetts would have become insular. The *coureurs du bois* would have been long gone, and cultural diversity would have been uncomfortable. Would Massachusetts accommodate or assimilate the First Nations? Mostly, urban-dwelling Francophone Massachusetts would have hoped the Indians would go away. Immigrants would have become a problem: too many foreign languages and cultures clashing with Massachusetts Franco-Americanism and competing for scarce jobs in a depressed economy. The government would have established massive public works projects in the Northeast, building the Boston–Montreal superhighway that would have created a new economic avenue between the two French-speaking areas of North America.

When World War II broke out, Massachusetts would have been neutral, but when France fell and Quebec rallied to the allied cause, Massachusetts would have enlisted too, sending money and supplies, gearing up war industries, and finally fighting alongside the Quebecois. After the war, much after, when Canada would have been rethinking its approach to federation and setting aside Nunavut, the First Peoples province, Quebec could have separated from Canada and joined Massachusetts to form a Francophone nation on the North American continent.

John H. Barnhill

Discussion Questions

1. After reading the detailed account of what really happened in the first Puritan settlements, what other chance events might have been "turning points" to make things turn out differently?

2. Why did the Puritans allow non-Puritan settlers to accompany them, and why did they choose them as leaders?

3. What was democratic about the early Puritan settlement, and what was nondemocratic? Why did the Puritans structure their democratic institutions the way they did?

4. Why do you think the Native American people in Massachusetts were taller on average than the English settlers?

5. What factors made some of the Native Americans friendly toward the English settlers? What factors made some Native Americans hostile to the English settlers?

6. Why did diseases like smallpox wipe out whole Native American towns and villages but have less effect on European settlers?

7. Although the English had firearms and armor, the English had little weapons-technology advantage over the Native Americans when there were skirmishes or armed clashes. Why was this so?

Bibliography and Further Reading

Ames, Azel. "The Mayflower and Her Log," FullBooks, http://www.fullbooks.com (accessed May 22, 2006).

Atkins, Scott. "The Beginnings, the Pilgrims," The American Sense of Puritan, http://xroads.virginia.edu (accessed May 22, 2006).

Boroughs, J. Jason. The Plymouth Colony Archive Project, http://etext.lib.virginia.edu (accessed May 22, 2006).

Brown, Richard D., and Jack Tager. *Massachusetts: a Concise History.* Amherst, MA:University of Massachusetts Press, 2000.

Bumsted, J. M., ed. *Canadian History before Confederation.* Homewood, IL: Irwin-Dorsey, 1979.

Cline, Duane A. "The Wampanoag/Pilgrim Treaty," The Pilgrims and Plymouth Colony: 1620, http://www.rootsweb.com (accessed May 22, 2006).

Eccles, W. J. *France in America.* New York: HarperCollins, 1972.

Harrold, Stanley. *American Abolitionists.* Boston, MA: Longman, 2001.

Landes, David. *Unbound Prometheus.* Cambridge: Cambridge University Press, 2003.

Moogk, Peter N. *La Nouvelle France: The Making of French Canada.* East Lansing, MI: Michigan State University Press, 2000.

Morgan, Ted. *Wilderness at Dawn.* New York: Simon and Schuster, 1994.

Newman, Richard S. *The Transformation of American Abolitionism.* Chapel Hill, NC: University of North Carolina Press, 2002.

Quinn, Arthur. *A New World.* New York: Berkley Books, 1995.

Temin, Peter, ed. *Engines of Enterprise: An Economic History of New England.* Cambridge, MA: Harvard University Press, 2000.

TURNING POINT

Thomas Hooker established a new settlement in Connecticut in 1636. What if this British Puritan was challenged by the Dutch in the area for control of the colony?

INTRODUCTION

Britain had been interested in the New England area as early as the late 15th century, when King Henry VII authorized John Cabot to explore the area during his expedition of 1498. His journeys laid the groundwork for future British claims in North America. Soon, early British explorers such as Captain John Smith and Bartholomew Gosnold began returning with favorable reports on the region. By the early 17th century, British mariners visited, and men like Sir Ferdinando Gorges promoted the region. The British, however, were not the only people interested in New England. They would have to compete with the Dutch and local Native American tribes for control.

Native Americans had already modified the New England area through hunting, forest burning, and planting and had developed extensive inter-tribal trading networks before the arrival of the British. Trade between the British and Native Americans started with the 16th-century European explorers in the region. Wampum, small purple and white beads made with polished shells by the southern New England coastal Native Americans, became the common medium of exchange with the British traders and their European manufactured goods. The Iroquois, among other tribes, used the beads for sacred purposes and were willing to provide beaver furs, highly demanded for European fashion, in exchange. The British also hoped to settle in the region and initially found little Native American resistance after a smallpox epidemic, to which the Native Americans had no immunity, struck the area's tribes in 1633 and 1634.

Many of the British colonists who initially emigrated to the area in the 17th century came seeking religious freedom in the New World. Many of those who came to New England were Puritans, so named because they wished to purify the Church of England (Anglican Church) of what they believed to be corrupt practices. They faced persecution under Archbishop William Laud in the 1620s, forcing many to flee first to the Netherlands and then to America. A group of Puritan Separatists known as the Pilgrims

KEY CONCEPT Dutch West India Company

Established in 1621 by the States-General of the Netherlands, the Dutch West India Company (or West-Indische Compagnie, WIC) was primarily a response to the phenomenal success of the East India Company and was given exclusive trading rights to the African coast, between the Tropic of Cancer and the Cape of Good Hope, and the American coast, between Newfoundland and the Straights of Magellan, in 1623.

More powerful than just a trading fleet, the WIC was overseen by a board of directors appointed by the States-General and given the power to conduct whatever business it saw fit, short of declaring war on its own. Originally the company had aspirations of taking Brazil from the Portuguese, but it spent decades mired in conflict and never enjoyed complete success. The company was influential in the development of early America as major trading routes around the mouth of the Hudson River led to the establishment of Fort Amsterdam, the center of New Amsterdam (now New York City) in 1626. General Peter Minuit bought Manhattan under direction from the WIC for the now famous price of 60 guilders. Fort Orange (1624) at what is now Albany, New York, and Fort Nassau (1624) on the Delaware River were two successful forts preceding Amsterdam, easily the most prosperous of them.

established Plymouth Colony in Massachusetts in 1620. Another group of Puritans established Massachusetts Bay Colony in 1630, and small settlements would later spread out into the surrounding countryside, including the area that would later become the colony of Connecticut.

The Dutch had gained their independence from Spain by the 17th century and were also interested in the Connecticut area because of its fertile soils and lucrative fur trading possibilities. In 1609, British explorer Henry Hudson entered the area of present-day New York on the ship *De Halve Maen (Half Moon)* in his search for a northwest passage to Asia at the behest of the Dutch East India Company. He navigated what became known as the Hudson River up to Albany, claiming the land for the Dutch company that employed him. The British seized Hudson's ship in protest of his incursion but that did not stop the Dutch from trying to profit from the area.

Dutch merchants competed for control of the area's valuable fur trade from 1611 to 1614. Notable early trading expeditions to the area included those of Dutch merchant Arnout Vogels and Dutch explorer and trader Adriaen Block, among others. Block became the first European to explore the Connecticut River, naming it the Versche (Fresh) River, and was instrumental in establishing trade relations between the Dutch and local Native American tribes such as the Pequots and the Mohawks. The States-General (Dutch Parliament) then awarded the newly formed New Netherland Company a 3-year monopoly on the fur trade in 1614. The company's charter was the first to name the area New Netherland. The company established the trading post of Fort Nassau on Castle Island (near present-day Albany) in that same year. The company never colonized and their monopoly was not renewed upon its expiration in 1618, opening the land to other Dutch traders.

The States-General chartered the Dutch West India Company, a national joint-stock private company, in 1621 and granted it a 24-year trading monopoly to colonize the area, as well as other Dutch possessions in the Western Hemisphere. The company-controlled colony of New Netherland was granted provincial status in 1623 and the first wave

Piracy was among the other interests of the WIC, and in 1628 one of the company's agents, Piet Heyn, captured a Spanish treasure fleet of silver and used the proceeds to further expansion, which would reach its height in the 1630s, after the WIC enjoyed victories against the Portuguese in Brazil. Thus the Dutch controlled land on the northeastern coast of Brazil.

Despite early successes, Dutch settlers on the Atlantic Coast never fully prospered. Only small numbers of people felt cause to leave their native Netherlands for the New World. The Dutch West India Company kept the States-General of the Dutch republic in control of the island of Manhattan, which

was initially ignored by the English, despite the settlement being on land they claimed, because of British wars with Spain and France. In 1664, the Dutch finally lost Manhattan to the British.

During this time the company experienced financial problems, losing its Brazilian lands back to Portugal, and after a reorganization of their contract in 1674, the Dutch West India Company limited its operations to mostly slave trading on the African coast. The Dutch West India Company never fully recovered from its setbacks and was eventually dissolved in 1798, after a century of debt and ineffectiveness, leaving its legacy as the first to settle the area that is today one of the most powerful cities in the world.

---

of settlers, 30 Flemish Walloon families, arrived aboard the *Nieu Nederlandt* (*New Netherland*) in 1624. The settlers then established Fort Orange (near present-day Albany). The next year saw the arrival of Willem Verhulst, the area's first commander. Additional colonists, livestock, and supplies followed in subsequent years. The company purchased tracts of land in the Connecticut River valley from its Native American inhabitants between 1607 and 1639 and would not allow land grants unless the Native Americans agreed to sell.

Company director-general Peter Minuit arrived in 1626 to take over the colony's administration, serving until 1631. He made the famous purchase of Manhattan Island from a local tribe for a small amount of trade goods valued at 60 Dutch guilders. He also began construction on Fort Amsterdam (present site of New York City) in 1626. He then established diplomatic relations with Plymouth Colony. Minuit also consolidated the settlers in far-reaching areas to Manhattan Island for safety. The Dutch established a commercial base rather than an expanding agricultural settlement and were able to maintain mostly good relations with the Native Americans in the colony's early years of slow growth. The company provided doctors, craftsmen, and soldiers, appointed director-generals such as Minuit to enact laws, and collected taxes, fines, and trading profits.

In 1629, the Dutch West India Company agreed to offer patroonships, which were large manorial estates, in order to attract settlers at no cost to the company under what became known as the Patroonship Plan. There was little initial interest because potential patroons also wanted access to the lucrative fur trade, which had quickly become the colony's economic foundation. In 1629, the company agreed to a revision known as the "Freedoms and Exemptions for the Patroons and Masters who would plant a colony and cattle in New Netherland," under which, among other concessions, patroons would be able to enter the fur trade through payment of a tax to the company. Dutch merchant Kiliaen van Rensselaer received the largest patroonship, consisting of the area along the Hudson River to Fort Orange. He named his colony Rensselaerswyck, and it quickly became the center of the fur trade. His was the only patroonship to survive; the rest were ultimately

KEY CONCEPT Patroonships

The Dutch West India Company instituted the Patroonship Plan in 1629 as a way to promote settlement of New Netherland at no expense to the colony. Any potential patroon who transported 50 families to settle in the New World would be eligible to receive a large manorial estate along a navigable river in the Dutch colony. The potential patroon would send a surveyor to claim his land and purchase the land from its Native American owners. The patroon would then register the claim with the company. The settler families would serve as agricultural tenants for a fixed number of years. The system would be feudal in nature, guaranteeing the patroon perpetual ownership and control of local offices and courts. Settler families could be required to pay the patroon with money, goods, or services.

abandoned and sold to the company. The patroonship system had died out by the mid-1630s.

The Dutch West India Company later abandoned its trading monopoly to more fully share the risks and expenses associated with colonization and to collect fees from other merchants, including some English settlers. The policies further expanded the colonists' trading rights and provided free land to potential settlers. They also allowed for smaller land grants and the development of small independent farms. These policies and fees were established under the 1639 Articles and Conditions and the 1640 Freedoms and Exemptions. Successful smaller traders and merchants took advantage of the new policies, as did larger Dutch firms, which would come to control the colony's trade.

The new benefits attracted more settlers, and New Netherland continued to expand. The colony ultimately encompassed parts of the present states of New York, New Jersey, Pennsylvania, Maryland, Connecticut, and Delaware. The northern border was the Connecticut (Fresh) River. The southern border included all of New Jersey. New Netherland's most important area was the land along the Hudson River from New Amsterdam (present-day New York City) northwest to Fort Orange (present-day Albany). New Amsterdam served as the colony's shipping hub. The Hudson, Connecticut, and Delaware rivers provided excellent transportation and navigation. The Dutch were the first Europeans to settle in the Connecticut area, when Director-General Wouter van Twiller established a small trading post called House of Good Hope at the future site of Hartford in 1633, but the Dutch had not made a serious effort to colonize the Connecticut area.

As the Dutch were expanding New Netherland, English settlers migrated into Connecticut from the Massachusetts Bay and Plymouth Colonies in search of fertile soil and trade opportunities, marking the beginning of a trend of westward expansion of the British colonies in America. They also left the Massachusetts Bay Colony due to religious, civil, and economic discontent. The British claimed that John Cabot's 1498 voyage, which predated that of Henry Hudson, gave them legitimate claim to the area despite the Dutch presence. Areas were chosen based on defense and access to pasturage.

The first three settlements along the Connecticut River were Windsor, Wethersfield, and Hartford. They were settled from 1633 to 1636. Many of

Thomas Hooker leading members of his congregation to Hartford, Connecticut. (Library of Congress)

these early settlers were rural Protestant farmers and servants. Most were English; however, there were some Irish, French, Dutch, Hebrew, German, and, later, Scots. Reverend Thomas Hooker led about 100 followers plus livestock from the Massachusetts Bay Colony and settled in Hartford along the Connecticut River in 1636. The Connecticut River was valued due to its navigability, peaceable Native Americans, and numbers of fur-bearing animals. This was the site where the Dutch had earlier established a trading post and fort, and it remained to be seen if they would now seek to expel Hooker and his followers from their new home.

TURNING POINT

Thomas Hooker (1586–1647) was born to Puritan parents in Marfield, Leicestershire, England, in July 1586. He graduated from Emmanuel College with a bachelor of arts in 1608 and a master of arts degree in 1611. Hooker claimed that it was at Emmanuel College that he became truly converted and dedicated to a religious life. Hooker became the rector of St. George's Church in Esher, Surrey, around 1620, where he developed a reputation as a gifted preacher. He married Susannah Garbrand on April 3, 1621. Hooker next resided in Chelmsford, Essex, where he became the lecturer at St. Mary's Church in 1626. Many credited his preaching with helping to restore order in the town, known for its alehouses and rowdy behavior.

Hooker later lost his position at St. Mary's in 1629 when Anglican Archbishop William Laud threatened him during a crackdown on Puritanism. He moved to the nearby small town of Little Baddow, where he established a grammar school in a nearby village and counseled area ministers. Continued threats from Laud forced Hooker and his family to flee to the Netherlands, where he once again entered the ministry at the English Non-Conformist church in Delft. He also lived in Rotterdam, where he served as an assistant to Dr. William Ames. Hooker became dissatisfied with the state of religion in the Netherlands and returned to England to join other Puritans sailing for the New World in search of religious freedom. In 1633, he sailed to Massachusetts aboard the *Griffin*, alongside noted Puritan leader John Cotton, to become a preacher in the New World. They arrived in Boston in the Massachusetts Bay Colony in September.

Hooker settled in Newtown (later renamed Cambridge), where a group of his former parishioners from Chelmsford had earlier settled. Hooker was chosen the town's pastor. Several years later, Hooker became one of the first Puritans of the Massachusetts Bay Colony to migrate beyond the colony's borders. Historians speculate on the exact reasons for Hooker's decision, but it is known that he disagreed with the colony's rule that political participation was restricted to male church members who owned property. Hooker believed all men should have the right to vote. The colony's leaders did not tolerate such dissenting views. Another motive for the exodus was the search for fertile land. After receiving permission from Massachusetts Bay leaders, Hooker left with a number of followers to establish a new settlement on the rich land along the Connecticut River, territory that had already been claimed by the Dutch.

The group established the town of Hartford in 1636 and Hooker served as a religious and political leader for the town in what became the colony of Connecticut. Hooker also played an instrumental role in the General Court of Connecticut's drafting of a constitution for the new colony. The result was the adoption of the Fundamental Orders, sometimes referred to as the first written constitution, in January 1639. Voting was opened to all adult males who had been accepted by a majority vote in their townships, a very democratic standard for that time.

ACTUAL HISTORY

The Dutch did not choose to challenge Hooker's presence and Hartford grew quickly due to its attractive location at the head of navigation on the Connecticut River and rich soil. It became the Connecticut capital in 1662 and has remained so ever since, sharing the designation with New Haven from 1701 until 1875. Hooker's reputation remained strong, even in England, and a number of his religious works were published. Hooker died of an epidemic sickness on July 7, 1647.

Early colonial life in Greenwich, Connecticut. (Victoria H. Huntley/Library of Congress)

Meanwhile, settlement expanded along the Connecticut River and the Atlantic coast, with many towns started by migrants from the three original settlements. The newer settlements included Branford, Fairfield, Farmington, Greenwich, Guilford, Middletown, Milford, New Haven, New London, Norwalk, Saybrook, Southold, Stamford, Stonington, and Stratford. The former Dutch presence in the Connecticut River valley led to a race for its control. A party sent by Massachusetts Bay Colony leader John Winthrop Jr. founded Saybrook in 1636, destroying a small Dutch fort in the area and erecting their own fort to prevent the Dutch from retaking control of the mouth of the Connecticut River. The Dutch were ultimately unwilling to press the issue against a more populated New England and lost control of the Connecticut River valley in the 1650 Treaty of Hartford.

The Puritan colonies of Plymouth, Massachusetts Bay, Connecticut, and New Haven united in 1643 in the New England Confederation to protect themselves from the nearby French, Dutch, and Native Americans. In 1662, the towns along the Connecticut River and the north shore of the Long Island Sound, including the separate colony of New Haven, were consolidated into the colony of Connecticut. The British had also established a number of other American colonies near New Netherland. Roger Williams had fled the Puritan leaders of Massachusetts Bay Colony in 1635 and established Providence Plantation along Narragansett Bay in the area that became the British colony of Rhode Island in 1663. The British also founded Maryland (1632), Pennsylvania (1681), Delaware (1701), and New Jersey (1702).

Although the Dutch had surrendered control of Connecticut, they had not given up on American colonization, and the colony of New Netherland continued to prosper. The Dutch focused on their main settlements on the sites of the future cities of New York, Kingston, and Albany. The new director-general, Peter Stuyvesant, arrived in 1647 to begin a 17-year administration, the longest in the colony's history. New Netherland captured the colony of New Sweden (present day Delaware), controlled by the Swedish West India Company, in 1655. The Dutch frontier expanded very gradually.

New Netherland enjoyed an ethnic and religious diversity unmatched by other European colonies in America, and this diversity expanded with the arrival of new emigrants from Europe. A large percentage of that population was not Dutch, including Germans, Finns, Swedes, and British. The colony also contained large numbers of African Americans, some of them slaves imported by the company. New Netherland had several thousand residents by the mid-1600s and about 9,000 residents by 1664. Expansion was delayed at times due to the struggles of the British and the Dutch with the local Native Americans.

The British fought the Pequot War in 1637 after the tribe attempted to gain a monopoly on trade with the Europeans. The Pequot had sought an alliance with the Massachusetts Bay Colony, but that failed to materialize and they ended up fighting the British instead. It was the first large-scale Indian war in New England and opened Connecticut to further British settlement. The Dutch fought their own wars between 1640 and 1664, notably after Willem Kieft became New Netherland's chief executive from 1638 to 1647, at a time when a buildup of grievances led to strained relations. He was noted for his rash Indian policies and led a series of wars (the Kieft Wars) against the local tribes in the lower Hudson valley region for control because the tribes were obstacles to immediate Dutch expansion.

King Philip's War, fought in 1675–1676, was the most serious conflict in the region and marked the last united Native American resistance to European settlement in the New England region. King Philip (Metacomet) was a Wampanoag Native and the son of Massasoit, a Native American who had aided the Pilgrims. He led the tribes of southern New England in an attack on the Massachusetts settlers who had been encroaching on their territory and hunting grounds. The Narragansetts of Rhode Island and the Nipmucks of Connecticut also participated in the fighting. The tribes suffered defeat by 1676. New England's Native American population was greatly reduced by 1700 due to epidemics and battle casualties, and only sporadic troubles remained along the remote frontiers.

In addition to Indian wars, the Dutch and British also fought a series of wars with each other in the mid- to late 17th century. The first Anglo-Dutch War of 1652 to 1654 was instigated when the British Parliament passed a series of Navigation Acts in 1651, in part to keep the Dutch out of colonial trade by declaring that all ships carrying trade between the

British Empire and other countries must be either British- or American-owned. The Dutch began attacking British shipping the following year.

In 1653, the British blockaded Dutch ports with the authority of Lord Protector Oliver Cromwell. The Dutch fleet, under Admiral Tromp, attempted to run the blockade and link with Admiral Witte de Witt, but failed, and the fleet suffered heavy damage. Cromwell sent a squadron of four warships to attack New Netherland, but peace arrived before they launched an attack. In 1654, the Connecticut General Court ordered the Dutch settlement in Hartford seized at the end of the first Anglo-Dutch War. The 1654 Treaty of Westminster ended the war in a stalemate.

The second Anglo-Dutch War was fought from 1664 to 1667. In 1662, the Netherlands had entered into an anti-British alliance with France. In 1664, British King Charles II (1660–1685) annexed New Netherland as a British province. He named his brother James the duke of York and Albany and future King James II (1685–1688), its lord proprietor. The duke then organized an expedition to attack New Netherland, sending a fleet under the command of Sir Richard Nicolls to seize the Dutch colony. Director-General Pieter Stuyvesant surrendered the poorly defended Fort Amsterdam in 1664 without firing a shot. The city of New Amsterdam and the colony were both renamed New York. The lack of decisive victory for either side resulted in a negotiated peace under the 1667 Treaty of Breda. The Dutch surrendered claim to New Amsterdam and retained Surinam. They also gained some favorable concessions on the Navigation Acts.

The third Anglo-Dutch War occurred after King Louis XIV of France sought to expand the French Empire and eliminate the Dutch trade rivalry. King Louis invaded the Netherlands in 1672. In 1673, King Louis and King Charles II of England joined together as allies in the war against the Netherlands under the 1670 Treaty of Dover. In America, Dutch soldiers under Captain Anthony Colve captured Fort James in 1673 and Admirals Cornelis Evertsen and Jacob Binckes forced the surrender of New York. The Dutch regained temporary control of its former colony, but the 1674 Treaty of Westminster restored the lands to British control under Governor Major Edmund Andros. The former Dutch colony of New Netherland left a legacy of place names and the multicultural character of the region.

The British now controlled the Middle Colonies along the Atlantic seaboard as well as New England. In 1684, King Charles II revoked the charter of the Massachusetts Bay Colony and created the Dominion of New England, consisting of New England, New York, and New Jersey, but the Glorious Revolution of 1689, when William and Mary ascended to the throne to replace the deposed King James II, ended the dominion. The region, including Connecticut, saw a rapid population increase in the 18th century, leading to dispersal. Connecticut's land was largely settled by 1750 and most of its towns were founded by 1800.

Initially, a number of Connecticut towns remained strongly Puritan, with voting restricted to church members. Religion and order initially remained priorities and there were a multitude of ordinances regulating personal behavior. The early Puritan zeal, however, began to fade by the mid-17th century. Many historians mark the Halfway Covenant of 1662 in the Massachusetts Bay Colony, which allowed children whose parents were church members to become members themselves even if they had not had a conversion experience, as a sign of this fading. In the 1720s through the

1740s, religion underwent a renaissance in the Great Awakening through such renowned preachers as Jonathan Edwards and George Whitefield. Religion, however, continued to gradually lose its grip on politics.

The Connecticut colonial government consisted of a general assembly and a governor and deputy governor, who were served by various assistants and commissioners. Towns worked cooperatively to govern common lands. Town residents elected selectmen to represent their interests at town meetings. A moderator ran such meetings but people spoke their minds freely. For most of the 17th century, it was here that residents dealt with town business and disputes.

New England's staple commodities were grains, meats, and timber. The region sold agricultural products to Newfoundland, the West Indies, and Europe via Boston and helped feed the New England fishing fleet. Cattle and hogs provided meat for consumption and sale. Forests provided timber, naval stores such as tar and turpentine, barrels, and potash used in soap making. Most farmers were subsistence farmers who lacked the manpower to engage in large commercial farming, even with the easy availability of land.

A series of European wars fought mainly in the early to mid-18th century often spilled over into America. These included King William's War (1689–1697), Queen Anne's War (1702–1713), King George's War (1740–1748), but the most significant was the French and Indian War (1754–1763). This clash for empire between the British and the French ended in a British victory. Under the 1763 Treaty of Paris, British territory now extended from Canada in the north to Florida in the south and from the Atlantic seaboard in the east to the Mississippi River in the west. France had been expelled from most of its American territory and was no longer a major power in North America.

The elimination of the French threat allowed the British to turn their attention to more fully governing their American colonies, ending a period of "salutary neglect." The British passed a series of laws and taxes that angered many American colonists who claimed that they had no representation in the British Parliament. They included the Proclamation of 1763, the Sugar Act (1764), the Stamp Act (1765), the Quartering Act (1765 and 1766), the Currency Act (1764), and the Townshend Acts (1767). Colonial protests and boycotts gained the repeal of certain unpopular measures such as the Stamp Act, but events such as the 1770 Boston Massacre continued to incite anger on both sides of the Atlantic.

The Tea Act of 1773 sparked the infamous Boston Tea Party, in which colonists dressed as Native Americans boarded a British ship and dumped its cargo of tea into Boston Harbor. The British government heavily punished Massachusetts through the Coercive (Intolerable) Acts in 1774. The American Declaration of Independence (1776) and the Revolutionary War (1775–1781) followed shortly thereafter. New York (the former Dutch colony of New Netherland) was a key British military stronghold during the war. The United States of America would win the war and officially gained their independence from Great Britain in the 1781 Treaty of Paris.

Meanwhile, the city of Hartford, Connecticut, founded by Thomas Hooker, continued to grow. In the late 18th century, it was a center of the Federalist movement, led by the Hartford Wits. The city gained prosperity through the New England whaling industry and would later become the country's leading insurance center.

ALTERNATE HISTORY

The Dutch could have been more alarmed at the presence of Thomas Hooker and his followers, viewing them as a threat to Dutch claims on the area along the Fresh (Connecticut) River. Although they had little presence in the area, the Dutch could have decided that they did not want to surrender control of the rich farmland and lucrative fur trade. Dutch settlers would then have used the trading post established near Hartford in 1633 as a base from which to attack Hooker's Hartford settlement. The Dutch at New Netherland would provide reinforcements and supplies for the small group. In the ensuing struggle, the Dutch could have killed Hooker and a number of his followers. Others could have escaped back to the Massachusetts Bay Colony, whose leaders would inform the British government of the assault.

A first Anglo-Dutch war would then have broken out in both Europe and America, with the Dutch fleet demonstrating their superiority. The Dutch would then regain control of the Fresh (Connecticut) River valley, quickly moving to strengthen the existing post and establishing new forts in the area to prevent the British from reentering the region. The rich land would also attract a number of Dutch settlers from New Netherland and from the Netherlands themselves. By mid-century, the Dutch would have established the new colony of New West India. Both Dutch colonies would have enjoyed much more rapid expansion and more support from the Dutch government and the Dutch West India Company. The company would also have become much more involved in the lucrative slave trade. By the middle of the 17th century, the Dutch government would have taken over control of its New World colonies from the company.

The Dutch would have been more involved in the New England Indian wars of the 17th century, including the Pequot War of 1637, which would have involved both the Dutch and the British. They also would have faced greater resistance from the tribes in the New Netherland area. King Philip's War, fought in 1675 and the most serious conflict in the region, would also have involved both British and Dutch settlers. King Philip would have led the tribes of southern New England in an attack on the Massachusetts and New West India settlers who had been encroaching on their territory and hunting grounds. The Narragansetts of Rhode Island and the Nipmucks of Connecticut also would still have participated in the fighting. The numbers of Dutch and British would still have ultimately overwhelmed the New England region's Native American tribes. The end of large-scale Indian wars in the region would have ended the temporary uniting of the British and Dutch against a common enemy and boundary disputes would have reemerged.

The 1650 meeting of the United Colonies of New England and the Dutch, represented by Peter Stuyvesant, at Hartford, designed to settle trade disputes and set territorial boundaries between the Dutch and English colonies, would have broken down because both sides would have been unable to agree on boundaries. Thus there still would have been a series of Anglo-Dutch wars for control of American territory in the mid- to late 17th century, but the outcome of those conflicts would have been much different. In America, the wars would have involved the Plymouth and Massachusetts Bay colonies against the Dutch in New West India as well as the British attacks on New Netherland.

The British Parliament would still have passed a series of Navigation Acts in 1651, in part to keep the Dutch out of colonial trade by declaring that all ships carrying trade between the British Empire and other countries must be either British- or American-owned. This incentive would have been even stronger with the larger Dutch presence in America. The Dutch would then begin attacking British shipping the following year and the second Anglo-Dutch War would have begun. In 1653, the British still would have blockaded Dutch ports at the authority of Lord Protector Oliver Cromwell, but they would have struggled against the powerful Dutch fleet in America. Cromwell's squadron would face defeat in their attack on New Netherland.

In revenge, the Dutch would have launched a powerful attack on the British New England colonies from the sea and from New West India. Although the Dutch were unable to take Britain's New England colonies, the 1654 Treaty of Westminster would have forced Britain to recognize Dutch claims to both New Netherland and New West India. King Charles II would not have been able to claim New Netherland in 1662 and grant it to his brother James, the duke of York and future King James II, and the colony would have remained firmly under Dutch control.

The third Anglo-Dutch War would have occurred after King Louis XIV of France sought to expand the French Empire and eliminate the Dutch trade rivalry. King Louis would still have invaded the Netherlands in 1672. In 1673, King Louis and King Charles II of England would still have joined together as allies in the war against the Netherlands under the 1670 Treaty of Dover. Under the 1674 Treaty of Westminster, however, the Dutch would have secured New Netherland and its surrounding countryside once again. Tight control of New Netherland and its expansion into the surrounding areas would have prevented the British from establishing the Quaker colonies of New Jersey, and, later, William Penn's Pennsylvania. They had already taken New Sweden (Delaware) in 1655, and would secure the now isolated colony of Maryland from the British. The Dutch would thus ultimately control the mid-Atlantic region, setting the stage for yet another war with the British for control of the New England region.

A series of European wars fought mainly in the early to mid-18th century often spilled over into America. These included King William's War (1689–1697), Queen Anne's War (1702–1713), King George's War (1740–1748), but the most significant was the French and Indian War (1754–1763). This war would now have been a battle between the French, English, and Dutch for control of the North American continent. The French and Dutch and their Native American allies would form an alliance and soundly defeat their common enemy, the British. Under the 1763 Treaty of Paris, France would have retained control of Canada and the Louisiana Territory, and the Dutch would have taken possession of the British colonies in New England, including Massachusetts. These colonies, including the former Puritan colonies, would then take on the cosmopolitan Dutch characteristics of multiculturalism and religious toleration. A seriously weakened Britain would retain control of its southern American colonies, from Virginia to Georgia. The Spanish would have sold Florida to the French.

The vulnerable position of the British southern colonies in America and the absence of Massachusetts, hot bed of Revolutionary activity, would mean that the British colonies would not rebel against the mother country. A final war in the early 1800s, however, would have forced Britain to abandon its North American colonies, including its claim on Oregon, and turn its attention elsewhere in the British Empire. This would allow the Dutch to gain control of the entire Atlantic seaboard with the exception of Canada and Florida. In 1803, the Dutch would purchase the Louisiana Territory and Florida from the French, paving the way for westward expansion. Canada would have remained a French colony until it gained its independence late in the 19th century.

The Dutch would then have come to the aid of the Mexican colonies of their old rival the Spanish, helping Mexico to become an independent country. In exchange, the newly independent Mexico would provide the areas of Texas and California to the Dutch, allowing for westward expansion to the Pacific. The colonies would have ultimately united into the country of New Netherland, which would have a separate government but which would still be linked to the Netherlands in much the same way that Canada is linked to Great Britain. Hartford would have grown into a thriving Dutch city where schoolchildren would learn of the British attempt to seize Dutch territory and the death of Thomas Hooker.

Marcella Bush Trevino

Discussion Questions

1. If the Dutch had been able to develop control of the Atlantic coast of North America from Georgia through New England by the late 18th century, what pressures might have developed to lead the Dutch colonies to demand independence?

2. Does the fact that the Dutch colonies in the Caribbean (Aruba, Curaçao, and Surinam) are still colonies in the 21st century suggest that Dutch North America would have remained a colony rather than becoming independent?

3. The Dutch retained slavery in their colonies in the Western Hemisphere until 1863. What pressures might have led to the abolition of slavery earlier if Holland had retained control of the plantation colonies of Virginia and Maryland? Is it likely that the issue of slavery would have divided the Dutch colonies and led to a local civil war as it did in the United States?

4. If the Dutch had retained control of North America but allowed immigration from Britain and other countries of western Europe, what sort of culture would have developed in what is now the United States? What do you think would be the dominant spoken language?

5. A large stimulus to emigration from England in the 18th and early 19th centuries was population pressure and lack of rural employment there.

If the Dutch controlled most of North America, do you think that English emigrants would have sought to move to Dutch North America, or would they have moved to other British colonies overseas?

6. If Holland had controlled an extensive empire in the Western Hemisphere, how do you think this might have affected Dutch neutrality in the First World War? Would the Dutch in that circumstance have been likely to remain neutral (as they did in fact)? What might have led them to join with Germany and Austria-Hungary as a member of the Central Powers, or with Britain and France as one of the Allies?

Bibliography and Further Reading

Bonomi, Patricia U. *A Factious People: Politics and Society in Colonial New York.* New York: Columbia University Press, 1971.

Boxer, Charles R. *The Anglo-Dutch Wars of the Seventeenth Century.* London: HMSO, 1974.

Bush Jr., Sargent. *The Writings of Thomas Hooker.* Madison, WI: University of Wisconsin Press, 1980.

Bushman, Richard L. *From Puritan to Yankee: Character and the Social Order in Connecticut, 1690–1765.* Cambridge, MA: Harvard University Press, 1967.

Cook, Sherburne F. *The Indian Population of New England in the Seventeenth Century.* Berkeley, CA: University of California Press, 1976.

Daniels, Bruce C. *The Connecticut Town.* Middletown, CT: Wesleyan University Press, 1979.

Leach, Douglas Edward. *The Northern Colonial Frontier, 1607–1763.* Albuquerque, NM: University of New Mexico Press, 1966.

Lewis, Thomas R., and John E. Harmon. *Connecticut: A Geography.* Geographies of the United States series. Ingolf Vogeler, general editor. Boulder, CO: Westview Press, 1986.

Nichols, William C. "A Biographical Sketch of the Life of Thomas Hooker," The Soul's Preparation for Christ. Ames, IA: International Outreach, Inc., July 16, 1994, www.intoutreach.org/biog.html (accessed May 22, 2006).

Rink, Oliver A. *Holland on the Hudson: An Economic and Social History of Dutch New York.* Ithaca, NY: Cornell University Press, 1986.

Russell, Howard. *Indian New England before the Mayflower.* Hanover, NH: University Press of New England, 1980.

Salisbury, Neal. *Manitou and Providence: Indians, Europeans, and the Making of New England, 1500–1643.* Oxford: Oxford University Press, 1982.

Selesky, Harold E. *War and Society in Colonial Connecticut.* New Haven, CT: Yale University Press, 1990.

Shuffelton, Frank. *Thomas Hooker 1586–1647.* Princeton, NJ: Princeton University Press, 1977.

Wilson, Charles. *Profit and Power: A Study of England and the Dutch Wars.* New York: Cambridge University Press, 1957.

TURNING POINT

Roger Williams founded Providence, Rhode Island, in 1635 based upon freedom of religion and separation of church and state. What if these views failed to succeed as guiding principles for America?

INTRODUCTION

Roger Williams (c. 1603–1683), the dissident minister who broke away from the Massachusetts Bay Colony to found the Providence settlement in 1635, held ideas on religion and the state that became irreconcilable with those of the governing officials of New England. Williams's arrival to New England was initially saluted with enthusiasm by the governor of the colony, John Winthrop, who defined him as a man of God. Yet Williams's uncompromising stances would soon set him apart from the New England establishment and were perceived as a threat for the Puritan polity that had been so laboriously consolidated in the past 30 years.

The dramatic social, demographic, and economic changes that took place in England during the 16th and 17th centuries led many people to migrate to North America. The doubling of the English population from the 1530s to the 1680s provoked unprecedented competition for food and goods, with the result that landless laborers and small tenant farmers were impoverished. Evicted from their farms by landowners who had required impossible rents or wanted to assimilate small farms into larger ones, these homeless people migrated from the countryside to English cities. Wealthy English citizens and officials were concerned that England was becoming overcrowded and thus encouraged the settlement of North American colonies as a solution to the surplus population.

In turn, the more disadvantaged sectors of English society regarded America as an opportunity to improve their condition. For those who created settlements in New England, however, these motives were inseparable from religious ones. The people who colonized New England were Puritans who believed that the English Reformation had not gone far enough in its renovation of the Church of England. As their name suggests, Puritans wanted to purify the Church of England, abolishing its hierarchies, freeing the church from political interests, and restricting its members to a community of people who were "saved."

Influenced by the ideas of French cleric John Calvin, one of the leaders of the continental Protestant Reformation, Puritans were tolerated under the reign of Elizabeth I (1558–1603). Yet, under James I (1603–1625) and, in particular, under Charles I (1625–1649), the situation changed for the worse, and both kings forbade Puritan clergymen to preach from their pulpits. Charles also refused to call Parliament into session for 11 years because it had a clear Puritan majority. He also appointed William Laud, a well-known opponent of the Puritans, as archbishop of Canterbury, the key post in the Church of England. Although Puritans were fleeing to New England shores predominantly for religious reasons, it is impossible to separate these entirely from economics. In fact, Puritans thought that work and economic success had a moral dimension.

The first group of Puritans came to North America in 1620 aboard the *Mayflower* and founded the Plymouth Colony. Yet the most influential group for the development of New England settlements was the Massachusetts Bay Company, whose members started to arrive in the 1630s. The Massachusetts Bay Colony quickly overshadowed the Plymouth Colony, which was officially incorporated in 1684. Contrary to the Plymouth Colony, the Massachusetts Bay Colony was dissenting but non-separating, wishing to reform the church from within. While still on board the *Arbella*, the ship that was taking them to New England, Winthrop preached the famous sermon A Model of Christian Charity, wherein he theorized the guiding principles to build a balanced Christian community. Winthrop described the immigrants to New England as chosen by God to preserve and show his glory to the entire world. Therefore, the Puritan experiment becomes, in one of the most quoted images of American literature, like a "city upon a hill."

The new settlement would have the eyes of the world scrutinizing its results. If it were not successful, it would give enemies of the Puritan creed arguments to speak against it. According to the Puritans, God had made a covenant with the Puritans when they were chosen to settle New England. Puritans had also made a covenant among themselves, deciding to work together toward the common good rather than their private goals. The type of community described by Winthrop in his sermon was to remain an abstraction rather than becoming a historical reality, and, in his journal, he devoted several passages to the contrasts that arose within the colonies, such as those with Williams himself and Anne Hutchinson (1591–1643).

Puritan New England was based on the close intersection of church and state, the kind of government known as a theocracy, from the Greek words *theos* (god) and *kratein* (to rule). Puritans governed all the northern colonies and imposed Congregationalism as the only official religion. In colonies such as Massachusetts Bay and New Haven, the right to vote was only given to church members. The strong link between church and state provoked the enforcement of rigid moral codes of social conduct. People who had premarital sexual intercourse were publicly humiliated, and those who were thought to have engaged in same-sex relationships were hanged. Idleness and drunkenness could constitute charges at a trial.

KEY CONCEPT   Congregationalism

Congregationalism, which began as a reaction against the Church of England in the 16th and 17th centuries, is a kind of Protestant church structure giving each congregation, or local church, freedom to organize and manage its own affairs. The fundamental principle is that each congregation has as its head Jesus alone and that the various congregations form one common family of God. Congregationalism eliminated bishops and presbyteries in its aspiration to eliminate hierarchies.

Robert Browne first defined the beliefs of the movement in 1582, and the first churches based on them were founded in the early 17th century in England, in Gainsborough and Scrooby. Soon, because of government opposition, these communities had to emigrate to Holland. The members of the Scrooby community who had emigrated to Holland

were part of the *Mayflower* expedition that took Congregationalism to America. Congregationalists were persecuted in England until the outbreak of the English Civil War (1642–1648) between the supporters of the Parliament (which had a clear Puritan majority), led by Oliver Cromwell, and the supporters of King Charles I. In addition to his refusal to call Parliament into session, Charles was regarded with suspicion because of his decision to marry a French Roman Catholic, Henrietta Maria. Catholic plots against Elizabeth I and the Gunpowder Plot during the reign of James I were still alive in people's memory. Cromwell won the war and Charles I was executed in 1649, making England a republic governed by Puritans for 10 years, the so-called Interregnum (literally "between two reigns") or Commonwealth Period.

Puritans believed that the state had the duty to protect the only true church on Earth. So, although they disliked political interference in religious matters, they believed that the church should influence politics and social affairs. The paradox of the Puritan experiment should be apparent: Escaping from England in search of religious freedom, Puritans did not even remotely consider that such freedom could apply to other religions as well. It was over this ground that the controversy with Williams was fought.

TURNING POINT

The turning point in Williams's life was his banishment from the Massachusetts Bay Colony, which occurred in 1635 after a series of religious and social disputes between Williams and Puritan officials. It was at this point that Williams could have given up his ideals of religious freedom, and of keeping church and state separate, to remain within Puritan orthodoxy and avoid banishment.

Soon after his arrival in the New World, Williams made clear that he was not going to conform with the institutions that his fellow Puritans had already established. He claimed that the king had no right to give to others the land that was occupied by Native Americans, and he considered the Charter of the Massachusetts Company as void. He refused a position in a Boston church, horrified because the congregation was not formally separated from the Church of England. Thus Williams put himself in open contrast with the majority of Massachusetts Bay colonists, who were not Separatists. When he took up the position of pastor in the church of Salem, a small village north of Boston, he preached against the right of magistrates to sanction citizens for violations to the first four commandments (you shall have no other gods before me; you shall not make for yourself an idol in the form of anything in heaven above or on the earth beneath or in the waters below; you shall not misuse the name of the Lord your God, for the Lord will not hold anyone guiltless who misuses his name; remember the Sabbath day by keeping it holy).

Williams's plea against legal punishment for the religious matters expressed in the first four commandments conveyed his persuasion that church and state should not be intertwined as they were in the Puritan structure. No court could have jurisdiction over the human conscience. Williams was anticipating the philosopher John Locke who, in 1689, said that it was necessary to separate church and state. Because the Puritan theocracy was based on the idea of the Covenant, Puritan magistrates required colonists to pronounce an oath of loyalty to the community. Yet Williams objected that oaths were a form of worship that could only be addressed to Christ, and that unregenerate men should not be considered part of a community anyway. The oath of allegiance to the church could not be rendered equal to an oath of citizenship in the colony.

All these remarks convinced Puritan authorities that Williams was a threat to the orthodoxy. In addition, when a dispute broke out between the Massachusetts Bay court and the Salem settlement concerning the possession of Marblehead, the court agreed to give Salem the piece of land on condition that they removed Williams as pastor. Williams considered this offer a bribe and denounced the proceeding to all the churches in Massachusetts, demanding the exclusion of the magistrates from church membership. The magistrates and their local churches replied by putting pressure on the Salem church for the removal of Williams, which, in the end, they obtained.

As a direct result of the Marblehead controversy and because of his uncompromising unorthodox beliefs, Williams had to appear several times before the General Court and, in October 1635, he was banished from the colony. The following January, to escape deportation to England, Williams fled from Salem to a Native American village in Narragansett Bay. In the spring of 1636, he was granted land by two chieftains at the head of Narragansett Bay and he founded the settlement of Providence, together with some of his friends and their families.

The area became a refuge for dissenters both from England and from Massachusetts, including Quakers, Jews, and Baptists. By 1643, there were four settlements in the Narragansett Bay region that had been settled by other dissenters, such as Anne Hutchinson. Williams went to England to obtain a patent (1644), uniting the Rhode Island towns of Portsmouth, Newport, and Warwick, with Providence. However, the relationships between the two components of

Disputes with Puritan officials, such as John Winthrop, led to the founding of Rhode Island. (Library of Congress)

The landing of Roger Williams at Rhode Island, greeted by Native Americans in 1636. (Library of Congress)

the colony would always be quite difficult and Williams was unable to resolve the tensions that divided the inhabitants. Disagreement arose between the towns of Providence and Warwick on the one side and the towns of Aquidneck Island on the other. There was also disagreement (on the island) between the followers of John Clarke and those of William Coddington. In 1651, while in England, Coddington managed to secure from the council of state a commission to rule both Rhode and Conanicut islands. This arrangement was strongly disapproved by Williams and his followers because it seemed to involve a federation with Massachusetts and Connecticut and a consequent threat to the liberty of conscience, not only on the islands but also in Providence and Warwick, which would be left unprotected.

The central point in Williams's life was his expulsion from Massachusetts. This event became for him the example of how intolerance as well as the pernicious unity of church and state could violate Christ's teachings. Williams constantly reminded Puritan theocrats of the evil they had done to him, at the same time considering his banishment as something to be proud of. He engaged in several theological disputes and was not intimidated by the importance of his opponents. A particularly bitter exchange occurred between Williams and the leading Boston minister of the time, John Cotton, first teacher of the Church of Boston.

His most famous book, *The Bloudy Tenent of Persecution* (1644), makes no mention of his personal experience but it is clear that that experience shaped his discussion of the evils of intolerance and oppression. Williams stated, according to *The Complete Writings of Roger Williams*, that "God requireth not an uniformity of religion to be enacted and enforced in any civil state; which enforced uniformity (sooner or later) is the greatest occasion of civil wars. . . . It is the will and command of God that . . . a permission of the most Paganish, Jewish, Turkish, or Anti-Christian consciences and worships be granted to all men in all nations and countries."

IN CONTEXT   Religious Persecution in America

Puritans were persecuted in Europe throughout the 16th and 17th centuries. Yet, once in the New World, they behaved no differently from their Old World persecutors, theorizing the need for a single religion to be present in their colonies. Puritans explicitly declared themselves against toleration of religious difference, expelling dissenters from their settlements. People who disregarded banishment and returned to their homes within the Puritan colony could face capital punishment.

This was the case of Mary Dyer, a dissenter turned Quaker, who was arrested several times before being banished for spreading Quakerism. When she defied the ban and returned to New England, she was hanged. Persecution of Quakers was not limited to New England, but was also widespread in Virginia. As Thomas Jefferson was to write in his *Notes on the State of Virginia* (1787), Quakers had "cast their eyes on these new countries as asylum of civil and religious freedom; but they found them free only for the reigning sect." To Jefferson, it was a mere coincidence that no capital execution had taken place in Virginia. Quakers found refuge in Rhode Island and, from the 1680s, in Pennsylvania, which was founded by the Quaker William Penn.

In colonial America, legal restrictions against Jews greatly varied from state to state. The early

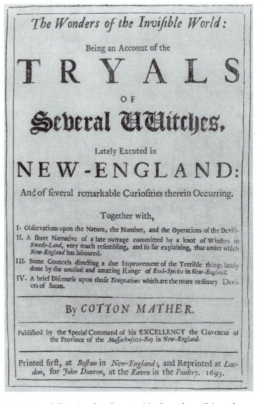

A 1693 publication by Cotton Mather describing the Salem Witch Trials. (Library of Congress)

Williams became fiercely committed to the ideas of freedom of conscience and the separation of church and state. It was not for other men to judge on matters of religion and conscience, only God could know the form of worship that men should practice. Human knowledge in the area cannot be complete. To Williams, Christians especially were to avoid persecuting other religious creeds. Throughout his life, Williams was committed to tolerance. His type of more personal religion came closer to the religious ideals held by American Enlightenment thinkers such as Benjamin Franklin and Thomas Jefferson than to Williams's contemporaries. Yet, when Quakers were gaining influence in the settlement, Williams attacked the teachings of George Fox, the founder of the Quaker movement, through the pamphlet *George Fox Digg'd out of His Burrowes* (1676). This raised doubts about his own adherence to the principle of freedom of conscience that he so forcefully advocated in his writings.

Williams's relationships with Native Americans were generally shaped by mutual friendship and understanding, although Williams found it hard to accept the polytheism of the Algonquian natives. Williams respected Native Americans and tried to treat them as equals, asserting that land should be bought fairly from them and not taken from them by "divine right."

IN CONTEXT   *Religious Persecution in America (Continued)*

Jews to arrive in America starting in 1654 were of Spanish, Portuguese, and Dutch descent and mainly settled in New Amsterdam. Although their condition improved when the colony passed from the Dutch to the English in 1664, becoming New York, the only New England colony that allowed a permanent Jewish community in the 17th century was Rhode Island. This was established in Newport, where the Touro Synagogue was built in 1773.

When the English Civil War began in 1642, the condition of Catholics in the American colonies became particularly difficult. That very same year, Virginia passed a law that prohibited Catholics to settle in the colony and was followed by Massachusetts Bay 5 years later. The Quaker state of Pennsylvania was more tolerant to Catholics. However, the first bishop for American Catholics was not appointed before 1790, 156 years after the first arrivals of Catholic missionaries.

Puritans also persecuted fellow Puritans. The most dramatic instance of this type was the Salem witchcraft trials in the Massachusetts village of Salem in 1692. This was a particularly difficult time for American colonies because the new British sovereigns, William and Mary, believed that tighter control should be exercised on the colonies. New England was also the target of attacks by the French who had allied themselves with several Native American tribes.

When a group of girls from Salem (now Danvers) started to have fits and convulsions, the doctor who examined them arrived at the conclusion that they were involved in witchcraft. Puritans considered witchcraft a pact with the devil to acquire evil powers; it was thus condemned as a sin and a crime. The girls in turn accused a black slave, Tituba, and two other women, Sarah Good and Sarah Osborne, as the people who had bewitched them. Although she initially maintained her innocence, Tituba eventually confessed that she was a witch like Good and Osborne. The village was seized by a climate of hysteria and paranoia, with every citizen becoming a potential suspect. Many of them were formally accused, tried, and hanged just on the basis of gossip. Those who refused to confess were executed as well. During the 10 months of trials that followed the confessions and the accusations, 19 people died because of their refusal to admit being witches. The trials ended when charges started to be made also against the most respected members of the community, and the colony's ministers expressed reservations on how the trials had been handled. The tragic events of the Salem trials inspired the 20th-century playwright Arthur Miller in his work *The Crucible*, where the trials become an allegory for the Communist witch hunt of the 1950s.

However, his banishment sentence did not mention his attitude toward natives because it was too antithetical to that of the Puritan establishment.

Since his arrival in the North American colonies, Williams wrote, according to *The Complete Writings of Roger Williams*, that his "soul's desire was to do the natives good, and to that end to have their language." His *A Key to the Language of America* (1643) described the customs and the languages of Native Americans and his renewed interest in their conversion to Christianity. Yet their conversion was not Williams's primary interest; he claimed that defining natives as "heathen" was "improperly sinful" and "unchristianly." For certain aspects, Williams found that native societies respected Christian values more than did Puritan communities: "There are no beggars amongst them, nor fatherless children unprovided for."

George Fox, founder of the Quaker movement, clashed with Roger Williams. (Edward S. Curtis/Library of Congress)

IN CONTEXT   Indian Wars

The phrase *Indian Wars* refers to the series of conflicts that originated between the United States and Native Americans from the colonial era to the Wounded Knee Massacre and the closing of the frontier in 1890. These conflicts, often overlooked in American history, caused the destruction of entire tribes of American natives, the shattering of their ways of life, and their removal to reservations. Although commonly used, the term is considered misleading because it conflates all Native Americans into a single entity, whereas, in fact, they were organized as separate peoples. Besides, the phrase simplifies the complex racial interactions that took place during these conflicts because native peoples often formed coalitions with whites against other Native Americans. The two most significant conflicts in Williams's time were the Pequot War and King Philip's War.

The Pequot War was the first major conflict of the Colonial era and broke out over the Pequots' attacks against several Massachusetts fur traders. The retaliation by Massachusetts was considered the beginning of the war that split the loyalties of Native American peoples, with the Mohican, Narragansett, and Metoac tribes siding with the colonists. The war ended with the Treaty of Hartford (1638), which stipulated the distribution of Pequot

Native American societies were also praised by Williams for being based on consensus rather than coercion. Williams ceased soon after his arrival to call native leaders kings, as the colonists had disparagingly done. He also disputed, according to *The Complete Writings of Roger Williams*, the widely held opinion that people of European descent were intellectually superior to Native Americans: "Nature knows no difference between Europeans and Americans in blood, birth, bodies, &c. God having of one blood made all mankind, *Acts 17*." This passage anticipates the belief held by American revolutionaries that "All men are created equal, and endowed by their Creator with certain inalienable rights," as stated in the Declaration of Independence.

Williams enjoyed the friendship of several native chiefs and he became a point of reference for the relations between colonists and Native Americans. Because of his relationships with natives, Williams was often used as mediator for commercial exchanges or to settle the conflicts that often arose between colonists and Native Americans. He was particularly useful during the Pequot War (1637) when he prevented an alliance between the Pequot and the Narragansetts and Mohicans against the very people who had exiled him. His help was fundamental in limiting the size of the Native American coalition, thus allowing the colonists to win the war. Yet Williams did not succeed in keeping the Narragansetts out of King Philip's War (1675–1676). After the war broke out, Williams met native chief Metacom to persuade him to stop the war, which could have tragic consequences for his people. The chief refused and the Providence settlement was attacked, forcing Williams to fight back.

ACTUAL HISTORY

Rhode Island's royal charter of 1663 guaranteed, according to *Master Roger Williams: A Biography* by Ola Elizabeth Winslow, all residents the right to "freely and fully have and enjoy his and their own judgments and

IN CONTEXT   *Indian Wars (Continued)*

prisoners as slaves to the tribes allied with colonists and of the Pequot lands to the Puritans. The war made the colonists so powerful that all native opposition was erased for an entire generation.

King Philip's War (1675–1676), from the Christian name given to the leader of the Wampanoag natives, Metacom, was instead a general Native American uprising to stop the continuous expansion of English colonists in America. By 1671, about 40,000 people of European descent lived in New England. The native population, double that of the Europeans before the Pequot War, was now about 20,000. European farms and pastures were endangering native cultivations. Many colonies came

under attack, including the Rhode Island settlements of Providence and Warwick, which caused great disappointment to the aging Williams. In the first phases of the war, natives managed to cause severe losses to the colonists, yet, in the spring of 1676, the fortunes of war turned to the whites, who were able to receive more regular supplies and who had broken the Native American front by allying themselves to the Mohicans. At the colonists' request, Britain also intervened to protect its colony. When Metacom was killed in August 1676, the war ended. King Philip's War caused the extinction of many Native American tribes, including the Narragansett, who had had so much contact with Williams.

consciences in matters of religious concernment." No person within Rhode Island "shall be in any wise molested, punished, disquieted, or called into question, for difference in opinion in matters of religion" that did not threaten the existence of the colony. When the college of Rhode Island (later to become Brown University) was founded in 1764, its charter assured that no religious test would ever be forced upon its academic community. Contrary to the Puritans who wanted religious freedom for themselves, the president of Brown, Francis Wayland, observed in the 19th century that Williams wanted it for the whole of humanity.

In the spirit of Williams, Rhode Island thus became a safe refuge for those persecuted for religious matters. It was also the first colony to pass a law to declare slavery illegal in 1652. America's oldest Jewish synagogue was built in Newport as well as the oldest Quaker Yearly Meeting. Williams's ideas would be more influential for the development of the American republic than those of the people who had banished him. When John Cotton commented on Williams's exile, he ironically explained that, in fact, Williams had been "enlarged," more than banished, to outside the colony, where he could have more space to do what he wanted.

What is certain is that, throughout American history and politics, Williams's legacy has certainly grown, as Edwin S. Gaustad has documented in several studies. Although his radical ideas may seem more appropriate for future eras than for his own, Williams's influence on American life was clear from the 17th century itself. Some historians have gone as far as claiming that Williams's arguments provided the theoretical basis for the philosophers of Europe and, through them, for the authors of the Declaration of Independence and France's revolutionary rhetoric.

The language of the Rhode Island charter of 1663 influenced other colonies, starting with New Jersey and Carolina. Gradually the threatening language of religious freedom and separation between church and state started to become more familiar and less frightening. Just a year later than the Rhode Island charter, New Jersey adopted a charter that not only contained the same legitimation of religious freedom but used the very same words of the Rhode Island one. In 1665, it was Carolina's turn to echo the words of the Rhode Island charter. In the 1680s, Pennsylvania was founded on the principle of religious liberty by a Quaker who had experienced persecution firsthand, William Penn.

The period immediately after the American Revolution witnessed an unprecedented dissemination of the idea of freedom of conscience also, thanks to the vast use of John Locke's ideas. Virginia was the state to start the debate that opposed the prominent figure of the American Revolution Patrick Henry (1736–1799) to the future fourth president of the United States, James Madison (1751–1836). Henry claimed that Christianity should be made the official religion of Virginia, although the other religions would be tolerated as well. Contrary to this view, Madison wrote in his petition A Memorial and Remonstrance that the state should not choose a religion to be its official one. In support of his argument, he invoked the torrents of blood that were shed in the Old World because of the attempts by different states to impose an official religion.

Madison then went on to claim in A Memorial and Remonstrance that the solution to religious tensions was "equal and complete liberty." Looking at "the contradictory opinions of rulers in all ages," Madison also concluded that state officials were not always the best of judges when it came to religious matters. Religion should never be used as the "engine of civil policy," otherwise America would become a copy of the English tyranny, which it had successfully defeated. On the contrary, Madison's America is described in terms that are often used to describe Williams's Providence settlement: a country that would protect "the persecuted and the oppressed of every nation and religion."

In 1786, Thomas Jefferson succeeded in having his Bill for Establishing Religious Freedom passed by Virginia legislators. Building on the Rhode Island charter, the law both prohibited all forms of persecution for religious beliefs and ordered that no one could be forced to practice another religion other than his or her own. Jefferson and Madison received strong support from Quakers, Baptists, and Methodists. As Edwin S. Gaustad has pointed out in Roger Williams, at a crucial moment in American history, "the heirs of Roger Williams joined with the heirs of European rationalism, or Enlightenment, to write religious liberty firmly into the legal structure of Virginia."

The Constitutional Convention in Philadelphia in 1787 officially stated for the whole nation that civil government and religion should stay separate. Article VI read that "No religious test shall ever be required as a qualification to any office or public trust under the United States." America would not elect a privileged faith for their citizens to follow. Adopting the Rhode Island model, the new nation would ask its citizens to pledge their allegiance "in civil things only."

Rhode Island, however, considered this statement too timid and refused to ratify the Constitution until 1790, when it was put under extreme pressure by the federal government's threat to sever commercial relations. Liberty of conscience in religious matters would be more explicitly affirmed in the first 10 amendments, also known as America's Bill of Rights, which were ratified in 1791. The first amendment started unequivocally with the prohibition for Congress to make a law regarding the "establishment of religion or prohibiting the free exercise thereof." So no official national church could be established in America, and minor religious groups such as Jews, Catholics, or Baptists could no longer be persecuted. This amendment gave all religious denominations the right to make proselytism for their churches.

The first scholar to revive Williams's reputation was the Baptist pastor Isaac Backus, who, in his *History of New England* (1777), gathered many important letters and rare documents of Williams. Backus thought it was vital to recover Williams's ideas and principles at a time of profound change for the country. No other individual contemporary of Williams had acted "so consistently and steadily upon right principles about government and liberty as Mr. Williams did." Backus wholeheartedly adopted Williams's views on the separation between church and state, writing that, when they "are separate, the effects are happy, and they do not at all interfere with each other: but where they have been confounded together, no tongue nor pen can fully describe the mischiefs that have ensued."

Backus's own intellectual biography resembles Williams's, in that he too had to fight the authorities of Massachusetts for his own right to religious liberty. In spite of what the First Amendment had established, Massachusetts and other New England states, except, of course, Rhode Island, still required citizens to pay taxes to the Congregational Church. Backus, as a Baptist, could be exempted if he applied for a special certificate. Yet, following Williams's ideas, he objected that the state should only look after civil affairs and compared this religious tax to the odious British tax on tea, which had given rise to the Boston Tea Party and the American Revolution. Massachusetts did not abolish this tax before 1833, and Connecticut did so just a few years before, in 1818.

Struggles for the recognition of Christianity as the official national religion continued throughout the 19th century. The National Reform Association, for example, was established in 1864 with the explicit intention of adding to the Constitution a preamble that would define the Christian character of the national government. The efforts of the National Reform Association were destined to fail, whereas the reputation of Williams increased. In his monumental, 12-volume *History of the United States* (1834), New England historian George Bancroft described Williams as a modern social and political thinker, the first to have theorized the establishment of civil government on the basis of the liberty of conscience. Educated at Harvard University, the cultural repository of the Puritan orthodoxy, Bancroft called for the name of Williams to be "preserved in universal history as one who advanced moral and political science" and as a benefactor of the human race. Rhode Island was praised too as a state small in size but large in those principles that guided its earliest institutions. The complete rehabilitation of Williams on the part of Massachusetts occurred in the 1936 when a legislative bill revoked the sentence of banishment of the General Court of Massachusetts Bay Colony.

Some historians have noted that Rhode Island lies at the periphery of New England. In response to this marginalization, Rhode Islanders have developed an alternative narrative of national origins, one that does not consider the arrival of the Pilgrims to Plymouth as the starting point for the new nation. In this alternative myth of origins, it is the persecuted Williams and his founding of Providence that mark the birth of American civic and religious liberty. From Rhode Island such liberty would spread to the whole country.

ALTERNATE HISTORY

To avoid being banished from Massachusetts, Williams would have had to renounce his ideal of liberty of conscience and his firm conviction that church and state should be two separate entities. Had he done so, early American thought would have lacked a formulation of two principles that, as the actual history shows, were founding beliefs for the American Constitution. Williams's banishment from Massachusetts became the central event in his life and the main reason for his writings, which theorized freedom of religion and the division of church and state. Without Williams to secure a royal charter, Rhode Island would not have set the example for other colonies to follow on freedom of religion and church/state separation. The colony would have probably been annexed by Massachusetts Bay and would not have become a safe refuge for those persecuted for their religious faiths.

Had the Providence settlement failed, America might not be the religious pluralist nation that it is today. Fundamental social conquests that we almost take for granted, such as divorce and abortion, may not have materialized had America remained a theocracy. Movements for the rights of women as well as gays, lesbians, transsexuals, and other so-called minorities may not ever have happened. The quintessentially American rhetoric of individual rights and the pursuit of happiness may have been obscured in favor of one centering instead on duty, responsibility, and community.

When compared to religious establishments in western Europe, the unofficial churches in the United States attract more active participants than state churches. The plurality of choices has prompted a high degree of competition among the different churches that has been one of the major reasons for growth. Over 200 religious groups are active in the United States, and the Web site of the organization Americans United for the Separation of Church and State claims that it is precisely the separation of church and state that makes religion strong. When religious institutions are dependent on government support, they lose their vitality, whereas relying on voluntary contributions makes churches more active. In addition, government contributions may make church leaders more reluctant to voice their opinions on moral and ethical matters because they may not want to engage in disputes with the body that funds them.

Without the separation of church and state, American society may have turned out profoundly different from what it is today. Most of the rulings of the Supreme Court headed by Chief Justice Earl Warren, which modernized America in the 1960s, would be unthinkable if church and state coincided. Because of the division of church and state, public education cannot enforce a particular creed or belief. The division between secular and religious institutions was at the base of the Supreme Court rulings that outlawed required prayers and Bible reading in public schools. Profoundly controversial at the time, these rulings did not ban voluntary Bible readings but prohibited schools from having compulsory devotional activities. Sexual education in school and campaigns for AIDS prevention in schools may also have been endangered if religious officials were also influential in making laws. Particularly the most conservative sectors of religious organizations condemn the use of condoms as encouraging sexual promiscuity. The only allowed prevention of AIDS is abstention from sexual intercourse.

Many important rulings of the Supreme Court could not have had a tangible basis under a theocratic form of government. If the views of the state had been the same as those of the church on the matter of contraception, *Griswald v. Connecticut* (1965) may have had a very different outcome. The ruling established that a state law prohibiting contraception by married couples was unconstitutional because it breached "a marital right of privacy." The same constitutional right of privacy was a decisive factor in the *Roe v. Wade* ruling (1973) that decriminalized abortion in the states that had laws making it illegal. The ruling read that the "right of privacy . . . is broad enough to encompass a woman's decision whether or not to terminate her pregnancy."

This right was reaffirmed and expanded upon in *Planned Parenthood of Southeastern Pennsylvania v. Casey* (1992). The ruling stated that the suffering of a pregnant woman deciding to abort "is too intimate and personal for the State to insist . . . upon its own vision of the woman's role, however dominant that vision has been in the course of our history and our culture." The state cannot use its power to impose traditional sex roles on women. For a state that is separate from the church, there is no natural role for women to take on. Landmark rulings such as *Griswald v. Connecticut* and *Roe v. Wade* are in stark contrast to two core principles of Christian churches; namely, that the only allowed form of sex is monogamous and between a married couple and that human life begins at conception. The fact that abortion and contraception are still, to a certain extent, taboos, and social conventions inhibit their practice, should make us even more aware of the importance for these issues of state/church separation. The discrepancy between law and accepted practice is due to the influence of religious institutions, and, were these institutions in charge of making laws, such a discrepancy would surely be solved with a clear ban on abortion and contraception. Still, in the 1960s, the Supreme Court declared that books, magazines, and films could not be forbidden as obscene unless they could be described as "utterly without redeeming social values."

Although divorce was recognized by Puritans in certain limited cases (adultery, long absence), the resolution of most cases in Puritan colonies reflected the gender hierarchy, favoring men and punishing women. Divorce laws became more favorable to women as church and state became increasingly separate and under the pressure of the women's movement. During the Revolutionary era, courts became more receptive to cases of divorce filed by women on the grounds of adultery, whereas reasons to petition for divorce were extended to include intemperance and cruelty. Cruelty went on to become the major reason to file for divorce, and its definition was modified during the 19th century to comprise mental cruelty. During the 20th century, no-fault divorce, which is granted without identifying wrongdoing by either party, was introduced. If the church had maintained legislative power, it is difficult to imagine these changes having been implemented.

The strict moral code of Puritans allowed little rights for those who were tried. Crimes were sins and thus subject to the unquestionable law of God. In the theocratic society of Puritan New England, punishments were given following Old Testament rules. The separation of church and state allowed the Supreme Court to transform the criminal justice system throughout the 1960s. In 1963, *Gideon v. Wainwright* established the right of the poor charged with criminal offences to have a lawyer appointed by the state. A year later, *Escobedo v. Illinois* allowed the accused to remain silent during interrogation and granted the right to counsel. Finally, in *Miranda v. Arizona* (1966), the court decreed that police had to inform suspects that they had the rights sanctioned by the two previous rulings and that any statements they made could be used against them.

Were church and state not separate, the American tax system would also be quite different. As a result of the theocratic system, colonial Americans had to pay taxes to support the churches favored by the state. The separation of church and state meant freedom for all religious denominations to raise funds for their institutions and for citizens to decide which church to finance. Furthermore, religious bodies are granted tax exemption as long as they do not engage in partisan politics. Although they are free to speak out on public issues such as abortion, gay rights, and euthanasia, churches cannot explicitly endorse one of two opposing political candidates without losing their tax exemption.

Without the example and the pressure exercised by men like Williams and by states such as Rhode Island, America today would probably resemble the nation designed in the manifestos of the Religious Right. The conservative groups that come under this common heading today oppose the separation of religious institutions and the state and call for a return of America to its Puritan past. They generally support sodomy laws to criminalize homosexual activity, creationism, abstinence programs, and school prayer while opposing euthanasia, same-sex marriage, abortion, feminism, sex education, secularism, and the exclusive teaching of evolutionary theory. That the separation of church and state in America is still a controversial issue is witnessed by the contrasting rulings of the Supreme Court in June 2005. The court upheld a 6-foot-high Ten Commandments monument on the grounds of the Texas Capitol, while judging that framed copies of the Commandments on the walls of two Kentucky courthouses were unconstitutional.

Luca Prono

Discussion Questions

1. If Roger Williams had not set the precedent for freedom of conscience, and each colony and then later each state had set an established state religion, how would it have affected U.S. history? Would the United States have been able to hold together as one nation, or would the different official religions have prevented unification in the period of the American Revolution?

2. If the concept of religious toleration or acceptance of nonofficial religions had never taken hold in North America, what would be different about the U.S. Constitution?

3. If the United States had organized around a single official religion for all of the states, how would that make life different in the 21st century?

4. How would the map of New England be different if Roger Williams had never established his separate colony and if Rhode Island had not been organized?

5. Does the separation of church and state make for more religion or for less religion in American life?

Bibliography and Further Reading

Americans United for the Separation of Church and State, http://www.au.org (accessed May 22, 2006).

Christian Coalition of America, http://www.cc.org (accessed May 22, 2006).

Delbanco, Andrew, ed. *Writing New England: An Anthology from the Puritans to the Present.* Cambridge, MA: Harvard University Press, 2001.

Delbanco, Andrew. *The Puritan Origins of the American Self.* New Haven, CT: Yale University Press, 1975.

Diamond, Sara. *Roads to Dominion: Right-Wing Movements and Political Power in the United States.* New York: Guilford, 1995.

"Famous American Trials. The Salem Witchcraft Trials of 1692," http://www.law.umkc.edu/faculty/projects/ftrials/salem/salem.htm (accessed May 22, 2006).

Forster, Stephen. *The Long Argument: English Puritanism and the Shaping of New England Culture, 1570–1700.* Chapel Hill, NC: University of North Carolina Press, 1991.

Gaustad, Edwin S. *Liberty of Conscience: Roger Williams in America.* Grand Rapids, MI: William B. Eerdmans, 1991.

Gaustad, Edwin S. *Roger Williams (Lives and Legacies).* Oxford: Oxford University Press, 2005.

Gilpin, W. Clark. *The Millenarian Piety of Roger Williams.* Chicago: University of Chicago Press, 1970.

Hall, Timothy L. *Separating Church and State: Roger Williams and Religious Liberty.* Urbana, IL: University of Illinois Press, 1998.

Juergensmeyer, Mark. *The New Cold War? Religious Nationalism Confronts the Secular State.* Berkeley, CA: University of California Press, 1993.

Martin, William. *With God on Our Side: The Rise of the Religious Right in America.* New York: Broadway Books, 1996.

Miller, Perry. *Roger Williams: His Contribution to the American Tradition.* Indianapolis: Bobbs-Merrill, 1953.

Morgan, Edmund S. *Roger Williams: The Church and the State.* New York: Harcourt, Brace and World, 1967.

Peterson, Mark A. *The Price of Redemption: The Spiritual Economy of Puritan New England.* Stanford, CA: Stanford University Press, 1997.

Library of Congress, "Religion and the Founding of the New Republic," http://www.loc.gov/exhibits/religion/ (accessed May 23, 2006).

Settle, Mary Lee. *I, Roger Williams: A Novel*. New York: W. W. Norton, 2002.

Faith and Values, "The Moral Majority Coalition," http://www.faithandvalues.us (accessed August 2005).

Theocracywatch, http://www.theocracywatch.org (accessed May 22, 2006).

Williams, Roger. *The Complete Writings of Roger Williams*. 7 vols. New York: Russell and Russell, 1963.

Winslow, Ola Elizabeth. *Master Roger Williams: A Biography*. New York: Macmillan, 1957.

TURNING POINT

John Wheelwright established Exeter, New Hampshire, in 1638, after being banished from Massachusetts. What if Wheelwright had found more tolerance among the Puritans?

INTRODUCTION

In January 1637, Puritan clergyman John Wheelwright offended the religious sentiments of the General Court of Massachusetts by the timing and contents of one of his sermons. After being pronounced guilty of sedition—rebellion against the government—and contempt, he was banished from the state. In 1638, he and a group of friends founded the town of Exeter, New Hampshire, and, for 5 years, he served as the minister for that town's residents.

Wheelwright was born in Lincolnshire, England, in 1592 or shortly thereafter to a financially comfortable yeoman, Robert Wheelwright, and his wife, Katherine, a woman from the well-respected Marbury clan. Wheelwright was graduated from the University of Cambridge in 1614 with a degree of A.B., and in 1618 with a degree of A.M. Oliver Cromwell, a college friend, noted Wheelwright's athletic ability, both in wrestling and in football.

On November 8, 1621, Wheelwright married Marie, daughter of Reverend Thomas Storey (or Storre), and he also took his own religious orders. In 1623, his father-in-law died and Wheelwright replaced him, serving as vicar of Bilsby, a town near Alford, until 1633.

Records show the birth of four children: John (1622); Thomas (1624); William (1627); and Susannah (1628). His wife died the following year and was buried on May 18, 1629. In 1630, Wheelwright remarried, this time to Mary Hutchinson. They had three children during their years in England: Katherine (1630), Mary (born and died in 1632), and Elizabeth (1633).

This was a time of great turbulence in England because passionate disagreements about religious doctrine broke out between those of the traditional Church of England and those called Puritans. It is important to note that Puritans did not necessarily call themselves by that term; rather, it was a term of derision foisted upon those who, in general, believed in:

- Further separation from the religious traditions and hierarchical government of the Roman Catholic Church
- Simplified worship, without elaborate music, rituals, festivals or religious clothing

- Their ability to personally interpret the Scriptures with the help of a lay preacher but without the need for governmentally appointed church services or clergy
- Strict Sabbath observances

As just one example, Puritans objected to the "surplice" worn by English clergy; the surplice was a white, loose fitting garment draped over the black clerical cassock. They objected to this garment because it was not mentioned in the Bible and because it was traditionally worn by Pre-Reformation Roman Catholics, whom the Puritans considered idolatrous. One Puritan woman broke into a church in Oxford before a service began and she tossed the surplices into a heap of dung. Another woman, accompanied by the town clerk and his wife, marched into a Litchfield cathedral and marred the garments with a bucket of pitch.

In 1633, those who believed in the traditional and ceremonial aspects of church worship gained a powerful advocate. That year, William Laud became archbishop. As a man who strongly believed in the sanctity of rituals, he punished those who objected to them, whether the rebellions were acts of vandalism or whether they were preachings or writings that Laud believed violated traditional beliefs of the Church of England.

According to Judge Smith, a clash between Laud and John Wheelwright occurred. Laud suspended Wheelwright from the Church of England, or "silenced" him. This left Wheelwright with two reasonable choices: to continue preaching and, most likely, end up in prison, or to emigrate.

Although taking away the pastor's livelihood and stature in the community was a punishment, Wheelwright was spared the full brunt of Laud's wrath. In 1636, Laud had William Prynne, Henry Burton, and John Bastwick tortured and imprisoned for espousing beliefs contrary to his own. On April 18, 1638, John Lilburne, who had distributed Puritan literature, was whipped at the cart-tail from the Fleet prison to the Palace Yard, Westminster; he then stood at the pillory and was afterward imprisoned.

William Laud, who suspended John Wheelwright, or "silenced" him. (Library of Congress)

After Wheelwright's suspension from the Church of England, he chose to leave for Boston, Massachusetts, to escape persecution endured in England and to find, he hoped, religious freedom. He and his family, including his widowed mother-in-law, Susanna, arrived at the colony on May 26, 1636, entering a community where ministers controlled every aspect of its citizens' lives. Wheelwright and his wife were admitted to the local church on June 12, 1636.

Wheelwright and Mary were also greeted by Anne Hutchinson, the wife of Mary's brother William. Anne was a woman involved in the heart of religious controversies in Massachusetts. She believed in the covenant of grace rather than the covenant of works, proclaiming that faith alone was needed for salvation. The covenant of grace placed the ultimate responsibility of salvation upon the individual, rather than on the church. Because the church, under Hutchinson's philosophy, was no longer needed to judge the acts of the citizens, this belief minimized the role of clergy in the theocratic colonies and was therefore unpopular with religious authorities.

Those who believed in the covenant of works called Hutchinson an antinomian heretic. This term was, however, incorrectly used; *antinomian* means "a belief that Christians are not bound by moral law," according to Winnfred King Rugg in *Unafraid: A Life of Anne Hutchinson*. In fact, what Hutchinson and Wheelwright espoused was an individual's freedom of religious belief. "What the Antinomians really taught," explains Hutchinson biographer Rugg, "was that holiness consisted in a state of heart, not in good works. They upheld a Covenant of Grace based on a direct revelation in the individual soul of God's grace and love, rather than a Covenant of Works. This did not discourage a decent life, observance of the Sabbath, sobriety of dress and manner, but it did put all such good works in a subordinate place as the fruits rather than the proof of a believing heart."

Wheelwright probably attended meetings at Hutchinson's home, where she and others would discuss these doctrines; it was said that 60 to 80 people attended these weekly discussion groups.

On October 25, 1636, religious authorities called for a theological conclave to discuss the Antinomian Heresy. Both Wheelwright and fellow pastor John Cotton were questioned, and both were exonerated.

Some wished for Wheelwright to become the "second teacher" of the church in Boston, but John Winthrop—a man who had served as the first governor of Massachusetts and who still held great stature in the Massachusetts Bay Colony—expressed reservations. Winthrop praised Wheelwright's godliness but stated that some of his beliefs might cause division in the congregation. Because of the lack of support from Winthrop, rather than serving as a minister in Boston, Wheelwright became pastor of the church at Mount Wollaston, a town later called Braintree and then Quincy.

At this point, definitive religious lines had been drawn. On the one hand, there were those who agreed with Hutchinson's views about the covenant of grace; those included Wheelwright and John Cotton, and the current governor, Henry Vane. On the other hand, there were those who believed in the covenant of works and who labeled as heretics those who disagreed with them. Because this group included former governor John Winthrop, a man who must have been humiliated when his tenure as governor ended by Henry Vane's successful election, the fight was about more than just religious doctrine; it was also becoming quite political.

TURNING POINT

In her critical essay, "Anne Hutchinson and the Economics of Antinomian Selfhood in Colonial New England," Michelle Burnham states that New England's Antinomian Controversy was the "earliest large-scale social, political, and theological crisis in the Massachusetts Bay Colony." John Wheelwright—who had fled England to escape religious persecution— found himself in the hub of that crisis.

Although Wheelwright was exonerated of antinomian heresies by the court in 1636, the mere fact that he was questioned had placed doubts in the minds of many about his strict and faithful adherence to Puritan doctrines. He nevertheless continued to minister to his congregation in Mount Wollaston.

In January 1637, religious authorities declared a "Solemn Fast Day" to be observed throughout the colony. One reason for this fast was to focus on the increasingly divisive nature of the debates between those labeled as antinomians and those who were considered "legalists." On this day of fasting, Wheelwright was invited to preach the sermon in Boston, where he had recently been rejected as its second teacher. Notably, he was asked to speak as a "private brother," which, to Wheelwright, may have served as a barbed reminder that he had not passed muster to minister in Boston.

Wheelwright's biographer, John Heard Jr., describes in *John Wheelwright: 1592–1679* the sermon as an "earnest exhortation, freely interlarded with Scriptural references in which neither chapter nor verse is omitted, of a good, fearless, and ardent clergyman. . . . Because of the far-reaching results which came thereof, this sermon has been the object of much study and discussion. The consensus of opinion appears to be that it contained nothing of an objectionable nature." Nevertheless, some Legalists did find his imagery objectionable and offensive, and this sermon did nothing to reduce the passionate debate or mitigate the increasing distrust among religious factions of the Massachusetts Bay Colony.

The particulars the Legalists objected to centered on Wheelwright's use of symbols such as swords and firebrands; they claimed that he intended their inclusion to promote further dissension. Although these icons were neither new nor unusual, the heated theological climate of the day caused them to stand out in Wheelwright's text, and they were examined closely. In March 1637, the court summoned Wheelwright to appear before the bench. He was handed a physical copy of his sermon and he was asked to accept this document as an accurate representation of his words, but he declined to do so; instead, he offered up his own copy, which differed from what they had presented to him.

At that point, the court temporarily adjourned. Shortly thereafter, more than 40 influential members of the community requested that future hearings about Wheelwright's pronouncements be held publicly; this petition was refused and questioning continued to occur behind closed doors. When Wheelwright asked the name of his accuser, he was told that his own sermon served as the accuser. After that, Wheelwright refused to answer any more questions. The court now faced untenable alternatives; if they dropped all charges, the Legalist movement would suffer, but if they convicted the minister without some appearance of proof, they feared that the antinomians might revolt. So, they decided to continue the trial in a public venue, as earlier requested. Not surprisingly, the courtroom was packed.

Members of the court, according to Heard in *John Wheelwright: 1592–1679,* repeatedly questioned Wheelwright about one certain phrase that he had used: "those under a covenant of works." Was Wheelwright, they wanted to know, referring to ministers? Each time, Wheelwright responded by saying that, "if he were shown any that walked in such a way as he had described to be a covenant of works, them did he mean." The court also persisted in an attempt to show that Wheelwright considered all who disagreed with him to be heretics, but the minister remained respectful throughout the trial and did not denigrate other clergymen.

Because members of this Massachusetts court acted as both prosecutor and judge, and because Wheelwright presented his own defense, he had little chance of acquittal. Furthermore, according to Heard in *John Wheelwright: 1592–1679,* the court framed the question in a convoluted manner: "Whether, by that which you have heard concerning Master Wheelwright's sermon, and that which was witnessed concerning him, ye do conceive that the ministers in this country do walk in and teach, such a way of salvation and evidencing thereof as he describeth and accounteth to be a covenant of works?" Thus phrased, Wheelwright was on trial for the sins of all clergy, rather than for his own actions, words, or beliefs.

Not unexpectedly, Wheelwright was found guilty of sedition and contempt of civil authorities, and a judge stated that, although the court had "appointed the fast as a means of reconciliation of differences . . . he [Wheelwright] purposely set himself to kindle them," according to Heard. Some of those who had not voted for a guilty verdict asked to have their names recorded as opposing it, but that request was denied. Some Legalists asked that Wheelwright be forbidden to preach between the conviction and the sentence, but that request was also denied, perhaps because it seemed uncomfortably close to the tactics of the Church of England.

On March 9, 1637, 60 citizens protested the verdict. This not only failed to help Wheelwright, it also caused the protesters to be punished. Sentencing for Wheelwright was delayed, though, because elections were nearing, and the Legalists were pushing for a John Winthrop victory and a Henry Vane loss.

Vane could reasonably count on the Boston vote, whereas Winthrop fared better away from the more metropolitan areas. Because people generally voted in Boston, ballot location appeared to favor Vane; the Legalist faction, though, managed to have the May 17 election moved to Newtowne (now Cambridge), which meant that Boston voters now needed to cross the Charles River to record their choice for governor.

Before the voting took place, Vane read a petition in favor of Wheelwright, which resulted in a near riot. Unfortunately for Wheelwright, not only was the petition ignored, Vane soundly lost the election to Winthrop, which meant that political support for Wheelwright, Anne Hutchinson, and their friends was now gone. Even so, it did not mean that Wheelwright's specific punishment was a foregone conclusion. After the election but before the August sentencing date, "A flood of papers now came forth: from the magistrates, to justify their course against Wheelwright; from him, qualifying or explaining passages in his sermon; and from the ministers, on all the tangled threads of the controversy," according to Heard. Some members of the court apparently hoped

Henry Vane, above, read a petition in favor of John Wheelwright, which resulted in a near riot. (Library of Congress)

IN CONTEXT The Protestant Reformation and the British Colonies

In 1517 Martin Luther, a German Catholic priest, nailed up a list of 95 criticisms of church practices, including taking cash donations in exchange for forgiveness of sins, a system known as the sale of indulgences. Luther intended his protest to produce reforms within the church. However, his followers became known as Protestants and set up independent churches, whereas the broader movement of reform came to be called the Reformation. The Catholic Church, based in Rome and headed by the pope, continued to exert its authority through the appointment of bishops, archbishops, and clergymen, and through organized monasteries and communities. Due to the fact that over hundreds of years devout Catholics had willed land, large estates, and other properties to the Church, with the wealth and positions held, the Catholic Church continued to wield great influence on civil governments. Even so, independent Protestant churches spread increasingly through northern and central Europe.

Another early leader in the establishment of independent Protestant churches was John Calvin. Born in France in 1509, he became an evangelical preacher in Paris in the early 1530s. He was soon driven out of France, and settled in Geneva, Switzerland. There his doctrines, known as Calvinism, and his system of church government, known as Presbyterianism, took

root. After a period of exile from Geneva, Calvin returned to establish a rigorous theocracy based in that city. Like the church he rebelled against, Calvin

Martin Luther, the instigator of the Protestant Reformation. (Library of Congress)

that a delay in sentencing would calm the community and allow more moderate factions of the court to emerge.

In preparation for an examination of Wheelwright's beliefs on August 30, 1637, the magistrates scheduled a day of humiliation on August 24; representatives of churches then met for 24 days. The sentencing did not occur, though, until the General Court hearing on November 2, 1637, when Wheelwright was given a chance to recant the essence of his sermon, but, according to Heard, "refused to yield either 'his opinions, his place, or his public exercisings.'" His punishment was then announced: banishment from the community within 14 days of the sentencing.

In that short amount of time and just as winter was approaching, Wheelwright needed to sell his farm and begin his journey to a new home outside of the Massachusetts Bay Colony. His choices were both limited and harsh, and this fleeing from persecution must have felt like a gloomy repetition of his forced departure from England. Much of the colony was raw wilderness, or nearly so; there were other settlements, but which of them would accept a chastised preacher who had just been banished from Massachusetts, the stronghold of all of New England?

was intolerant of dissenters, and he had the independent Spanish preacher Servertus arrested and burned at the stake for his views.

At the same time as Luther established his evangelical faith and Calvin spread his reformed churches on the continent of Europe, King Henry VIII declared the Catholic Church in England independent. In 1534, the king dissociated the Church of England from the Roman Catholic Church and assumed the power to appoint bishops and archbishops. Dissenting from the established Church of England, various pastors, such as John Cotton in the next century, began to form new, congregational-based groups. From among these groups, strongly influenced by Calvinist doctrine, the Puritans emerged. The Puritans of Massachusetts and surrounding colonies, like Calvin in Switzerland, hoped to establish a society governed by religious principles. The variations in views by preachers such as John Wheelwright, Roger Williams, and Anne Hutchinson led the founders of Massachusetts to attempt to enforce conformity by expelling such independent thinkers, who went on to form settlements in New Hampshire and Rhode Island.

Thus, by the time of the settling of the British colonies in North America, numerous sects and variations of Protestant thought contended for membership. Congregationalist variations on Puritanism dominated in New England. New Netherlands, first settled by the Dutch, had strong Dutch Reformed churches representing a Lutheran influence. Many other groups, including anabaptist sects (those who rejected oaths and infant baptism in favor of adult baptism), such as the Mennonites, formed in Switzerland in the 16th century, had settled in the British colonies to avoid persecution. In the 17th century, George Fox established the Society of Friends in England, and his followers, known as Quakers, settled in Pennsylvania and southern New Jersey. In Virginia, and to an extent through most of the British colonies, the Church of England or Episcopal Church continued to flourish alongside the various other groups. John Wesley, an ordained Church of England priest, traveled to Georgia in 1835 as a missionary. Returning to England, he experienced a reawakening of his faith and established an evangelical branch of the Episcopal church, which came to be known as the Methodist Episcopal or Methodist Church.

Thus, by the late colonial period of the mid-18th century, the British colonies had a great diversity of religion, including not only numerous Protestant sects but Roman Catholicism and, here and there, small groups of Jews who also found the religious diversity and emerging tolerance of the colonies somewhat hospitable to their faith. The only way such groups could survive without disastrous conflicts between each other was to develop some form of official toleration of religious variation. Such toleration of dissent and different opinions came to characterize the American political and religious landscape through the next centuries.

ACTUAL HISTORY

The predicament that faced Wheelwright and his family, who had come to the Massachusetts Bay Colony in hopes of escaping religious persecution, was cruelly ironic. The fact was, though, that colonial Puritan leadership suppressed nonconformity in belief and deed even more harshly than those who led the Church of England. As early as 1631, religious leaders in Massachusetts determined that its residents could only belong to the Congregationalist Church. "Thus," writes Lyon Gardiner Tyler in *England in America, 1580–1652*, "through church influence, the limitations on thought and religious practice became more stringent than in the

ANOTHER VIEW   John Cotton and Henry Vane

In general, those in positions of Puritan authority had the most to gain by the suppression of beliefs that did not conform; strictly enforcing governing beliefs bolstered their clout and influence. Two men who did not fit this precise mold were John Cotton, one of the most influential Puritans of the day, and Henry Vane, who served as governor of the Massachusetts Bay Colony in 1636.

Cotton was a well-respected minister, admired both for his intellect and for his religious purity. In a culture where consensus was central, people did not generally value bold or original ideas; although Cotton did preach theologies that were on the edge of standard Puritan beliefs, he did not attempt to engage others in picayune debates and he was not, prior to the Antinomian crisis, a figure of controversy. Vane was the son of an important man in the English court, and it was perhaps his standing in the motherland that gave him the courage to explore the more radical aspects of Cotton's theology.

It is entirely possible, though, that, without the addition of a third person to this mix, Cotton's beliefs—and Vane's fascination with them—would not have caused any noticeable ripples of dissension in the colony. But a third person there was— Anne Hutchinson—whose beliefs did not conform to traditional Puritan thought.

Hutchinson's gender automatically placed her at greater risk of suspicion when theologies were being examined. Furthermore, she was vocal in her views, and she associated with people, such as Cotton, Vane, and Wheelwright, who were prominent in the Massachusetts Bay Colony. Therefore, to quote Winship in *Making Heretics: Militant Protestantism and Free Grace in Massachusetts, 1636–1641*, "what energized the free grace controversy was not simply suspect doctrine, but that doctrine's visibility and claims to authority." It is reasonable to question whether it was Wheelwright's connection to his sister-in-law, rather than his own sermons, that caused

mother-country, where the suffrage took in all freeholders, whether they were adherents of the established church or not. . . . While suffering from persecution in England, they (Puritans) had appealed to liberty of conscience; and when dominant in America the denouncers of persecution turned persecutors."

Wheelwright did have some reasonable options after being banished from Massachusetts. He had received messages from settlements in Rhode Island, urging him to relocate there. Why he chose not to accept one of those invitations and move to a relatively stable environment is unknown; author John Heard speculates that Wheelwright decided to risk the dangers inherent in wilderness living rather than once again face persecution from an established religious community. It is also likely that Wheelwright disapproved of the comparatively tolerant religious atmosphere in Rhode Island; although he clearly did not fit in well with the more extreme requirements of the Massachusetts Bay Colony, he was still, by and large, a traditional Puritan, merely a heretical one, at least in the opinion of the leaders of Massachusetts Bay.

Rather than settle in Rhode Island, then, Wheelwright decided to relocate to New Hampshire; at that time, the population of that entire colony was about 1,000—or, if spread out equally across the region, one person for every 9 square miles of land. Under the best of circumstances, travel was difficult in 1637 and, that year, winter conditions were especially severe, even as early as November. Even so, Wheelwright arrived safely in authorities to closely examine his beliefs. No matter the impetus, the covenant of free grace needed to be repressed to bring consensus back into balance, and Wheelwright was too close to that fire to escape attention.

Ultimately, Wheelwright was banished. Underlying that form of punishment was the notion that the person exiled could no longer directly influence members of his former community—and, to some degree, that occurred as the result of Wheelwright's expulsion. A number of prominent people followed Wheelwright into New Hampshire, a pattern that also transpired when charismatic leader Roger Williams left Massachusetts for Rhode Island. Williams, who had fled England as a controversial figure because of his religious beliefs, initially preached in the Salem, Massachusetts, area. Like Wheelwright, he became at odds with Puritan authorities and, when he left Massachusetts, he led a community in Rhode Island that became known for religious tolerance.

Although Puritan lawmakers in Massachusetts would have been horrified at the following interpretation of events, it was their driving out of men such as Williams and Wheelwright that served as a backhanded blessing of the founding of communities that did not follow such a strict set of doctrines; Puritan authorities in Massachusetts actually were partly responsible for the eventual breakdown of religious consensus. Perhaps if they had chosen another form of punishment for dissidents, they could have maintained control for a longer period of time. Execution or imprisonment may have been more effective; this would have served as a powerful deterrent to those considering their own heresies. Ironically, even compromise may have better served their purposes; negotiation may have dulled the edges of differences instead of sharpening them into fiery debate. By choosing banishment, Puritan authorities in effect dispersed powerful and influential people throughout the colonies, which eventually decentralized the Massachusetts Bay Colony.

New Hampshire and he survived the winter by staying with a pioneer named Edward Hilton, one of only a few non-natives who lived by the Squamscott River; on April 3, 1638, the exiled pastor—with the assistance of funds provided by a group of friends—bought a tract of land by Squamscott Falls from a Native American named Wehanownowit Sagamore.

Early that spring, Wheelwright's wife, Mary, her mother, Susanna, and their expanding family joined him. A daughter, Rebecca, had been born in 1635; Mary in 1637; and a son, Samuel, in 1638. Later children included Hannah (1640) and Sarah (whose birth date has been listed as 1657, which, if accurate, means that Mary Hutchinson Wheelwright gave birth at the age of 52). The family wasn't entirely alone in their journey, either. Friends and supporters soon joined them.

Out of the total purchase of land located near Squamscott Falls, Wheelwright received 80 acres, but his family was far from being settled or feeling secure about their new living arrangements. In September 1638, Massachusetts authorities notified those in Wheelwright's settlement (Exeter) that they were displeased by community support of the shunned preacher. This pronouncement seemed to have little effect, though; by January 1639, a church was built for the community—which was only the third settlement established throughout New Hampshire—with Wheelwright named pastor.

ANOTHER VIEW   Dissension in Exeter?

Logic dictates that people who followed John Wheelwright to Exeter, New Hampshire, supported him and it also suggests that they would form a cohesive community. One historical record, though, implies dissension as early as 1639, the year that Wheelwright established his church in Exeter. That same year, the settlement of Dover, New Hampshire, applied to become part of the Massachusetts Bay Colony, which was the strongest and most powerful settlement in the colonies. Dover's application appears noncontroversial and it was accepted.

Even though no formal documentation exists, records from 1639 tantalizingly suggest that Exeter applied for the same arrangement, which raises intriguing questions. First, did this really happen? It is by no means certain; clerical errors happen throughout time and place. If such an application was made, though, it suggests that not everyone in Exeter was as supportive of Wheelwright as mainstream history texts indicate. Who, then, filed this supposed application?

Did one of the pioneers already living in that region resent the intrusion of this Puritan settlement?

What is known is that Wheelwright lodged with Edward Hilton during his first hard winter in Exeter; perhaps Hilton lived in isolation to escape intensely religious community living—or perhaps one of the other, admittedly few, wilderness dwelling inhabitants felt that way and therefore applied for Exeter to become part of the Massachusetts Bay Colony, in order to remove themselves from Wheelwright's influence. If Exeter became part of Massachusetts, then Wheelwright, laboring under a sentence of banishment, would need to leave that community, as well. Conversely, perhaps they agreed with the beliefs of those who banished Wheelwright from Massachusetts and did not want him to spread his "heretical" beliefs into New Hampshire. Another question is whether they knew the process whereby Exeter could be admitted into the Massachusetts Bay Colony. There are no facts to support any potential answers.

Even so, conjecture continues. Perhaps, as author John Heard suggests, the impetus came out of a sense of spite borne by someone living in Massachusetts desirous of driving Wheelwright

Wheelwright and his associates attempted to purchase the town of Hampton, as well, but they were blocked in their efforts by Massachusetts officials. They then began focusing their efforts on establishing a governmental constitution. Thirty-five signatories certified the document, which they called a combination for self-government.

This charter did not list what would happen if someone did not abide by its conditions. Rather, it spelled out how to select town officials, taxation methods, and treatment of forest lands; it named items—specifically, gunpowder, weapons, and liquor—that could not be sold to Native Americans; and it established tribunals and jury trials.

According to James Duane Squires, author of *The Granite State of the United States: A History of New Hampshire from 1623 to the Present*, "This document proclaimed a democratic republic, subject only to God and the King of England. Exeter differed from the other towns of early New Hampshire in that it was from the beginning distinctly a religious settlement." Wheelwright was largely responsible for the creation of this agreement. Heard, when comparing this legislation to the sketchy documentation drafted when men headed to California, said in *John Wheelwright: 1592–1679* that Wheelwright's "concept of community legislation was farther-sighted and more advanced."

farther from civilization or back to England. Word of Wheelwright's church may well have reached parties who passionately despised what they saw as the heretical nature of the banished pastor's beliefs; they may have wanted to wrest the church from Wheelwright's control or obtain even more revenge.

If this person was from Massachusetts, he didn't necessarily even need to know Wheelwright to resent Exeter's relative freedom. According to Heard, "Speaking generally, the theocracy in Massachusetts disliked the religious tolerance and easy-going attitude that characterized New Hampshire from the beginning."

One would imagine that only Wheelwright supporters or those who were themselves disgraced in Massachusetts would head to Exeter with the preacher. What other motive would any of them have to start this petitioning process?

It is possible that a feud occurred in the early days of settling Exeter. Life was brutally difficult there, and surely these pioneers sometimes felt hungry and exhausted; it is easy to speculate that they also became argumentative and fractious.

While laying the groundwork for their community, it is conceivable that someone disagreed with conditions listed in the settlement's bylaws and may have filed the petition out of pique. Some of the better-educated and well-connected citizens had defended Wheelwright during his heresy trial and then followed him. Any one of them might have known the mechanics of the petitioning procedure. Perhaps, after this person cooled down or after Wheelwright reasoned with him, he withdrew his request, if indeed, it was ever made.

Another possibility is that some residents believed that, if Massachusetts wanted to take control of Exeter, they would do so under their own conditions. Would it not be better, then, if the settlement proactively requested this situation, thereby controlling events and preserving some of their own priorities and wishes?

Regardless of whether this application was ever filed, and, if it was, by whom, nothing of substance occurred because of it. There was an application filed in 1641, though, with long-term ramifications for John Wheelwright and his family and supporters.

Wheelwright's thinking may well have been advanced, but the settlement was still quite isolated; contact and barter with outside communities was impractical and it was also quite rare. Residents lived in rough-hewn log cabins and they supplemented their meager diets with salmon in season; they also raised sheep and cattle and farmed vegetables and grains, while small grist mills and saw mills provided for their basic needs. Under Wheelwright's leadership, though, the community grew; by 1641, two political parties existed in Exeter.

Although the creation of a second political party indicated growth and expansion, a more ominous side effect for Wheelwright and his contingency loomed. Members of one of those parties wished to merge with Massachusetts; 13 of its adherents—11 of whom had signed the community's bylaws—applied for such a move. They included conditions in their petition, though, the specifics of which are lost, and the application lay dormant for 2 years. In 1643, 22 men signed a petition containing no provisional conditions, and the application was granted. Exeter, New Hampshire, was now officially part of the Massachusetts Bay Colony.

Wheelwright must have anticipated this eventuality. On September 24, 1641, he, Samuel Hutchinson, and Nicholas Needham had acquired title from Sir Ferdinando Gorges to property located in Wells, Maine, and several men left Exeter to establish the settlement. By the spring of 1643,

ANOTHER VIEW   Consensus versus Diversity

John Wheelwright and his family survived the Antinomian crisis and the subsequent banishment; he was reaffirmed into the traditional Puritan faith during his lifetime; and, overall, whenever historical texts mention Wheelwright, they tend to portray him as a courageous—albeit somewhat inflexible—man who stood up for what he believed and who was willing to accept the consequences. Nevertheless, claims made against Wheelwright had significantly damaged his reputation in the eyes of many of his contemporaries and they forced him to uproot his family and suffer through many indignities and hardships. Surely they also derailed Wheelwright's personal ambitions, whether he desired financial success or advancement in the Puritan hierarchy.

It's important to understand why the religious community reacted so strongly to his beliefs and words. In his book *Making Heretics: Militant Protestantism and Free Grace in Massachusetts, 1636–1641*, Michael P. Winship discusses the mindset of a typical Puritan for whom the Reformation "shattered Western Christendom" and for whom "the unity of the saints remained a powerful ideal. As Massachusetts magistrate John Endicott put it, 'God's people are all marked with one and the same mark ... and where this is, there can be no discord.' In pursuit of that freedom from discord

---

Wheelwright joined them and, on July 14, he bought 400 acres along the Ogunquit River. Wells, by contrast to Exeter, was relatively settled as a community. Nevertheless, life was primitive, not even the wealthiest had crockery, glassware, knives, forks, spoons, or chairs. Once again, Wheelwright found himself the pastor of a frontier settlement.

In a bold move, occurring as early as September 1642, someone petitioned Massachusetts authorities to allow Wheelwright to return to the colony; rather than finding resistance, a softer answer arrived. On May 10, 1643, the court granted him permission to spend 2 weeks in Massachusetts during any time within the next 3 months. What occurred, specifically, during this brief return to Boston is not known.

The famous Dr. Cotton Mather was an initial supporter of John Wheelwright. (Library of Congress)

In April 1644, Wheelwright personally pursued that avenue as he wrote the General Court a letter recanting his former beliefs. "I confess," it reads in part, "that herein I have done very sinfully, and do humbly crave pardon of this honored state," according to Heard in *John Wheelwright: 1592–1679*. After receiving a response that would allow him safe conduct, he wrote to Governor John Winthrop directly. In this letter his tone is again submissive, but he also attempts to justify his actions and innocence. Without debating specifics, on May 9, 1644, the court lifted his sentence of banishment and he returned to the colony without recorded incident.

On April 12, 1647, he signed a contract as pastor of Hampton; that document compliments Wheelwright and endows him with a lot, farm, and annual salary of £40. In 1654, his congregation determined to officially clear his name, so, on May 1, Dr. Cotton Mather read a petition

ANOTHER VIEW   *Consensus versus Diversity (Continued)*

Puritans proved among the most zealous heresy hunters."

Consensus, then, rather than diversity, was a predominant communal value. Although no Puritan in Massachusetts had any living memories of the Reformation, many could recall how their religious community, while still located in England, banded together against the dominant church and how many friends and family members were persecuted for their beliefs; many of these colonists must have also felt maltreated, and their memories and wounds were still fresh.

Another factor further fueled the drive for consensus. Although Massachusetts was a relatively settled community when compared to most of the colonial expanses, the focus of daily life was still group survival rather than individual freedoms. To Winship, this entire Antinomian controversy was rooted in this value system, and he called the crisis a "heavily contingent series of events revolving around the maintenance and breakdown of consensus."

Of course, the ideal of doctrinal consensus would not need to be defended or protected if that concept was universally accepted. In reality, although dominant beliefs widely prevailed, a subgroup of some influence did not espouse these prevailing viewpoints, and thus the tension continued to rise. Escalating this phenomenon was the fact that those in the dominant culture, perhaps after being treated with hostility in England, responded by harshly treating those appearing "less pure" in their religious beliefs.

stating that Wheelwright was an orthodox minister. Also in 1654, Wheelwright received a raise of £10, but his salary appears to end the following summer. He continued to perform ministerial duties, though, until 1656, when he returned to England. There he spent time with Oliver Cromwell, whom he knew in Cambridge; perhaps he also visited Henry Vane, the former governor of Massachusetts who had supported him but who had returned to England upon the loss of his government position in the colonies. Wheelwright did correspond with the Hampton church while living in England, discussing his conversations with Cromwell in a letter written on April 20, 1658; he must have parted ways with Hampton on a cordial note.

In 1660, when Charles II ascended the English throne, the political climate in England changed in a manner unfavorable to Puritan thought, and, in 1662, Wheelwright came back to Boston, never again to return to his homeland. He became pastor of Salisbury in 1662, where he remained for the rest of his life, and where he died on November 15, 1679. His tombstone, erected by his descendants in 1927, reads:

> In Memory of Rev. John Wheelwright
> Born in England 1592
> Vicar of Bilsbury, England 1623
> Came to Boston Massachusetts 1636
> One of the founders of Exeter, New Hampshire 1638
> Commissioner to England for the Colonies 1657 to 1662
> Died in Salisbury Massachusetts 1679

Here ends the personal history of Wheelwright: son, student, husband, father, pastor. Fleeing from persecution in England, he faced similar challenges in the colonies. What part he played in his own troubles and which were strictly the result of intolerance of even the slightest nuances and deviations of belief cannot be determined for certain and will remain a matter of speculation. His influence on New Hampshire—and American—history, though, is significant. Here is but a brief summary of what has transpired in Exeter since Wheelwright's departure:

In 1774, on the cusp of the Revolutionary War, two provincial congresses were held in Exeter, and the third assembled there on April 21, 1775, "to consult on what measures shall be thought most expedient to be taken at this alarming crisis," according to James Duane Squires in *The Granite State of the United States*. As many as 5,000 men joined New Hampshire militias in response to this crisis; according to Squires, "This electrifying outburst of military support for the patriot cause was in part a natural result of the sturdy individualism of New Hampshire people." At least 108 of these patriotic men left Exeter parade grounds on April 20, 1775.

When the fourth provincial Congress met in Exeter in May 1775, New Hampshire solidified its intent to fight for independence by creating an army of 2,000 men. In November 1775, Congress advised Exeter citizens to name which representatives could best serve the needs of their people "during the continuance of the present dispute between Great Britain and the colonies," according to Squires in *The Granite State of the United States*, solidifying Exeter as the central point of government for New Hampshire. Besides serving as the governmental focus during the war, men from Exeter also participated in naval patrols

On January 5, 1776, governmental representatives ratified New Hampshire's first constitution while convening in Exeter's town house; in 1788, New Hampshire's first convention, formed to ratify the U.S. Constitution, met in the same location.

When it came time to disperse war pensions, the state appointed Exeter's John Taylor Gilman as their official agent. He compiled lists of disabled former soldiers and certified their eligibility to receive aid. On November 18, 1783, the first New Hampshire meeting of America's first veteran association, the Order of the Cincinnati, met in Exeter. Revolutionary War officers with 3 years of experience could join, as could their descendants. As for Gilman, he became treasurer of New Hampshire after 1783. In 1794, he was elected governor for a term of 1 year and reelected 13 times.

On May 1, 1783, John Phillips formally dedicated the Phillips Exeter Academy, endowing the educational facility with $60,000. Upon his death, Phillips gifted the academy with another $60,000—collectively the largest gift given, to that point, to any educational facility in the United States. One of the academy's earlier students was Daniel Webster, who later became an attorney, statesman, senator, congressman, and presidential candidate. Robert Todd Lincoln, son of the president, was also graduated from Exeter Academy.

In 1822, poet James M. Whitfield was born in Exeter. Whitfield, a free Negro, published his work in now-famous publications such as William Lloyd Garrison's *The Liberator* and Frederick Douglass's *The North Star* and *Frederick Douglass's Paper*. In 1850, Daniel French was born in Exeter. French is a sculptor best known for his Abraham Lincoln statue in the Lincoln Memorial.

Initially formed as a refuge for a banished preacher and his small band of followers, Exeter, New Hampshire, served as a focal meeting point during the Revolutionary War, and to this day it houses a premiere facility that has educated some of the country's elite youth. It is tempting to imagine the reaction of John Winthrop and other adversaries of John Wheelwright were they able to see the evolution of Exeter, the town founded when they forced one of their own to find refuge in its wilderness.

ALTERNATE HISTORY

"The election will take place in Boston."

These seven simple words, if spoken in 1637, could have altered the direction of American history. That year, the challenger to the office of the governor of the Massachusetts Bay Colony—John Winthrop—requested that voting take place in the town of Newtowne (renamed Cambridge in 1638), rather than at the more traditional and central site of Boston.

How might history have changed if the incumbent, Henry Vane, and the challenger, John Winthrop, had received the news that the May 1637 gubernatorial election would indeed take place in Boston? Vane wanted the election to occur there because the majority of its residents supported him as governor. Because Winthrop and the Legalist faction fared better in more rural areas, they wished to move the election away from Boston—and, by choosing Newtowne, they would add a physical barrier to Vane's supporters, who would then have to cross the Charles River to vote for their candidate.

In reality, the election was moved to Newtowne. If, however, the voting site remained in Boston, Henry Vane—a supporter of John Wheelwright—would have stood a much better chance of winning. Vane had read a petition in favor of Wheelwright before the voting occurred; he garnered little support for the shamed pastor, and a near riot ensued. Surely, though, if Vane had the courage to read this petition in "enemy" territory; that is, in front of a large throng of Winthrop supporters, then he certainly would have done so in Boston—and the words of likely winners carry far more weight than those humiliated with rejection and loss of status.

Vane and Wheelwright, surrounded by supporters, might have changed the momentum of the election. A Vane win, in turn, would have bolstered official support for Wheelwright.

Even with a Vane win, of course, the August sentencing date for heresy would still have loomed for the convicted Wheelwright. Political support behind the scenes, though—and perhaps even openly stated support—might have swayed the judges to order a less harsh punishment for Wheelwright. Negotiation and compromise would seem more likely with Vane as governor; and even though Wheelwright frequently displayed obstinacy, it is possible that Vane might have persuaded him to apologize publicly for any misunderstandings to avoid a sentence of banishment. Perhaps he could have appealed to Wheelwright's loftier and more idealistic side, explaining that, with his presence in Massachusetts, Vane and Wheelwright could collectively continue spreading their religious beliefs; perhaps the governor could have pleaded to Wheelwright that the cruelty of banishment could be fatal to Mary, Wheelwright's often pregnant wife, or to Susanna, her aging mother, and so theocratic and political reconciliation was in order.

Even the strongest modern-day supporters of Wheelwright would not suggest that this Puritan minister stood up for freedom of religion; instead, he strongly believed in his own interpretation of religious thought. Nevertheless, had Wheelwright—a convicted heretic—been allowed to stay in the Massachusetts Bay Colony, it is conceivable that other citizens of that influential colony might have felt freer to express dissenting thoughts without fear of dire consequences.

How might this have changed history?

By pardoning Wheelwright, Massachusetts officials would be showing more tolerance toward dissension and differences of opinion. Meanwhile, Roger Williams, who was an important figure in the settling of nearby Rhode Island, believed strongly in freedom of religion. Moreover, many settlers in New Hampshire wished to band together with Massachusetts to gain the benefits of its more civilized ways of life; this collusion of thought and/or governmental cooperation would help spread the influence of more tolerant thinking, at least in New England, and perhaps throughout the rest of our country as it expanded westward. This altered way of thinking surely would have prevented, or at least mitigated, some of our country's darker moments that were partially caused by intolerance and prejudice.

During 1692, for example, 55 years after the Wheelwright heresy examination, several young women in the town of Salem, Massachusetts, accused neighbors of being witches. Ultimately, 19 people were hanged and one was pressed to death; large stones continued to be placed on his chest in an attempt to obtain a confession, but he refused to respond to the accusations and the weight of the stones crushed him to death. Hysteria ruled during the accusation, trial, and punishment stages, and few people dared question the proceedings. Although all is speculative, it is possible that, had Wheelwright, his sister-in-law Anne Hutchinson, and Vane triumphed in their attempts to forward alternate interpretations of theology, then perhaps minority voices could have continued to prevail in the colonies, which included Salem in 1692.

People accused of witchcraft in Salem were almost exclusively women. If more tolerant thinking had prevented the ruin of those accused, this triumph for women, coupled with a different ending to the Hutchinson story, could have sparked the suffrage impetus 2 centuries earlier than it did. It is unrealistic to imagine that any one woman—even one as strong, intelligent, and forthright as Anne Hutchinson—could have single-handedly changed the relationship between genders in the Puritan society or significantly altered the role of women in society. However, had Wheelwright prevailed, and, perhaps even more important, had Henry Vane remained in power in the colonies, it is unlikely that Hutchinson would have suffered the same fate that she did, which was permanent banishment. Her influence would therefore have continued to chip away at traditional gender roles in Massachusetts.

Hutchinson surely would have continued to hold Sunday meetings in her home to discuss matters of theology; these were attended by 60 to 80 women each week. Even if no other woman in that group became as emboldened as Hutchinson, the words of this passionate leader would have influenced her listeners; the notion of independent thought and belief would have been passed along—and who knows what cumulative effect this might have had on gender equality, especially over a few generations. Might that factor alone have changed, or at least mitigated, the results of the Salem witch trials? Is it possible that women of that era—and men, as well—would not have been so easily caught up in group hysteria? On a broader and more long-term scale, perhaps women would have earned the right to vote and own property much earlier than in actual history.

An atmosphere of religious tolerance and one with more equality between the sexes could also create an atmosphere of acceptance in other areas. That might have led to better understanding among races, cultures, and ethnicities in the United States. It is possible that a culture of tolerance and equality could have even prevented the early economic base of our country from relying on slave labor.

Roger Wilkins, author of *Jefferson's Pillow: The Founding Fathers and the Dilemma of Black Patriotism,* points out the extreme irony that George Washington and Thomas Jefferson, two men who greatly influenced the founding of our country that was officially based on freedom and equality, were slave owners; Washington and Jefferson were, in fact, freed up to do their works of historical significance in large part because slaves fueled the labor in their homes and on their plantations. These two historical figures were, therefore, according to Wilkins, "cushioned by slavery." The author also points out that it would take a "secular saint" to go against prevalent culture, thereby relieving Washington and Jefferson from any preponderant burden of guilt; but an atmosphere of tolerance from the 17th century on, both religious and otherwise, might have prevented the institution of black slavery from ever taking such a deep-rooted hold in the United States.

It is also possible, if slavery was a reality during the pre-Revolutionary War era, that when the founders of our country wrote the Declaration of Independence and the Constitution, slavery might have been banned in those documents, given an atmosphere of significant tolerance and genuine belief in equality for those of all races, genders, and ethnicities. If that had occurred, then the lives of countless people could have been lived in freedom rather than in bondage, and the poignant deaths of more than 618,000 Civil War soldiers would have been prevented.

Given a long-term history and culture of harmony, tolerance, and equality, rather than one more tainted with religious repression and enslavement based upon race, the entire structure of our society would be quite different—and the United States might be serving as a peaceful role model for the rest of the world. Energies previously spent debating minor and seemingly meaningless points of religious doctrine would have been better spent solving problems of society, whether that meant reducing hunger, improving educational opportunities, or attending to environmental issues.

Furthermore, a more tolerant and accepting society would choose its leaders on the ethical standards of a particular person, rather than by the gender, race, age, or religion of the candidate. The resolution of issues would therefore be more encompassing. To quote Adrienne

Redd in her Proposal for Radical Tolerance, "A group of people trying to solve a problem has more success when there are differing points of view. Similarly, the strongest society is not the one that isolates its fragile prosperity and ideological purity, but which is open to creativity, experimentation, and risk."

As with any speculative questions about events obscured by the past—and, by this point, the idealistic notions being presented here are quite speculative and perhaps humanly unobtainable—the answers will never be known. It is unlikely that, had any one event—or any one person—experienced a different outcome, the broad scope of American history would be dramatically different. Nevertheless, the wheel of history would have tilted in another direction. For example, if Wheelwright, Vane, and Hutchinson had prevailed, then perhaps the repressiveness in the Massachusetts Bay Colony might have eased, and men and women would have more quickly seen freedom of belief and inclusiveness as desirable alternatives to theocratic rigidity and exclusivity based upon religious doctrine. The more quickly tolerance and equality were embraced as cultural values, then the more impact they would have on the forming of the new and influential nation.

Kelly Boyer Sagert

Discussion Questions

1. Why do you think John Wheelwright recanted from the beliefs that caused his banishment, to ask for readmission into the Massachusetts Bay Colony? What do you think of his choice? What, if anything, could he have done differently?

2. The English king was certainly watching over the actions of the colonies. How do you think that influenced the actions of those in charge, especially governors John Winthrop and Henry Vane? Perhaps if Massachusetts authorities had been more yielding, then banishments based on doctrine would not have occurred. Do you think it is possible that, under those circumstances, the colonists would have learned to live in relative peace with one another? If so, would they have felt the need to separate from England? If not, how might it have changed history?

3. In the Alternate History suggested here, the colony of Massachusetts develops more religious freedom than it did in fact. To what extent would this development have improved the status of women in Massachusetts and other colonies? What factors would be at work to prevent such improvement?

4. If religious freedom had developed in the colony of Massachusetts early in its history, to what extent would this development have affected conditions in other colonies, such as New York and Virginia? What factors would favor such intercolonial influence? What factors would have tended to prevent or limit such influence?

Bibliography and Further Reading

Breen, Louise. *Transgressing the Bounds: Subversive Enterprises among the Puritan Elite in Massachusetts, 1630–1692*. New York: Oxford University Press, 2001.

Buckingham, Rachel. "Anne Hutchinson: American Jezebel or Woman of Courage?" http://www.inclinehs.org/english/ventreenglishpaper.htm (accessed August 2005).

Burnham, Michelle. "Anne Hutchinson and the Economics of Antinomian Selfhood in Colonial New England." *Criticism* (Summer 1997).

"Digby Finds the Sweet Spot Again," http://www.kiddingonthesquare. com/the_state_of_america (accessed August 2005).

Dow, Joseph. "History of Hampton," http://www.hampton.lib.nh.us/ hampton/history/dow (accessed August 2005).

Ellis, George E. *The Puritan Age and Rule in the Colony of Massachusetts Bay 1629–1685*. Boston: Houghton Mifflin, 1888.

Independence Museum, "Exeter—Its History," http://www. independencemuseum.org/aim_exeter.htm (accessed August 2005).

Hazlett, Charles A., *History of Rockingham County, New Hampshire and Representative Citizens*. Chicago: Richmond-Arnold, 1915.

Heard, John, Jr. *John Wheelwright: 1592–1679*. Boston: Houghton Mifflin, 1930.

Web Roots. "History of the Town of Hampton, NH: Chapter XIX. The Interwoven Pastorates: Rev. Stephen Bachiler, 1638–1641—Rev. Timothy Dalton, 1639–1661—Rev. John Wheelwright, 1647–1656— Rev Seaborn Cotton, 1657–1686," http://www.webroots.org/library/ usahist/nh/hoh-nh10.html (accessed August 2005).

Kahl, Jeffrey M. "The Antinomian Controversy and the Puritan Vision: A Historical Perspective on Christian Leadership." *Quodlibet Journal* (September 2004).

Kiefer, James E. "William Laud, Archbishop and Martyr," http://justus. anglican.org/resources/bio/76.html (accessed August 2005).

Osgood, Herbert L., *The American Colonies in the Seventeenth Century*. New York: Columbia University Press, 1904.

Plant, David, "Puritans and Puritanism," http://www.british-civilwars. co.uk/glossary/puritans.htm (accessed August 2005).

Rugg, Winnifred King. *Unafraid: A Life of Anne Hutchinson*. Boston: Houghton Mifflin, 1930.

Squires, James Duane. *The Granite State of the United States: A History of New Hampshire from 1623 to the Present*. Washington, DC: American Historical Association, 1956.

Tyler, Lyon Gardiner. *England in America: 1580–1652*. New York: Harper and Row, 1904.

Weymouth, D.G. "Person Sheet: Rev. John Wheelwright," http://www.weymouthtech.com/Genealogy/ps50/ps50_442.htm (accessed August 2005).

Winship, Michael P. *Making Heretics: Militant Protestantism and Free Grace in Massachusetts, 1636–1641.* Princeton: Princeton University Press, 2002.

TURNING POINT

The Dutch colony of New Amsterdam surrendered to the British in 1664. What if New York was never established and the colony remained under Dutch control?

INTRODUCTION

On a misty morning in September 1609, Henry Hudson, a British sailor working for the Dutch, weighed anchor off the coast of what is today Sandy Hook, New Jersey, and began a momentous journey up the river soon to be named after him, the Hudson.

Eighty-five years earlier, an Italian named Giovanni da Verrazano had seen the beginning of the same river (which he called The River of the Steep Hills), but chose to ignore it. The Dutch would not. The Dutch would soon create a colony in the land explored by Hudson and name it New Netherland. And very importantly, the British would eventually also make a claim to the same territory. This would lead to tension, political intrigue, crisis, and a momentous historical event. And Peter Stuyvesant, the leader of New Netherland at the time, would be at the center of it all.

The Hudson River area was, according to the early Dutch settlers, a land with rocky headlands, high cliffs, grape vines, hazel nuts, and a river and bay where whales sometimes beached themselves on shoals and sandbars, where oysters abounded—some with pearls. It was a wild, heavily forested country. The Pilgrims had not yet even landed at Plymouth Rock. To the south, the British had a small colony called Virginia. In short, this was a land of opportunity for the Dutch. There were furs, timber, and the possibility for farms and fishing and a fantastic deep-water port.

At this time, the Netherlands in Europe was growing as an economic power. The Dutch hoped that New Netherland would add to their wealth. To accomplish this, private companies, rather than the government itself, administered New Netherland through exclusive government-approved charters. In the beginning, the companies only wanted trading outposts for furs, but in 1621, authorities in the Netherlands granted the Dutch West India Company the exclusive right to do business in America. This company wanted to expand operations by creating a colony.

IN CONTEXT   Indian Reaction to Hudson According to the Dutch

One of the later Dutch colonists, Adriaen van der Donck, claimed that some of the natives, standing on the shore watching Hudson's ship (the *Half Moon*) slowly make its way up the river, thought the ship was a strange fish. Others, wrote van der Donck, thought it was a sea monster or a ghost from either heaven or hell. Some thought the men on board were devils. Hudson and his shipmates also had mixed feelings about the Native Americans. They had to fight off some of the natives they encountered near the mouth of the river, firing at them with small cannons and muskets, but they found the natives up river to be loving and gracious.

This colony, established in 1624, was to be a "company" outpost, run like the military, and the man in charge was to be known as the director-general. The colony went through several directors before Peter Stuyvesant arrived. The company fired all of them for one reason or another. The most famous of them was Peter Minuit, known for his purchase of Manhattan Island from the natives and for his moving company headquarters, which he called New Amsterdam, to lower Manhattan. The most infamous of the directors was Willem Kieft.

Kieft started a brutal war with the Native Americans and outraged the colonists, driving them to argue with authorities in the Netherlands for more self-rule. Eventually the colonists convinced the Dutch West India Company to give them some limited say in governing the colony and to replace Kieft. This replacement would be the more honest, upright, but tougher Peter Stuyvesant.

Willem Kieft was the most infamous of the New Amsterdam director-generals. (Charles Beschler Co./Library of Congress)

A rugged, proud, physical man, and a devout, strict follower of John Calvin, Stuyvesant had worked his way up from a clerk's job in Amsterdam to the governorship of the Caribbean islands of Curaçao, Aruba, and Bonaire. In March 1644, he led an invasion fleet to the Spanish-held island of Saint Marten in hopes of retaking the island for the Dutch. The invasion failed and a cannon ball smashed into Stuyvesant's right leg. His men carried him back to the ship where the ship's surgeon amputated his leg without anesthetic and then cauterized it either with a hot iron or with boiling water. The company physicians forced him to return to the Netherlands to recuperate, and there doctors fitted him with a wooden leg.

The Dutch West India Company then decided to put Stuyvesant in charge of the always-difficult colony of New Netherland. His job was to bring order and make a profit. And so on May 11, 1647, a cloudless spring day, he stood at the waterfront of New Amsterdam and briefly addressed the crowd. The soldiers in the fort had saluted him with

IN CONTEXT　　　The Dutch Struggle for Independence from Spain

The Netherlands at this time was in the process of asserting its independence from Spain. In 1567, the Dutch had begun the Eighty Years War, revolting against the abuses of the Spanish King, Philip II, who laid claim to the territory. The king had sent the Duke of Alba to enforce his rule, including the enforcement of the state religion of Spain, Catholicism. But the Netherlands was in large part Protestant. The Duke of Alba would send troops to various towns where they would set up a Council of Blood, which would execute people and confiscate their property. Then in 1579, the Netherlands declared itself an independent country in a document known as the Union of Utrecht agreement. William, the Prince of Orange, led the resistance. After much bloody fighting—which included help from England for the Dutch side—the Dutch and Spanish finally, in 1609, the year of Henry Hudson, agreed to a truce (though the Spanish would not formally acknowledge the Netherlands as an independent country until 1648).

their four brass cannons—in fact, they had used all of their powder to do so. The crowd was loud and jovial; many of them had been drinking. (At one time, one quarter of all the buildings on Manhattan had been bars and taverns.) However, he was not what the colonists had expected: he was not a man who would allow them more freedom. They soon, at least in written notes and letters, would simply call him "The General." They considered him pompous and authoritarian. And he said of them: "The people are grown very wild and loose in their morals," according to Hendrick Van Loon in *Life and Times of Pieter Stuyvesant*.

Stuyvesant's insistence on loyalty to the company and his sense of morality almost immediately alienated him from the colonists. As a result, the colonists resisted the changes Stuyvesant wanted to make. The company had been inept in its management and the colonists resented it. They had gone to America to make their fortunes and they felt that the company's rules and its many taxes and fees kept them from prosperity.

Part of the problem with loyalty, as Stuyvesant saw it, was that the colony was too diverse. Kieft had reported that there were numerous different languages spoken in the colony and several different religions. Although society back in the Netherlands was one of the most tolerant in Europe at the time, Calvinism was still the official religion, and Stuyvesant found it hard to tolerate other religions—though he had no problem with people of different faiths worshiping privately. The most troublesome of the non-Dutch colonists were the English. Some of them had sworn allegiance, but others—especially those in the eastern portion of Long Island, refused to accept Dutch sovereignty.

A 1936 poster depicting Peter Stuyvesant directing a bucket brigade to put out a fire in 1656 in New Amsterdam. (Library of Congress)

KEY CONCEPT — Calvinism

Calvinism is a Protestant religion started by John Calvin (1509–1564). He was born in France but moved to Geneva, Switzerland. Like other Protestants, he was rebelling against what he believed was the corruption of the Roman Catholic Church. He believed in a literal reading of the Bible and in predestination. Calvin's teachings glorified work and discipline. His doctrine first appeared in the Netherlands in about 1545 and the Calvinist creed was often preached in open air services. In the Netherlands as well as in New Netherland, the Dutch Reformed Church represented Calvinism. This was the religion of Peter Stuyvesant.

While Stuyvesant was having difficulties with the colonists, more serious trouble was brewing with the British. The New England colonies were growing in power and scope and were beginning to encroach upon the Dutch territory. In 1650, Stuyvesant was able to negotiate a treaty, the Treaty of Hartford, with the New England colonies. This treaty set agreed-upon boundaries. Later, the British would ignore this treaty.

TURNING POINT

Then, 3 years after Stuyvesant had arrived, there began the first of several wars between England and the Netherlands. This first occurred between 1651 and 1654. Primarily a naval war, it spilled over into America when the New England colonies (excluding Massachusetts) attempted to invade New Netherland. British leader Oliver Cromwell sent four ships loaded with troops to Boston. Their goal was to attack New Amsterdam and annex the colony. To help, the New England colonies were recruiting men to bolster the invasion.

But just as the British ships, loaded with 900 men, were ready to leave Boston harbor for the Dutch colony, word came from England that the war was over, and the invasion was called off.

The year after the war (1655), two important events occurred. First, Stuyvesant decided to attack the Swedish colony located on the Delaware River. Legally, the Dutch considered the Swedish colony to be an encroachment upon Dutch territory; economically, many of the Dutch felt that the Swedes were stealing away part of the fur trade. Second, while Stuyvesant was on the Delaware successfully negotiating a Swedish surrender, he learned that a native war had broken out to the north.

It had begun, possibly, as an intertribal war that became a Dutch and Native American war

British leader Oliver Cromwell planned an invasion of New Amsterdam that was later called off. (E. Scriven/Library of Congress)

because of panic and poor judgment on the part of the Dutch. Or possibly it started as a native retribution for the attack on New Sweden. In any case, Stuyvesant resisted calls for revenge and was able to ransom back most of the Dutch prisoners and to make peace. The war served to reinforce Stuyvesant's fear that New Netherland was vulnerable to attack from both the natives and the British.

For the next 9 years, life in New Netherland improved, despite an ominous change in government in England in 1660. Cromwell died in 1658 and Parliament elevated Charles II to the throne in 1660. Ignoring Dutch claims, Charles gave New Netherland to his brother James, the Duke of York, in 1664. James intended to make good on his gift.

Until then, Stuyvesant continued to encourage the development of an education system in New Amsterdam, to encourage farming, to improve defenses, and to make New Amsterdam look and function like a city. Some of the roads in the city were paved with cobblestones. A wharf was built on the East River. The city was tidied up. Some of the houses were now built with bricks instead of wood and thatch. And to help with the defensive capabilities of Manhattan, Stuyvesant started a new village in the northern part of the island: New Haarlem, known today as the Manhattan neighborhood of Harlem. And he worked on the defensive wall to the north (today Wall Street, home of the New York Stock Exchange).

Stuyvesant was well aware of the desires and intentions of the British, but his attempts to obtain help from authorities back in the Netherlands were to no avail. They were sure that there would be no problems with England and even went so far as to order him to cut the number of soldiers he had in order to save money. He attempted negotiations with New England, but to no avail. It only made him more convinced that the British would soon attack. And despite pleas, the Netherlands refused to send him military reinforcements.

In March 1664, James, the Duke of York, formally received his gift. In April 1664, James arranged with Colonel Richard Nicolls to sail a small invasion fleet of four ships to America. His mission was to assert royal authority in America—including New Netherlands. Then in late August, Stuyvesant returned from a trip up the Hudson to Fort Orange. Disturbing news awaited him—Nicolls was on his way.

Stuyvesant and the citizens of New Amsterdam made desperate attempts to strengthen the fort. But everyone soon knew the truth: the Dutch West India Company had refused to resupply the colony with munitions and it was estimated that they had about a half a day's worth of powder for the cannons. In addition, the harvest had been bad that year and they were short on bread; they could not sustain a long siege. Nevertheless, Stuyvesant refused to give up. "I would much rather be carried out dead," he said later, according to Van Loon in *Life and Times of Pieter Stuyvesant*.

Could New Amsterdam have been an Italian colony? Giovanni da Verrazano explored the Hudson River region 85 years before the Dutch settlement, but chose to ignore it. (Library of Congress)

Meanwhile, Nicolls anchored his ship, *The Guinea*, in Gravesend Bay, not far from what is today Brooklyn. Nicolls sent troops to the ferry at Brooklyn to cut off the Dutch coming from and going to Long Island. The next day, Nicolls's fleet anchored near Governor's Island, in plain sight of the fort in New Amsterdam.

Stuyvesant sent a note asking him his intent. Nicolls answered the next day, saying that he was demanding the town in the name of the king, and if they refused, then the Dutch would bring down the devastation of a war upon themselves. Soon a rowboat approached, flying a white flag, carrying John Winthrop from the New England colonies, with terms of surrender. The terms were generous. People could keep their property and pretty much continue their lives as before—except that now their loyalty would be to the king of England instead of the Dutch West India Company.

When people from the town demanded to see the terms, Stuyvesant refused and tore the paper into pieces. Later, when they insisted, he gave them the torn pieces and they learned the truth.

Nicolls, deciding to force the issue, moved his ships into close range. People from the town, including Stuyvesant's 17-year-old son, had signed a petition, asking him to surrender. Stuyvesant, alone with a single gunner, then stood at the battlement of the fort, a cannon aimed at the British. Two of the Calvinist ministers from the town came to his side and talked to him, finally convincing him to come down. Nevertheless, he tried, by note, one more time to convince the British to leave—to no avail. And then, on September 8, 1664, it was over. The British flag now flew over the fort.

Hereafter, declared Nicolls, New Amsterdam was to be known as the city of New York. Thus the turning point in history is, what would have happened if Stuyvesant had not surrendered and the colony remained New Amsterdam?

The turning point: the surrender of New Amsterdam. (National Archives)

ACTUAL HISTORY

Within months of the British takeover, Stuyvesant returned to the Netherlands to defend himself. The Dutch West India Company blamed him for the loss of the colony. He argued, rightly, that the true problem had been neglect by the company. It was not easy to convince the authorities. They delayed him for 3 years. Finally, in the spring of 1668, he returned to his wife and family and his home in New York.

His farm was at Great Bouwery (the Dutch word for farm) Number One. There he had built a chapel and when he died in August 1672, he was buried near it. His chapel has today been replaced by St. Mark's Church in the Bowery, and his grave is still there.

The same year that Stuyvesant died, another war between England and the Netherlands broke out. This time a Dutch fleet entered New York harbor and overwhelmed the English forces on August 9, 1673. They remained in power for 15 months, renaming New York as New Orange. The peace treaty in 1674 between the two countries called for both to return any territory formerly belonging to the other. Because Britain had possessed New York City prior to the war, the territory reverted to the British.

But British or Dutch, it made no difference. What was on the mind of New Yorkers was still the same: freedom. The history of New York City until after the American Revolution revolves around people agitating for more freedom and for unfettered possibility—just as they had under the Dutch. The new British governor, Sir Edmund Andros, did make improvements that helped gradually to move the city toward the economic power it became in the 19th century.

Perhaps most importantly, he built what came to be known as the Great Dock on the East River. This expanded the maritime and commercial power of the city. He further strengthened the economic power of the city by giving it a number of monopolies. But Andros made enemies—especially with the English cities on Long Island, which felt they were the victims of New York's monopolies. And many felt that he was abusing his power. As a result, James recalled Andros in 1682. The English sent a new governor, Irish Catholic Thomas Dongan.

Dongan instituted more self-government by creating an elected, representative assembly. This assembly wrote the Charter of Liberties and Privileges. But then Charles II died and in 1685 James became James II, King of England. He refused to accept the charter and decided to combine all of the New England colonies plus New York into a single entity called the Dominion of New England. In 1688, he sent back Edmund Andros as the governor of the dominion (with the capital in Boston). Andros left the lieutenant governor, Francis Nicholson, in charge of New York.

Then life became even more complicated. James II was forced to abdicate the throne. The Whig party in England was afraid that James would force the nation to become Roman Catholic. To solve their problem, they turned to Protestant Netherlands. Their plan was to install Dutch royalty as king and queen of England: Prince William of Orange and his wife, Mary. The Dutch, encouraged by the English Parliament, landed an army in England. James fled to France. But now, what was New York to do?

In Boston, they arrested Andros and sent him back to England. Nicholson remained in power. But when New Yorkers heard the news, they forced Nicholson to leave. They set up their own government, led by Jacob Leisler. As usual, some of the people were happy with the new leader, and some were not. But whatever Leisler's shortcomings may have been, he was decisive. He was the first in America to try to deal with an essential problem: contention for territory between the English colonies and the combined forces of the French and Native Americans. He called the first colonial congress after the French and natives attacked Schenectady, massacring the people living there. This was the first time that the colonies considered acting in a united way. But nothing came of his attempts. And nothing good—for Leisler—came of his time in power.

England once again sent a new governor, Henry Sloughter, who promptly had Leisler executed.

Before the next crucial event in history—the American Revolution—several important events happened in New York.

The decade of the 1690s in New York might be called the "pirate years." Some New York merchants would invest in a privateer—a type of government-sanctioned pirate—who would then attack enemy French ships for their cargo. The crew and the investors would then split the money. The most famous of the privateers, William Kidd, also known as Captain Kidd, lived in New York City. When Kidd started attacking British ships in addition to French, British authorities caught him and hanged him (twice, the first time he broke the rope). They then tarred his body and put it in a cage that swung over the River Thames in London.

In the early 1700s, trade in New York City increased—including the trade in slaves. An event of true shame happened in 1741. A number of fires were set in the city, as they had been during a slave revolt in 1712. Whether there actually was another revolt or not is still uncertain. But many in the city jumped to the conclusion that there was a plot between blacks and poor whites to set fire to the city and to rise up in violent revolt. It became like the Salem witch trials. City officials ended up executing, by hanging or by burning at the stake, 32 blacks and 4 whites and imprisoning many others.

Also during this period in time, New York took on more of the elements of a true city. The city's first college, King's College (now Columbia), opened in 1754. During the 1730s, the city created a volunteer fire department and a rudimentary police force. In 1725, William Bradford started the city's first newspaper, *The Gazette*. In 1733, John Peter Zenger started a competing paper, *The Weekly Journal*. Zenger was quickly sued for seditious libel, but he won in a dramatic trial, and thus helped to secure freedom of the press in America.

Outside of the city and the colony of New York, another important event was going on that would eventually lead to the American Revolution: the French and Indian War.

Just as the Dutch and the English contended for territory in America, so did the French and the English. The French were in Canada and had explored down the Mississippi River and the Ohio valley, claiming all of that territory. The British had no intent to allow themselves to be boxed in. Thus began an expensive, bloody war that would run from 1754 until 1763. The result would be the removal of France from America and a huge debt for England—which they would try to pay for by taxing the colonies.

While the war was going on, New York profited. English troops were primarily arriving through the port of New York. Commerce boomed and the port was busier than ever—despite a troubling inflation. Then, when most of the British troops left after the war, a depression hit the city. That was bad enough, but to make things worse, the British decided to recoup their losses and pay for the troops still there by taxing the colonies. Soon the famous phrase, "taxation without representation," could be heard, not only in New York City but also throughout the American colonies.

One of the new tax laws, the Stamp Act of 1765, aroused great passions in New York City and in most parts of the American colonies. Massachusetts called for a meeting of representatives from all of the colonies, known as the Stamp Act Congress, to agree upon a unified stand against the tax. They decided to hold it in New York City in October 1765. Representatives from 9 of the 13 colonies met at City Hall and declared that the tax was a denial of their rights as free British citizens. Merchants decided to put economic pressure on the king (George III) and parliament by refusing to import British goods until the Stamp Act was repealed.

The common people also took things into their own hands and created their own type of pressure: the Sons of Liberty. Rowdy, sarcastic, intimidating to the British and to the New York establishment, radical in their demands for freedom (the original Dutch colonists would have loved them), they burned the royal governor in effigy and ransacked the house of the British artillery captain—among other things.

When the Stamp Act was finally repealed in 1766, New Yorkers threw a huge party with barbecued oxen, rum, and 25 barrels of beer. Again, the original Dutch settlers would no doubt have been proud of them.

A 1768 distant view of New York City with King's College, now Columbia University, in the background. (Thomas Howdell/Library of Congress)

KEY CONCEPT   The Federalist Papers

The Federalist Papers were a series of written arguments concerning the Constitution. They were first published in the *Independent Journal* in October 1787. The arguments were signed by someone calling himself "Publius." In fact, Alexander Hamilton, John Jay, and James Madison wrote them. In May 1788, they were published together in book form under the title *The Federalist*. Their goal was to convince the states to ratify the new Constitution, especially the state of New York.

IN CONTEXT   The Duel between Alexander Hamilton and Aaron Burr

One of the most dramatic events in the early history of the American government and New York City was the duel between Alexander Hamilton and Aaron Burr. Aaron Burr was born in New Jersey and graduated from the College of New Jersey (today, Princeton). At the beginning of the Revolution, Burr approached General George Washington asking for a commission as an officer. Washington turned him down, but Burr was able to distinguish himself in battle, and eventually the Continental Army gave him the rank of lieutenant colonel. He briefly was military secretary to Washington but didn't get along with Washington and so was fired. After the war, Burr practiced law in New York and won a number of state elections. In 1800, he became Thomas Jefferson's vice president, though Jefferson dropped him from the ticket in 1804.

Alexander Hamilton was born in Nevis, British West Indies. He was sent to New York for an

---

The celebrating was premature. England found new ways to tax the American colonies, and in 1775 fighting broke out in Massachusetts at Lexington, Concord, and Bunker Hill. Then, on July 4, 1776, came the Declaration of Independence. George Washington, the commander-in-chief of the Revolutionary Army, knew where the British would mass their power: New York City.

He led his ragtag army there in 1776. On June 29, the British began an amphibious invasion, the largest ever (at that time) by the British: eventually over 400 ships (with 1,200 cannons), 32,000 troops, and 13,000 sailors. The Americans were forced to abandon the city (someone set fire to it as they were leaving) and they were chased by the British across the state of New Jersey. Finally, in the dead of winter, Washington was able to win two battles, those at Princeton and Trenton. The Americans were not able to return to New York City—victorious—until November 25, 1783, now known as Evacuation Day, the day the last British troops left New York City. Washington was invited to a banquet at Faunces Tavern where 13 toasts—for the 13 colonies—were given.

For a while, New York was the capital of the country. In fact, George Washington was sworn in as the first president of the United States on April 30, 1789, at Federal Hall in New York City.

The years between the end of the Revolution and the end of the Civil War would see New York City become the dominant economic city in the country. In 1791, a group of brokers met under a buttonwood tree on Wall Street and a year later created the New York Stock Exchange. And in 1817, then governor of New York, DeWitt Clinton, proposed building the Erie

---

education, graduating from King's College (Columbia). He decided to remain in America and at the start of the Revolution raised a company of soldiers; the Continental Army gave him the rank of captain. The army soon promoted him to lieutenant colonel and placed him on Washington's staff. After the war, he was one of the New York delegates to the Continental Congress. He argued for a strong federal government and was one of the authors of the Federalist Papers, which helped to convince the country to accept the Constitution. President Washington appointed him to his cabinet as secretary of the Treasury. The country was badly in debt. He presented a system in 1790 to make the country solvent. In order to get his plan passed, he had to make a deal with the state of Virginia: the capital of the United States would be moved to an area on the Potomac River (Washington, D.C.) in return for their vote. Virginia, of course, accepted, and New York City was no longer the country's capital. In addition, Hamilton created the Federal Bank. His plans

worked and indeed the United States survived its financial crisis.

Unfortunately, both Burr and Hamilton moved to New York City and lived near each other on Wall Street. Politically, the two men were at odds for years. Then in 1804, Hamilton argued publicly against Burr, who was running for governor of New York. A newspaper reported that Hamilton said Burr could not be trusted. Despite the fact that Hamilton tried to make it clear to Burr that his words only applied to politics—not as personal slander—Burr challenged Hamilton to a duel.

Hamilton had been against dueling since his son had been killed in a duel 3 years before. Nevertheless, he felt he could not back down.

They met on the bank of the Hudson in New Jersey, 10 paces away from each other. Hamilton had said that he would let Burr take the first shot, and he did. The shot mortally wounded him and Hamilton never shot his weapon. He died the next day. Burr left the city just before his indictment for murder.

Canal. Clinton realized that agriculture was shifting westward and that soon the heartland of the country would find it more convenient to ship its goods down the Mississippi River to the Port of New Orleans than ship through New York. A canal connecting the Great Lakes to the Hudson River, he argued, would solve the problem. He was ridiculed for his idea; detractors called it the "big ditch." But it was successfully completed in 1825.

The big story of New York City during the 1800s and early 1900s was immigration. By 1860, the population of the city was over one million. Potato famines in Ireland and in Germany brought waves of Irish, German, and Jewish immigrants through the port of New York. Many of them remained in the city. Even more immigrants came in the later years of the 19th century and in the early years of the 20th century. These included east Europeans, Italians, Russian Jews, Chinese, and people from the Caribbean. The Statue of Liberty was completed in 1886, and Ellis Island was opened in 1892.

In the 20th century, the city started to take on its modern, urban look. The Brooklyn Bridge began construction in 1860, but the Williamsburg Bridge opened in 1903, the George Washington Bridge in 1931, and the Triboro Bridge in 1936. The first subway began operation in 1904; the Holland Tunnel opened in 1927 and the Lincoln Tunnel in 1937. This was also the century of great skyscrapers: the Chrysler Building opened in 1930, and the Empire State Building in 1931.

Finally, symbolic of centuries of aspiration, hard work, success, and American values, New York completed the highest skyscrapers in Manhattan—the World Trade towers—in 1973. They were destroyed by terrorists in the 21st century on September 11, 2001.

ALTERNATE HISTORY

How would the world be different if on that day in 1664, Peter Stuyvesant had not handed over New Amsterdam to the British?

If the Dutch West India Company had been more concerned with New Netherland as a long-term investment rather than as an object for immediate profits, it could have easily provided Stuyvesant with the necessary munitions, troops, and vessels to withstand the British attack.

What about attacks coming from the New England colonies? In reality, it would have been even more difficult for the New Englanders to take Manhattan; Stuyvesant had been preparing for attacks from the north—whether it was from the natives or from the New England colonists. And he was a patient negotiator; he likely would have convinced at least some of the natives to fight with the Dutch.

More importantly, the Dutch fleet sailed up the Thames in London in 1667 and successfully attacked the British fleet. The Dutch would have had enough leverage to force Britain to restrain their colonists.

In reality, after Stuyvesant surrendered New Amsterdam, James gave parts of New Netherland to people who had done him favors, thus creating New Jersey (in addition to what would become New York State). In this alternative history, these colonies never would have existed.

The fact that the Dutch were in America would certainly not have altered the ambitions of the French. And so, there would still have been a French and Indian War. How involved would New Netherland have been? Would they have shared the cost of the war with England? It is doubtful that they would go into debt to further the ambitions of the English. Certainly, they would have defended their own borders, but not the borders of British colonies.

Would the American Revolution still have happened? One of the prime triggers of the war—taxation due to the French and Indian War—would still have existed and so the Revolution would probably have happened. But the way it was fought would obviously have been different. Without New Amsterdam (New York City), the British would have probably used Boston for the 1776 invasion, despite the fact that the rebels beat them there at the beginning of the war. Or they could have used the port at Philadelphia to stage the war.

New Netherland would have divided the southern colonies from the northern colonies, but communication between northern colonies and southern colonies probably would have been better for the American rebels than for the British. The Dutch would also have been more likely to grant the rebels movement through New Netherland than the British. By the time of the Revolution, the Dutch were economically tied to the rebels; they were conducting trade with them and had even lent them money. At best, New Netherland would have been neutral territory during the war, but probably the Dutch sympathies—like their money—would have been with the rebels. So the outcome would probably have been the same, with the rebelling colonists victorious.

The outcome of the Revolution may have been the same, but this division between the New England states and the other states would likely have altered the settlement of the American West. After the

Revolution, the Confederation Congress in 1785 created the Northwest Territory out of the land ceded to it by Britain in the Treaty of Paris (the formal treaty ending the war between England and the United States). This territory would eventually become the states of Ohio, Indiana, Michigan, Illinois, Wisconsin, and parts of Minnesota.

It was primarily ex-Revolutionary soldiers from the New England states who first settled in the Northwest Territory, trekking across the mountains of Pennsylvania to Pittsburgh and then down the Ohio River in rafts to settle in the Ohio Territory. This was a convenient way for the new government to pay off debts to members of the Revolutionary Army. The new U.S. government also needed money to pay its other war debts. Yet, as can be expected, it was very sensitive to the idea of taxing people. And so it decided to raise money through land sales.

Unfortunately, to get to the Northwest Territory, the New Englanders would have had to go through New Netherland. The fur trade, primarily because of a growing shortage of beavers, was starting to dwindle in the east. The fur trade in the Great Lakes region (Ohio, Michigan) was still viable in 1785 (though it would all but end by 1800).

This would have put the Americans in competition with the Dutch. The Dutch may not have been able to stop the migration west through New Netherland (and thus stop the competition), but they likely would have slowed it down by detaining intruders. The Americans could have gone from New England to Delaware by boat, if necessary, and from there westward. This would have been more costly and more time consuming. No doubt, the westward migration would have happened, but not as quickly.

With New Amsterdam on the American continent, another important—crucially important—situation would have been altered: the problem of slavery.

The Netherlands banned Dutch involvement in the slave trade in 1814, but they did not ban slaves in their colonies until 1863. Thus New Netherlands might have kept slaves until the middle of the American Civil War (1861–1865). The persistence of slavery in New Netherland through this period would have altered the development of the Underground Railroad.

The Underground Railroad was a loosely organized network of blacks and whites who helped slaves in the Southern states to escape to the North—often to British Canada (where slavery had been outlawed in 1807). This was a dangerous endeavor. Federal law did allow slave masters to go into Northern states to retrieve their "property." Often, the slave masters would hire bounty hunters to track the fleeing slaves. In addition, there was a $500 fine for anyone who helped escaping slaves. In 1850, the government passed the Fugitive Slave Law, which raised the fine to $1,000 and added a prison sentence.

If slavery were legal there, New Netherland would not have been a safe haven for slaves. And yet, many of the Underground Railroad routes (in actual history) went through New Jersey and New York State. However, if New Netherland had followed the pattern of developments in nearby English-speaking New England, the Dutch colony might have abolished slavery as early as 1800 to 1829, about the same time that the state of New York did in actual history. In that case, New Netherland would have represented a haven and escape route for slaves escaping from the South as much as it did in actual history.

One of the most famous members of the Underground Railroad was Harriet Tubman, who in actual history worked out of New York State. She was a former slave who had escaped from bondage in Maryland. She first went to Philadelphia, and then moved to Auburn, New York. She was so successful that her former owner put up a $40,000 bounty—a very large sum of money at that time—for her capture.

Not having New York or New Jersey as part of the United States would also have had an impact on the Civil War. Though there were no battles fought in either state (the war took place primarily in the South with the major exception of Gettysburg, Pennsylvania), together these two states provided nearly 20 percent of the Union troops for the war. Still, the Union Army outnumbered the Confederate Army by nearly two to one, so the existence of New Netherland would not have had much of an impact on the final outcome of the war. However, if slavery had been present in New Netherland until 1863, it is quite possible that the sectional division over slavery between the slave states of the South and the free states of New England, the Ohio valley, and Pennsylvania would not have developed to the point of a Civil War between the states at all.

The presence of New Netherland on the North American continent would have changed history in another way: the history of immigration. New Netherland was already—even in the days of Peter Stuyvesant—known for drawing a diverse group of people from many countries. To some extent—especially in the 1800s—New Netherland would have competed with the United States for immigrants. Eventually, of course, the Dutch would have had to put limits on the number of people coming to the colony—they only had so much room.

There are other ways immigration would have been altered by New Netherland. For one thing, the Statue of Liberty, a gift from France to the United States, would probably be in Boston harbor. Immigrants most likely would have come through Boston, making it the most populous city in America. And another actual migration to New York City—this from within the United States—would not have happened: the migration of southern blacks to Harlem.

Around the time of World War I (though it had begun to some extent earlier) black Americans from the South began to migrate north, going from rural regions to urban areas.

In an alternate history, the Statue of Liberty could very well be in Boston harbor rather than New York harbor. (Library of Congress)

They were leaving the South because of violence, oppression, and lack of opportunity. In actual history, by 1910, over 60 percent of African Americans in New York were from the South. One of the most famous destinations was the Manhattan neighborhood of Harlem, created by Peter Stuyvesant as a line of defense against attacks by natives and New England colonists coming from the north.

During the 1920s, one of America's great cultural events occurred in Harlem, the Harlem Renaissance. It was a great coming together of black writers, activists, intellectuals, painters, actors, and musicians. Writers included Langston Hughes, Countee Cullen, Claude McKay, Zora Neale Hurston, and James Weldon Johnson. Painters included Aaron Douglass, and sculptors included Sargent Johnson. In this alternative history, none of this would have happened. Social activist, writer, and intellectual, W. E. B. Du Bois lived in Harlem. He helped to found the National Association for the Advancement of Colored People (NAACP) and was the editor of their magazine, *Crisis*. Supreme Court Justice Thurgood Marshall also lived in Harlem.

Harlem was also a home to jazz. Of course, jazz did not begin in Harlem or even in New York City, but it was home or a major working place for many famous musicians (Duke Ellington and Ella Fitzgerald, for example) as well as a place for musical innovations. In fact, one important strain of jazz, bebop, was invented in Harlem in the late 1930s and early 1940s. It was in Manhattan jazz clubs like Minton's Playhouse in Harlem and Monroe's Uptown House that musicians such as Dizzie Gillespie, Charlie Parker, and Thelonious Monk created bebop—a type of jazz that has influenced all modern styles of jazz. If New Netherland had remained in Dutch possession into the 20th century, the 1920s flowering of African American culture might have occurred somewhere else, perhaps in Chicago, St. Louis, or Boston.

The existence of New Netherland may have had a profound effect on World War II. Germany began attacking neighboring countries in 1939. By May 1940, despite the Netherlands' declared neutrality—Germany had seized the Dutch homeland. All during this time, the United States was also neutral and did not enter the war until December 1941. But with New Netherland as a close neighbor, the Americans may have entered the war earlier, especially if Nazi Germany had sought to take possession of and occupy Dutch colonies in the Western Hemisphere. The U.S. government would no doubt have regarded such a move as a severe threat to national security. Public opinion would likely have been in favor of joining the fight because many Americans would undoubtedly have had close relations with people in New Netherland—on a personal as well as on a business level.

Certainly, the immediate effect of an earlier declaration of war would have been an earlier buildup of the military. This would also have included an earlier strengthening of the U.S. Navy. As a result, perhaps the attack on Pearl Harbor wouldn't have been as crippling as it was. The war in the Pacific as well as in Europe would likely have ended sooner. The Germans would have had less time to build up defenses in France, and so the Battle of D-Day would not have been as bloody.

> If on that fateful day of September 8, 1664, Peter Stuyvesant, hard nosed, profoundly religious, and unwaveringly loyal to the Dutch West India Company, could have held out, if he could have stood up to the British attempt to take over the colony of New Netherland, American history would no doubt have been altered. Sometimes, as in the American Revolution, the change in history would have been minor. And at other times, like during World War II and even the Harlem Renaissance, the effect would have been profound.

William P. Toth

Discussion Questions

1. If the Dutch had been able to retain New Netherlands or New Orange (including what is now New Jersey), and if the English colonies still succeeded in gaining their independence in the American Revolution, would the United States have gone to war with Holland to try to gain control over New Netherland? When do you think such a war would have happened?

2. If the Dutch had retained New Netherland or New Orange, including what is now New Jersey until the 1860s, how would this development have affected the sectional crisis in the United States over slavery? Would Dutch control of this mid-Atlantic region have prevented or made more likely a Civil War between the Northern states and the Southern states?

3. If New Netherland or New Orange had sponsored an Erie Canal to open the Midwest to traffic through the Hudson River from the Great Lakes region in the 1820s, how could that have affected political and economic control of the area of Ohio, Indiana, Illinois, and Michigan?

4. Suppose that the Dutch had retained control of the mid-Atlantic region into the 20th century. What effect would that development have had upon the effort of the United States to remain neutral in World War I? Remember that Holland was neutral in that conflict.

5. Suppose that the Dutch had retained control of the mid-Atlantic region, along with Aruba, Curaçao, and other possessions in the Caribbean until 1940. How would such control have affected the outcome of World War II, after Nazi Germany invaded Holland?

Bibliography and Further Reading

Bliven, Bruce, Jr. *New York: A Bicentennial History*. New York: W. W. Norton, 1981.

"British History On-Line," www.british-history.ac.uk (accessed August 2005).

Burns, Ric, James Sanders, and Lisa Ades. *New York: An Illustrated History*. New York: Knopf, 2003.

Burrows, Edwin G., and Mike Wallace. *Gotham: A History of New York City to 1898*. Oxford: Oxford University Press, 1999.

Condon, Thomas J. *New York Beginnings: The Commercial Origins of New Netherland*. New York: New York University Press, 1968.

Donck, Adriaen van der. *A Description of the New Netherlands*, www.americanjourneys.org/texts.asp (accessed August 2005).

Ellis, Edward Robb. *The Epic of New York City*. New York: Coward-McCann, 1966.

Elson, Henry William. *History of the United States of America*. London: Macmillan, 1904.

Findling, John E., and Frank W. Thackeray. "The Surrender of New Amsterdam, 1664." In *Events That Changed America through the Seventeenth Century*. Edited by John E. Findling and Frank W. Thackeray. Westport, CT: Greenwood Press, 2000.

"Henry Hudson's Third Voyage 1609: The New World," www.ianchadwick.com/hudson/hudson_03.htm (accessed August 2005).

Kessler, Henry H., and Eugene Rachlis. *Peter Stuyvesant and His New York*. New York: Random House, 1959.

Lancaster, Bruce. *The American Revolution*. New York: Houghton Mifflin, 2001.

Mackey, Thomas A. "Interpretive Essay." In *Events That Changed America through the Seventeenth Century*. Edited by John E. Findling and Frank W. Thackeray. Westport, CT: Greenwood Press, 2000.

Mushabec, Jane, and Angela Wigan. *A Short and Remarkable History of New York City*. New York: Fordham University Press, 1999.

New Netherland Project, www.nnp.org (accessed August 2005).

Rink, Oliver A. *Holland on the Hudson: An Economic and Social History of Dutch New York*. Ithaca, NY: Cornell University Press, 1968.

Shorto, Russell. *The Island at the Center of the World*. New York: Vintage Books, 2005.

Van Loon, Hendrick. *Life and Times of Pieter Stuyvesant*. New York: Holt, 1928.

TURNING POINT

Sweden first claimed the Delaware area in 1638. What if the Swedish colonies prospered and were able to repel invasions from the Dutch and British?

INTRODUCTION

Sweden in the 1630s stood as one of the dominant powers in Europe. The greatness of Sweden was created by one man, King Gustav Adolf, who is best known to history as Gustavus Adolphus, commonly referred to as Gustavus. Gustavus did much to modernize the Swedish army and navy, and he developed a keen interest in establishing colonies in the New World, like the other major European powers, including England, France, Spain, and the Netherlands.

As a major European power, Sweden's Gustavus was able to negotiate with King Charles I of England, who agreed "that the early explorations of the Swedes gave Sweden a prior claim to lands lying along the Delaware River Valley" in today's New Jersey and Pennsylvania and, "in 1634, ceded to Sweden all rights in the area," according to historian Ralph K. Turp, writing in *West Jersey: Under Four Flags*. Four years later, on March 16, 1638, two Swedish ships, the *Bird Griffin* and the *Key of Kalmar* (or *Kalmar Nyckel* in Swedish) arrived off the mouth of the Delaware River in the New World. The two ships carried the Swedes into a tributary of the Delaware, which was named the Christina River (today's Brandywine Creek), after Gustavus's daughter, Queen Christina, who ruled after his death.

With the Swedish expedition was Peter Minuit, who had purchased Manhattan Island for the Dutch, and subsequently served as governor of the new Dutch colony, now in New York State. However, Minuit had a falling out with the Dutch and had offered his services to the Swedes—without telling the Dutch. He informed his former employer, the Dutch West Indies Company, that the Swedes had actually stopped at the Christina only to take on fresh water. (On ocean voyages, drinking water was stored in large wooden barrels, or casks, and became badly spoiled by the time the ships reached the New World).

Minuit bargained with the Native American Lenni-Lenape tribe to purchase land for the Swedes to settle, and by March 29, he had already

A modern-day replica of the *Kalmar Nyckel,* one of the ships that brought Swedes to America. (Loretta Carlisle)

arranged a deal with the natives. The resulting agreement called for "as much . . . of the land in all parts and places of the river, up the river and on both sides as Minuit desired," according to C. A. Weslager in his book, *New Sweden on the Delaware.* In order to hold the new colony, commonly called New Sweden, Minuit directed the building of Fort Christina (today's Wilmington, Delaware), which most likely was a log stockade with some cannon. Based on the research of historians, the Swedish soldiers were probably armed with matchlock muskets and pole arms, like the pike. Officers may have worn cuirasses, or breast plates, as would the pikemen and any cavalry, who would also have been armed with swords and pistols. Minuit thus helped establish the new Swedish colony and its defenses, but his leadership was cut short. In May 1638, Minuit was lost at sea when his ship was lost on the return trip to Sweden.

Throughout this early period, neither the Dutch in New Netherland (New York), nor the British in Virginia made any effort to oust the Swedes: the reputation of King Gustavus, now called "the Great," was

KEY CONCEPT The Fur Trade in North America

From about 1600 to 1850, some 250 years, the fur trade was one of the earliest and most important industries in North America. Native Americans traded furs for such goods as tools and weapons. Beaver fur, which was used in Europe to make felt hats, became the most valuable of these furs. The earliest fur traders in North America were French explorers and fishermen who arrived in what is now eastern Canada in the 1500s. Trade started after the French offered the natives kettles, knives, and other gifts as a means to establish friendly relations. The natives, in turn, gave pelts to the French. By the late 1500s, a great demand for fur had developed in Europe. This demand encouraged further exploration of North America, and the trade in beaver increased rapidly in the early 1600s. Such furs as fox, marten, mink, and otter were also traded. The fur trade prospered until the mid-1800s, when fur-bearing animals became scarce and silk hats became more popular than felt hats made with beaver. The territorial claims of fur traders played a part in establishing the border between the United States and Canada. For example, the areas of trade controlled by U.S. and British traders helped determine the border in the region of the Great Lakes.

simply too formidable. Mans Kling, in Minuit's absence, was made governor of New Sweden and commanded Fort Christina's 21-man garrison. The Swedish colony did well, and even more, the Swedes began to make an initial, fruitful alliance with the Lenni-Lenape tribe, or the "Delawares" as the English would call them. As with their French allies to the north in New France (Canada), the Swedes focused on friendly relations with the Native Americans. At least at first.

One reason for the friendliness with Native Americans was the importance of the fur trade, the trade in beaver skins, or pelts, which became the first big business in North America. It was the luck of the Swedes that the land they held contained some of the Native American trails that connected New France with the Atlantic Ocean. The Lenni-Lenape, traveling to the seashore markets for the summers, would bring along their furs for trade with the Swedes. Karla Messenger, former president of the Lenni-Lenape Historical Society, explains that the Lenni-Lenape, in addition to trading furs, gave the new settlers "everything, including food and medicine" to help them survive in their new environment.

During the next 15 years, New Sweden enjoyed a remarkably stable political life, supported in large part by the economy that benefited from the fur trade. Peter Hollander Ridder took over from Kling as governor in April 1640 and served until 1643, when he was recalled to administrative duties in the Kingdom of Sweden. His replacement was Johann Printz, a former Swedish lieutenant colonel. Printz had had a troubled past back in Europe. The New Sweden governorship was Printz's chance to redeem himself from a terrible military blunder in which he had disgracefully surrendered a key fort. In the New World, Printz was not personally fond of the Native Americans, but he followed, at first, the directives of the Swedish South Seas Company, which governed the colony for the queen (Gustavus's daughter who now reigned over the Kingdom of Sweden). As historian Turp writes in *West Jersey: Under Four Flags*, "the natives were to be given fair and equable treatment at all times and under all circumstances."

Reproductions of the log cabins occupied by New Sweden governor Johann Printz. (Loretta Carlisle)

It was not only the fur trade that made the Lenni-Lenape vital to the Swedish settlers—the Native Americans' friendship with the Swedes also probably helped keep the neighboring Dutch settlers from encroaching into New Sweden. But as time went on, the friendship was strained, and friction between the Swedes and Native Americans developed. On June 11, 1644, Printz reported to his superiors that the "Indians murdered a man and wife in their beds, and a few days afterwards they killed two soldiers and a workman," according to Turp writing in *West Jersey: Under Four Flags*. However, it is not possible to assess how Printz's attitude toward the tribe may have influenced this hostile behavior; his own prejudice can be summed up in one quote: "With the help of God not a single savage would be allowed to live on [the Delaware] River," according to Turp in *West Jersey: Under Four Flags*. In spite of Printz's personal feelings, and occasional violence, the Native Americans still presented more of an opportunity for the Swedes than a threat. They were not at war, but neither were they friends anymore.

In spite of the fact that New Sweden rarely had more than 400 full-time settlers, the colony eventually spread throughout much of today's Delaware, Pennsylvania, and parts of New Jersey. Printz erected a handsome house (fortified with cannon) at what he called New Gothenberg, the Printzhof on Tinicum Island. Printz also fortified the region now in New Jersey when he built Fort Elfsborg near today's city of Salem. In addition, Printz built a network of fortified wooden blockhouses on the frontiers of New Sweden, including one at Upland (now Chester), along with two others in the vicinity of today's Philadelphia, known then as Wiaco, which

---

KEY CONCEPT   The Rule of George III

George III (1738–1820) was committed to taxing his American colonies, and forcing the colonists to bend to British rule to the point of the colonial rebellion that culminated in the American Revolution that broke out in 1775. George obstinately continued the war until the final American victory (with French help) at Yorktown, Virginia, in 1781. Yet George's rule over his British colonies was also affected by his own personal disposition: George suffered from porphyria, a maddening disease that disrupted his reign as early as 1765. The defeat at the hands of the American colonists cost George dearly; his sanity was stretched to the breaking point, and he ended up dying blind, deaf, and mad at Windsor Castle, England, on January 29, 1820.

---

apparently had its own soldiers to guard the Delaware River there. Thus Governor Printz created a series of strong points to defend the colony from the Dutch, who, under their aggressive governor Peter Stuyvesant, began to object to Swedish encroachment on what they felt was their land.

In 1647, Printz was recalled to Sweden because of his autocratic ways. Perhaps the worst part of his legacy had been his tactics with the Lenni-Lenape. Later, Printz's attitude toward the Native Americans would have dire effects on New Sweden. Johan Rising replaced Printz as governor. In 1651, the Dutch sailed from New Amsterdam (today's New York City) and built Fort Casimir at what is now New Castle, Delaware. This post was meant to checkmate New Sweden's Fort Christina. Because of their naval superiority in the region, Stuyvesant and the Dutch could control the seas—but without a friendly port in the area, Stuyvesant could not maintain a naval squadron in isolated territory far from New Amsterdam. Realizing how the Dutch Fort Casimir would affect Swedish control of the Delaware, the Swedes, under Governor Rising, attacked after the Dutch ships had left. Without any naval support, and with limited ammunition, the Dutch commandant had to surrender the fort. Because it fell to the Swedes on Trinity Sunday in 1651, Rising renamed it Fort Trinity.

Realizing the ill effects of Printz's policy toward the Native Americans, Rising held a meeting, or powwow, with the natives to try to repair the damage the high-handed Printz had caused. He met them at the Printzhof on June 17, 1654. Tentative efforts were made by Rising to arm the Lenni-Lenape, but the amount of weapons and ammunition offered indicated they were only intended for hunting. As with Printz before him, Rising underestimated the military potential of the tribe's warriors.

Concerned about the plans of the Dutch, Rising sent two settlers on a spying mission to New Amsterdam. Hans Manson and Jacob Sprint, mostly likely guided by Native Americans, managed to find their way to the Dutch colonial capital, where they learned that Stuyvesant was planning an invasion of New Sweden. Indeed, it would have been easy to see the Dutch ships in New Netherland's harbor being fitted for an invasion; Stuyvesant planned on many of them to attack New Sweden. Stuyvesant did not move, however, until he had received word that peace had been made between the warring Netherlands and England back in Europe, which reached him on July 16, 1654. He could not risk a larger British squadron attacking his fleet, if England were still at war with the Netherlands.

ANOTHER VIEW   Hurricanes in the North Atlantic Ocean

An untimely hurricane could also have been a turning point in history at this time. All the colonial powers in the New World knew only too well the ravage of hurricanes that struck the Caribbean islands, where the first colonies had been established, as well as the east coast of America from Florida all the way up through New England. The Delaware Bay and New Jersey shore are the graveyards of perhaps hundreds of ships lost during fierce storms. According to the National Geographic Society, Spain's colonial ambitions were particularly hard hit by one such hurricane: "Spanish ventures in the New World were bedeviled by hurricanes in the 17th and 18th centuries. In late July 1715, a fleet of 11 Spanish

TURNING POINT

On August 30, 1654, Stuyvesant appeared with his fleet of ships, carrying a few hundred soldiers. Stuyvesant was faced with the strategic need to take an entire colony with several important factors weighing in the scales against his success.

One of these factors was the Swedes' relationship with the Lenni-Lenape. Stuyvesant was not sure whether the Native Americans would side with the Swedes and fight against the invading Dutch. The turning point in the history of Colonial America and the United States came as soon as Stuyvesant reached New Sweden's Fort Trinity, the next day on August 31, 1654. As the Dutch prepared their ships for battle, they also disembarked soldiers into the surrounding area to launch a ground assault on New Sweden. Would the Lenni-Lenape stop them?

The antipathy shown to the Native Americans by Swedish Governor Printz, and Rising's inability to repair relations, much less trust and arm the Lenni-Lenape tribe as a military ally, now had come back to haunt New Sweden. The Native Americans let the Dutch invade New Sweden without interference. The turning point could have yielded a very different history had the Lenni-Lenape tribe been armed by the Swedes as an ally, and helped New Sweden repel Stuyvesant's land forces.

ACTUAL HISTORY

The actual historical record shows Stuyvesant facing New Sweden with hundreds of soldiers low on supplies and eager for an attack. Swedish Governor Rising, although he had taken Fort Casimir in 1651, seems to have been devoid of the aggression needed to defend New Sweden. Even with advance knowledge of the invasion Rising had probably received from spies sent north, he apparently had done nothing to prepare for a siege. In fact, when the Dutch attacked, Rising surrendered without a fight: He did not have enough forces to fight the Dutch. The Dutch had been able to operate not only on the river, but also used the

ANOTHER VIEW   *Hurricanes in the North Atlantic Ocean (Continued)*

ships left Havana, Cuba. They were carrying gold and silver worth more than $300 million in today's U.S. dollars. Fleet commanders knew they were going to sea in the middle of the hurricane season, but Spain was desperate for cash after years of warfare. On July 30, a killer hurricane caught the treasure fleet off Florida, smashing the ships and scattering them along the coast from Cape Canaveral to present-day Fort Pierce. More than one thousand people died, and Spain's badly needed treasure, ended up on the bottom of the ocean." Thus, by chance, Peter Stuyvesant's Dutch fleet could well have been knocked out by a hurricane, leading to the rise of New Sweden.

overland assault—without any interference from the numerous Native Americans.

The Dutch terms of surrender were mild enough: Rising and his officers, rather than being executed, were transported by the Dutch back to Sweden. However, the Dutch then carried out a program of calculated atrocities toward the Swedish settlers, a terror campaign to prevent any future resistance. Historian Turp writes in *West Jersey: Under Four Flags*, that "many of the men were arrested and put aboard ship. The women were abused and raped; their possessions were carried off and their cattle slaughtered." Thirty of the Swedish soldiers were also taken back to New Amsterdam. Apparently feeling he had made his point, and realizing he

The Delaware River proved to be a critical factor in the settlement and survival of New Sweden. (Edward S. Curtis/Library of Congress)

could not keep such a fleet in the area, especially in hurricane season, Stuyvesant then made an agreement with the Swedish colonists. Today's Swedish Colonial Society, in a "Brief History of New Sweden in America," remarks that "Swedish sovereignty over New Sweden was at an end, but the Swedish presence was very much in evidence. In fact, Governor Stuyvesant permitted the colonists to continue as a 'Swedish Nation' and be governed by a court of their choosing, be free to practice their religion, organize their own militia, retain their land holdings, and continue trading with the native people." Concerned about the fear that the British might intervene in his conquest, Stuyvesant seems to have considered his attack as a way of overwhelming the Swedes, rather than attempting to add the colony to New Netherland.

Yet an even more important reason existed for Stuyvesant to get the Delaware colony settled down: The Native Americans around New Amsterdam had attacked the settlement. (New York City's Wall Street marks the historic site of the wooden palisade the Dutch put up to protect New Amsterdam, the southern tip of Manhattan Island.) With the Swedes cowed, Stuyvesant had no choice but to hastily return to New Amsterdam; his own family had to be protected by French mercenaries in his absence. He left behind Captain Dirk Smit with some 60 soldiers to control the conquered population, as well as the local Native Americans. Surprisingly, with Stuyvesant and his army gone, no Swedes rebelled against their new rulers, at least not openly. Jean Jacquet, who replaced Smit, informed his superiors that some Swedes (and by inclusion Finns) were secretly planning against Dutch rule, but apparently nothing came of it.

With New Sweden subdued, Stuyvesant went back to New Amsterdam to rescue the town from the Native American attacks; he was kept busy with isolated raids that continued.

Although the Netherlands had a large navy, suddenly it could not provide Stuyvesant with much immediate support to quell the Native Americans and also keep the conquest in Delaware under control. In 1658, hostilities between the Dutch and Swedes erupted in Europe where the Dutch intervened in the Baltic (today's Lithuania) to keep the Swedes from taking it over. Conflict with the Swedes was not the Netherlands's only problem.

In 1660, King Charles II became king of England, and the maritime rivalry between the British and the Dutch renewed. It was again a war motivated by the Dutch and British competition over maritime trade. As British General Monk, who had made possible Charles's becoming king, put it when the war began, "what matters this or that reason? What we want is more of the trade that the Dutch now have," according to David Howarth in *British Sea Power: How Britain Became Sovereign of the Seas*. Then, a British squadron under James, Duke of York, the king's brother, sailed to the New World. On September 8, 1664, Stuyvesant was forced to surrender New Amsterdam to James, who renamed it New York. By October 1, the British arrived in the Delaware River and New Sweden and its new Dutch rulers capitulated as well.

All those settlers who agreed to British rule, as Weslager wrote in *New Sweden on the Delaware*, "were permitted to remain and enjoy all the rights of Englishmen." The Swedes had no reason to support the Dutch, and the

IN CONTEXT   Later Swedish Emigration to America

The end of Swedish control of the Delaware colony in 1654 did not mark an end to Swedes coming to the New World. Two hundred years later, a tidal wave of Swedish emigration began in the mid-1840s, when the first organized emigrant groups started to arrive in New York City harbor. These farmers headed to Iowa, Illinois, Minnesota, and other mid-western states, and were followed during the period up to 1930 by almost 1.3 million countrymen. Today, the Swedes still rank seventh among the European immigrant groups. In proportion to the population of their home countries, only the British Isles and Norway surpassed Sweden in the number of immigrants. The effect of this exodus from Sweden reached its climax around 1910, when 1.4 million Swedish first- and second-generation immigrants were listed as living in the United States. When compared to Sweden's population at the time of 5.5 million, approximately one-fifth of all Swedes had their homes in America before World War I.

conquest by the Duke of York was complete. British conquest of New Amsterdam, and New Sweden incorporated into it, was ratified at the Treaty of Breda in 1667, bringing peace between the maritime rivals.

Thus the era of Swedish influence in the New World passed first to the Dutch, then relatively quickly thereafter to the British. And the United States we know today, founded mainly on a British culture, government, and language began to grow, culminating in the British American colonies' war of independence a century later in the late 1700s, and the rise of the United States of America as a superpower 2 centuries later in the late 1900s.

ALTERNATE HISTORY

Had governors Printz and Rising acted differently toward the Lenni-Lenape, the outcome could have been uniquely different when Stuyvesant began his invasion of New Sweden on August 31, 1654. With the aid of the Native Americans, the Dutch land assault would probably have failed, leading to a quick retreat by Stuyvesant. Native Americans had often come to the aid of other colonial powers in the Americas. The French, for example, had gone to great lengths to appease the thousands of natives who lived along the Great Lakes and to the west. Tribes like the Pottawatomies and Miamis, who might have been fierce foes, loyally followed the French into battle, both against the other natives and against the British.

The Swedes had settled right astride the main trade routes of the Middle Atlantic region of North America, over which the natives had to travel, (Minquas, Susquehannock, or Lenni-Lenape), to bring their fur pelts to market. By settling where they did, the Swedes became the main source of all the European goods upon which the natives were growing increasingly dependent, from fish hooks to hatchets. There was really no other source for the natives to trade with: to both north and south they faced not only much longer trips but also bloody encounters with hostile tribes like the Iroquois in New York. At least at first, if the Native Americans were to get what they desperately needed, they had to deal with the Swedes.

Therefore, the Swedes, in commercial terms, had a stranglehold on the natives. Without relations soured by Printz, in the alternate history, the Lenni-Lenape have little recourse but to support the Swedes against the Dutch. The Swedes, like the French, could have turned the natives' trade dependence (with some human charity and understanding added) from a mere business alliance into a true friendship, affecting the entire history of the region, and perhaps far into the future too. From the cargo manifest that historian Turp recorded in *West Jersey: Under Four Flags,* we know that the Swedes trusted the natives with firearms, albeit in limited supply. However, Governor Rising could have overcome his prejudice and fear and armed the Lenni-Lenape fully as a military ally.

The fact that the Dutch were far more numerous than the Swedes would not have been a decisive factor: With trust and more armament, the addition of the Native Americans to the Swedish force would have been more than enough to push back the Dutch. And the natives were predisposed to not trust the Dutch. In 1659, a Mohawk leader complained of the Dutch in New Amsterdam, saying that the Mohawks were only trusted as long as they had beaver furs.

Assuming a Swedish victory on August 31, 1654, Stuyvesant would return to New Amsterdam in defeat. But he may not have given up on the idea of the Dutch invasion of Swedish Delaware and very well may have planned another attack. Yet that plan would be thwarted as well because, in reality, Swedish Queen Christina had ordered two ships with supplies bound for New Sweden. Therefore, even if Stuyvesant sailed south again in 1654, he would very conceivably have met an even more hostile reception. Indeed, with the Native Americans at their side, the Swedes, reinforced by two ships, could repel the Dutch again.

Lenni-Lenape scouts would have notified Governor Rising as soon as the Dutch sails were sighted in the mouth of Delaware Bay; swift runners and messenger canoes would have carried word back to him at the Printzhof. Immediately, forts at the mouth of the Delaware River would have beat the call to arms, turning out the militias. With more colonists having been inducted into the militia, there would have been enough to man the strategic blockhouses as well as give military advice to the natives. Although war canoes would have been smashed by the cannon from the Dutch ships, the natives were wily enough to avoid any such suicidal attacks. Instead, any effort by the Dutch to come into shore for fresh water or food would have been met from the (then) densely forested shores of the bay and river with dozens of arrows from Lenni-Lenape warriors, waiting in ambush for just such an attempt. Decidedly, the Dutch would not have taken over New Sweden.

Thus repelled again, Stuyvesant would have received word by now of the massive Native American attack on New Amsterdam. With fear of an impending massacre in New Amsterdam, Stuyvesant, with his battered army, would have had to make all haste to sail down the Delaware, weather past Cape May, and put on all sails to head for New

Amsterdam. The spectacle of the shattered Dutch army would have had a devastating effect on the Dutch under siege by the natives. With the guns of his fleet, Stuyvesant would have been able to drive any natives out of New Amsterdam: Native Americans would not march forward and be blown into body parts, as some colonial forces would do. However, Stuyvesant would have been almost totally unable to help the Dutch plantations that stretched up the Hudson River and north into Albany. The Dutch colonists would have felt the full tithe of vengeance that the natives would exact for previous atrocities.

Even more, it is unlikely that New Sweden would have let the chance slip to carry the war to New Amsterdam. Rising would have sent his Swedes and Native American allies hot in pursuit of the retreating Dutch. Thus, coming from the south along Native American trails, the Swedes and natives from New Sweden would have joined forces with the tribes already besieging Stuyvesant. It would not have been long before the cornered Stuyvesant would have been trapped within the wooden palisades of New Amsterdam. Any foraging parties by the Dutch faced ferocious Native American attacks. Any real supplies—certainly not enough to support civilians and soldiers—would only have been gathered by armed parties from the ships. Before long, starvation would have become a real fear for the Dutch. Moreover, if the troops and sailors were still aboard ship, it would only have been a matter of time before "ship fever," or disease, broke out onboard and quickly spread to the people in New Amsterdam. Thus, not only privation but disease would be deadly forces within New Amsterdam's walls.

Furthermore, the hurricane season was wearing on: every week would have put the Dutch ships in more peril. Because few of the ships under Stuyvesant appear to have been Dutch naval ships, but rather merchant ships, their captains would have been even more reluctant to risk them in New Amsterdam during hurricane season. Moreover, as winter approached, the merchants would have wanted to sail to the warmth and trade of the West Indies.

If Stuyvesant continued to hold out at New Amsterdam, it would be unlikely he could compel many of the Dutch ships to remain to support him once late October came. If he was determined to try to hold out without the ships, he might possibly have clung to New Amsterdam during the winter—but he would have had to abandon the Dutch up the Hudson River valley to their fate at the hands of the natives. Yet, if disease had broken out in New Amsterdam, not even this option would have been open to him. And if disease had not broken out before the ships had left, it would have over the winter when the population was weakened by meager supplies. Therefore, Stuyvesant, rather than accepting the surrender of Swedish Governor Printz as he did in actual history, would have been faced with surrendering his sword to the giant Swede. Instead of sailing home in triumph, Stuyvesant would have sailed to the Netherlands in disgrace.

The prospect of retaking a New Amsterdam—now thoroughly incorporated into New Sweden—would have been a daunting task for the Dutch. Worse for the Dutch, the Swedes in Europe had become a real threat to the Netherlands. Historian Frederick L. Nusbaum wrote

France's Louis XIV, the main power broker in European relations during the time of the New Sweden settlement. (Library of Congress)

in *The Triumph of Science and Reason, 1660–85,* "Sweden had become an army. War had been profitable and Sweden, in close alliance with France, did not fear the enemies which its conquests made for it."

Although in 1662, France's Louis XIV signed an alliance with the Dutch, it seems unlikely that he would have risked war with England over any Dutch attempt to reconquer New Amsterdam, which, after all, was within the area that the English claimed in North America. Moreover, Louis XIV would not have wished the Dutch to move against New Sweden, which would have alienated Sweden from France in Europe. When France declared war against England in January 1666, Sweden was neutral and both England's Charles II and Louis XIV were anxious to keep it that way. Thus, with New Netherland in Swedish control, it is highly unlikely that the Duke of York would ever have sailed to North America at all. How could he take New Netherland from the Swedes, whose neutrality his brother the king was desperate to keep at all costs?

With the Swedes firmly established in the former Dutch colonies, and the French holding New France (Canada) to the north, it would have eventually become difficult for the British colonies to sustain themselves. Much of the fighting done during the wars between France and England in North America (1689–1763) depended vitally on the participation of the Middle Atlantic colonies and New York. Indeed, the strategic Lake Champlain–Lake George water route flows north to Canada (New France) by the Richelieu River through New York. From 1755 to 1759 in the French and Indian War, this formed a major battle front for the British attempting to attack New France from the south—from New York. Yet, if New York had been in Swedish hands, this vital avenue would have been cut off. By the same token, the second major path of attack was westward from Pennsylvania into the French Ohio valley and Great Lakes. With the Swedes in possession, this avenue would have been blocked too.

Although it is true that the two attacks which defeated New France, in actual history in 1758 at Louisbourg and in 1759 at Quebec, sailed directly from England, these occurred with the British prime minister William Pitt being able to depend on the full resources of British North America. With so much of North America in Swedish and French hands, would there have been any British North America left by 1758? The colonies of New England were always the poorest, and with the least number of men enrolled in the militias. Could they have fought off many years of Swedish and French attacks? That seems highly doubtful, since during that entire period England's main military effort was always directed toward Europe.

The southern English colonies in Maryland, being so culturally similar to Pennsylvania, would most likely have joined New Sweden as a matter of course. This may have been likely as well for Virginia, for even by the middle of the 17th century its economy was inextricably tied to the other colonies through trade in indigo, tobacco, and cotton. Until the 1740s, North and South Carolina and Georgia were plagued by serious Native American attacks, abetted by the Spanish in Florida. Since 1715, Spain had been an ally of France and, with New Sweden, would have been an ally of the Swedes as well. Economically, Georgia was among the poorest colonies and had only been settled by James Oglethorpe in 1732 to serve as a buffer from Spanish attack for the Carolinas. However, the loyalty of the Carolinas to England was in reality tenuous at best. Given the existence of a powerful French and Swedish alliance covering much of the eastern part of North America, the economic interests in the southern colonies, as well as the people on the frontier, may have had serious doubts about retaining loyalty to England, whose help was far away. By 1758 there simply may have been no British North America.

With no British rule, there may not have been an American War of Independence. Indeed, George Washington would likely have been the governor of Swedish Virginia because governorships had been an important part of Swedish administration since at least 1719. The Swedish form of government prevalent at home by then would have been applied to New Sweden. Each Swedish American city would have been governed by a magistraten, or a borough council. Anxious to respect the colonial administrations—the Swedish would never have enforced rule as had King George III at the time of the American Revolution—most likely an American government would have evolved as a mix of Swedish and American political systems.

The only period that might have caused friction between New France and New Sweden came during the Napoleonic Wars, when Sweden sided with England against France. However, since Napoleon abdicated in April 1814, it is unlikely that, given the intense fighting in Europe, many troops could have been spared for North America. Most likely both New France and New Sweden would have taken a "wait and see" attitude to see how events in Europe turned out.

The next American crisis of national proportions would have been the Civil War, which broke out in April 1861 over the Southern states' defiance of the federal government over the issue of slavery. However, assuming Sweden did not attempt to bend Americans to its will as had George III in the Revolution, there may not have been any federal government in Washington, D.C., nor President Abraham Lincoln to fight the Civil War. With no Civil War, would African slavery have persisted? The initial answer must be a qualified yes. However, with the growth of American industry, now coupled to a French ally in the North, the South would have been increasingly an economic backwater in a growing industrial North America. Furthermore, neither the Swedes nor the French viewed slavery with the easy morality with which the American religious establishment did in the South during English rule. Strict Swedish Lutheranism as well as French Catholicism would have frowned on it. Given that an underdeveloped, Southern plantation economy would continue to exist in the midst of growing industrialization, and strong opinion among its business partners on the issue of slavery, it would very likely not be a question of if slavery would have ended in the South, but when.

In terms of government, it is likely, that some movement toward self-government would have emerged in Swedish America during the same era. The Swedes, with their tradition of commitment to local management of affairs, would have viewed this as a logical development. Even today, the Swedish government notes in "Local Government in Sweden," at www.sweden.se that "Local self-government has a long tradition in Sweden. The first legislation in this field is generally considered to be the Local Government Ordinances of 1862, which separated Church of Sweden tasks from civil ones." Most likely, a new Dominion of New Sweden would have been born around the turn of the 20th century, with representatives sent to sit in the Swedish Parliament, or Riksdag.

In actual history, Sweden adhered to its neutrality during World War I, which began when Germany invaded France and Belgium in August 1914. However, had the alliances continued in alternate history, Sweden would have been drawn into the war on the side of England, France, and Russia. This would be especially so since having a rich colony in North America, which would have greatly increased its share of maritime trade, Sweden would have been just as adversely affected as the United States was by the German policy of unrestricted submarine warfare. Indeed, it would be this German aggression that would be one of the major reasons for the American declaration of war on Germany in April 1917. By 1918 then, some two million Swedish American soldiers would have helped compel the Germans to surrender in November 1918. Actually, had Sweden entered the war in August 1914, the massive influx of American troops might have ended the war far sooner.

Moreover, with Swedish involvement in European affairs, rather than neutrality, Swedish America would likely have maintained its involvement too, instead of retreating into diplomatic isolationism. With an internationalist Swedish American participation, the League of Nations would have gained strength during the 1920s. When Adolf Hitler gained power in Germany in January 1933, he would have been faced by a France strongly allied to a powerful Dominion of New Sweden. It is possible Hitler would have been stopped short in his European aggression that began World War II.

With a sudden passing of Hitler, Germany would have returned to its experiment with democracy. After the Great Depression of the 1930s, a peaceful Germany would have taken its place in the middle of a quiet Europe. The fascist Benito Mussolini, who took power in Italy in March 1922, would have been isolated and, without the support of Hitler, most likely would have been removed from power even sooner than he was in 1943. Without a Nazi Germany in 1938, Josef Stalin of the Soviet Union would not have turned from England and France to embrace an alliance with Hitler in 1939. Rather than experiencing a period of isolation, which only increased Stalin's paranoia and fear of encirclement, Soviet Russia, even under Stalin, may have evolved along much more liberal and capitalist lines in an alternative Europe. With no World War II bringing Russia's Red Army into the center of Europe, there would—almost certainly—never have been a Cold War. In short, the entire 20th-century history of Europe would have been different, and infinitely safer and more prosperous for all.

And what of Swedish America? What changes would have occurred during the 20th century under a distant Swedish monarchy? Quite possibly, few if any. Western civilization was trending toward a homogenization that was already visible in entertainment and dress in 1900. There is little reason to believe that things would have developed any differently in a Dominion of New Sweden. With Swedish rule always moderate and respectful of American ways, there would have been no need to declare independence, any more than Australia and Canada or New Zealand ever declared themselves free of Great Britain. Although the Swedish language may have gradually been subsumed by English, Swedish would still exist in a government where American documents would be in Swedish and English, and Swedish would have been compulsory in American schools.

In terms of economy and social welfare, Swedish Americans may have enjoyed a higher or different standard of living than Americans do today. During the 20th century, at the cost of the world's highest tax burden, Sweden built up what is often called the world's most generous general social welfare system, with such elements as virtually free (that is, tax-financed) schools, child care, health care, pensions, elder care, social services, and various economic security systems. Although Sweden has always been a solid market economy, the Social Democratic governments in power for most of the 20th century borrowed many ideas from socialism. Swedish prosperity has been redistributed among the population to a greater degree than in perhaps any other country. Given Swedish socialism, with far more people in America to share the cost—the individual burden would have been far less. Because of the socialized health care of Sweden, the people of Swedish America would have been ahead of where we are now in the two most critical areas of health services: infant mortality and life expectancy. According to national statistics, in 2003 infant mortality was 6.8 per every 1,000 live births in the United States—but only 3.4 in Sweden. Life expectancy in Sweden was 80.0 years for both men and women at birth, whereas in the United States it was only 77.1 years.

Thus, in 2005, instead of celebrating the 229th anniversary of American independence, Americans would have been celebrating the 350th anniversary of the salvation of New Sweden from the Dutch. Instead of hailing the Star-Spangled Banner, Americans would be saluting the yellow and blue flag of Sweden and King Carl XIV Gustaf would be in Philadelphia, founded by a William Penn grateful to be able to find freedom of religion in New Sweden. And all this develops because one day in August 1654, in Delaware Bay, the Native American tribe Lenni-Lenape came to the aid of a few hundred besieged Swedes.

IN CONTEXT   Swedish Socialism in America?

The rugged individualism of the early Americans, their sense of self-sufficiency and independence, became ingrained in the national culture. Such traits do not necessarily fit well with socialism, a social and economic philosophy that places the betterment of society as a whole over the progress of any one individual. Thus one could question whether the American character would thrive in a Swedish socialist setting. Yet, in actual history, the United States veered very close to socialist ideals in the Progressive era of the early 20th century. And the New Deal social and economic programs instituted by President Franklin Roosevelt during the Great Depression of the 1930s mirrored many aspects of socialism. Today's Social Security, welfare, Medicare and Medicaid programs in the United States can rightfully be labeled as socialistic. So, in a sense, despite their capitalistic individualism, Americans may have been open to a form of Swedish socialist government in New Sweden in the 20th century.

John F. Murphy Jr.

Discussion Questions

1. What other aspects of American culture would be different today had the country grown up as a colony of Sweden?
2. Would American business be the same today under a Swedish socialist system?
3. Do you agree that World War II might have been averted had an alternate Sweden and Swedish America played a larger world role after World War I?
4. Why did the governors of New Sweden fail to seek permanent and friendly relations with the Lenni-Lenape tribe?
5. What other turning points in the actual history of New Sweden might have yielded other alternate histories?

Bibliography and Further Reading

Acrilius, Israel. *A History of New Sweden.* Philadelphia: Historical Society of Pennsylvania, 1874.

Ahnlund, Nils. *Gustavus Adolphus The Great.* Michael Roberts, trans. Westport, CT: Greenwood, 1999.

American-Swedish Historical Museum, www.americanswedish.org (accessed July 2004).

Balesi, Charles J. *The Time of the French in the Heart of North America, 1673–1818.* New York: Alliance Française, 1992.

Brzezinski, Richard. *The Army of Gustavus Adolphus.* Oxford, UK: Osprey, 1997.

"Brief History of New Sweden in America," www.colonialswedes.org (accessed July 2004).

Goldstone, Robert. *The Road between the Wars, 1918–41.* New York: Fawcett, 1980.

Howarth, David. *British Sea Power: How Britain Became Sovereign of the Seas.* New York: Carroll and Graf, 2003.

"Immigrants to New Netherland," www.rootsweb.com (accessed July 2004).

"Infant Mortality and Life Expectancy for Selected Countries, 2003," www.infoplease.com (accessed July 2004).

Koedel, R. Craig. *South Jersey Heritage: A Social, Economic, and Cultural History.* Lanham, MD: University Press of America, 1979.

Liddell Hart, B. H. *Great Captains Unveiled.* New York: Da Capo Press, 1996.

Murphy, John F., Jr. "First People In Delaware County," *Delaware County Magazine* (March/April 1991).

Murphy, John F., Jr. "Shipwrecks off the South Jersey Coast," *Atlantic City Press Magazine* (May 1977).

Mahan, Alfred Thayer. *The Influence of Seapower upon History, 1660–1783.* Mineola, NY: Dover, 1987.

Nusbaum, Frederick L. *The Triumph of Science and Reason, 1660–85.* New York: Harper and Row, 1953.

Shirer, William. *The Rise and Fall of the Third Reich.* New York: Fawcett, 1960.

"The Home of the People," and "Local Government in Sweden," www.sweden.se (accessed July 2004).

Taylor, Alan. *American Colonies: The Settling of North America.* New York: Penguin Books, 2001.

Trevelyan, G. M. *History of England, Volume II: The Tudors and the Stuart Era.* New York: Anchor, 1953.

Turp, Ralph K. *West Jersey: Under Four Flags.* Pittsburgh, PA: Dorrance, 1975.

Weslager, C. A. *New Sweden on the Delaware.* Moorestown, NJ: Middle Atlantic Press, 1988.

Wolf, John B. *Louis XIV.* New York: W. W. Norton, 1968.

TURNING POINT

*James, Duke of York, granted the charter for New Jersey in 1664.
What if James had died before establishing the colony, thus
affecting the future course of the United States?*

INTRODUCTION

The presence of the Dutch colony of New Netherlands and its absorption
of New Sweden, as well as the spreading of settlers down the Delaware
River, had become a serious thorn in the side of British North America.
Although largely Dutch, small pockets of Swedes, Finns, and Germans
had emigrated or had been absorbed from Swedish settlements and had
founded Pavonia, which later became Hoboken and Jersey City. Although
not yet involved in a declared war, the restored English monarchy of
Charles II, after the experiment with the Commonwealth under Oliver
Cromwell, used the threat of Dutch merchant vessels cutting into English
trade and nationalistic jingoism left over from the English Commonwealth's
victory over the Dutch in 1654 to promote privateering attacks on Dutch
East India Company ships. The tension was deliberately increased with
attacks on Dutch slave-trading entrepôts (trading centers) in West Africa
and a fleet sent to take the New Netherlands.

Charles II's brother and heir, James Stuart, Duke of York, acting as lord
high admiral, received a royal patent giving him possession of all Dutch
colonial land before the invasion fleet sailed. James sent a fleet of four
ships, approximately 450 soldiers and armed sailors and acting as his
proxy, Colonel Richard Nicolls.Nicolls, an experienced professional soldier and devoted royalist, consulted with the governors of the New
England colonies, coordinated actions based on their intelligence and
resources, and carried off a remarkably efficient attack. The capital city of
New Amsterdam was blockaded by the English ships, and Nicolls
demanded surrender of the Dutch governor, Peter Stuyvesant. Under
pressure from the Dutch clergy and frightened townspeople, Stuyvesant,
who realized he had little chance of avoiding a bloodbath if the town
chose to fight, handed over the colony to Nicolls on September 7, 1664.

Nicolls, who was empowered by James to assume the post of deputy
governor immediately, assured the Dutch residents that the Duke of York
had every intention of continuing their freedoms as they had been
enjoyed under the Dutch. In particular, Nicolls promised that New York,

James Stuart, Duke of York, became James II, king of England. (Library of Congress)

A portrait of Charles II, king of England, painted between 1670 and 1676. (Library of Congress)

as he promptly renamed the colony, would keep the religious toleration granted by the Dutch, even to Jews, and that settlement by a variety of religious and ethnic groups would be welcome. Acting on his own authority, Nicolls quickly began sorting out land grants for two major groups in the southern part of the colony, which he called Albania, recruiting a number of Quakers who planned to move into the western region on the Delaware River, and giving eastern lands to New Englanders, mostly Congregationalists in search of better land for farming than the rock-strewn soil of Massachusetts. Nicolls was handling the settlers well, insisting that they come to an agreement with the Lenni-Lenape tribes to establish an acceptable modus vivendi in the region. He reiterated his promise of religious toleration, town meetings, and a minimum of one church in every town, chosen by the population living there and to be paid for by a locally determined tax.

Then Nicolls received word from London. . . .

Without telling Nicolls, or consulting with anyone else, James met with two of his courtier friends, Sir George Carteret and Lord John Berkeley. Both men had been staunch supporters of the Stuarts, and James in particular. Carteret had kept the island of Jersey loyal to King Charles I during the Civil War and was personally extending credit to keep the Royal Navy at sea during the second Dutch War. What James was about

ANOTHER VIEW   Local Diversity and Religious Cultures

In actual history, the heritage of a single church in each town, at first financed by local taxes, left New Jersey with a system in which each township would determine its own church, leading to a patchwork of communities nominally committed to religious freedom but with great insularity. Each community tended to attract adherents of its dominant faith. Quakers, Anglicans, and a wide variety of Protestant sects took hold, and even after taxation to support churches was abandoned, the heritage of powerful local government remained characteristic of the state.

Retaining the coastline and ports of New Jersey, as well as the eastern shoreline of the Delaware River that provided access to the Port of Philadelphia, in the alternate history Greater New York–New Jersey would became the dominant colony of England in North America, outstripping Pennsylvania and Virginia in economy and importance. With a rich agricultural hinterland and its hundreds of quasi-independent religious enclaves, the downstate counties would provide an ameliorating influence on the commercial, quick-dollar, materialistic culture of New York City.

to do was a cheap, easy, and painless way to reward two stalwarts. On June 23, 1664, months before Nicolls had actually taken possession of the New Netherlands, James gave the two men 4.8 million acres, covering 7,500 square miles of the area. This chunk of land, measured from 41° 40' north on the Delaware River, extending in a straight line to the Hudson, passed into the hands of the two men. James, misunderstanding the map, believed that the area was an island, which, to flatter Carteret, he named New Jersey. In another provision of the land grant, that was less a misunderstanding and more James's personal greed, Carteret and Berkeley got the land, but the rights of government and tax revenue stayed with New York, which remained in James's hands.

TURNING POINT

The spring of 1664 was particularly warm, and an excellent breeding ground for the city of London's large population of rats. The old medieval city, with no building codes or public sanitation, was a morass of open sewers, rotting garbage, and rodent dens. Everyone expected the heat to raise the stench to levels that would cause anyone with means to leave for the countryside, and miasmic fevers were expected to strike the elderly and children, but no one was expecting the plague. It hit early (the real plague appeared in late summer 1664, after the royal family had gone to an estate outside London, rather than in June, in this alternate timeline), and James hardly noticed the deadly flea bite among the others he had acquired at the theater.

On June 21 he collapsed while playing cards with his mistress, Arabella Churchill. Royal physicians quickly diagnosed him with the bubonic plague. This was the septicemic variety, and James died in less than 48 hours from a massive blood infection. On his deathbed, James attempted to make a dying conversion to the Roman Catholic Church, but the frightened servants in attendance believed that his ramblings were the hallucinations of the high fever. Thus the Duke of York died a communicant of the Church of England. In this alternate version of history, the absence of a royal Catholic threat to the Church of England has far-reaching consequences, not just for New Jersey, but for the future history of what becomes the British Empire.

Having left only two infant daughters, Mary and Anne, all of James's property went to King Charles II, including the recently conquered New Netherlands. Careful management of the funeral and subsequent Church of England sermons assured that James was remembered as a loyal brother, faithful husband and father, and daring lord high admiral. Meanwhile, the surviving royal family went on an extended tour of the midlands, far away from the plague.

ACTUAL HISTORY

James gave away New Jersey in June 1664, despite the pleading arguments of Nicolls, who pointed out that James had just crippled New York geographically by cutting the colony off from the Atlantic coastline at all points but New York City. Furthermore, he had created a situation in which New York would be hemmed in by hostile Native American tribes northward up the Hudson and by poor quality farmland in the south.

James also made the decision to keep governmental authority in his own hands, while giving the actual real estate of New Jersey to Carteret and Berkeley, but he did not make this clear to them. Most proprietors undertook colonization grants with the understanding that they would invest in the infrastructure and development of a colony before reaping the rewards of increased revenue, but James had no available capital to invest in land clearing, port building, or construction of a New York merchant fleet, having spent his royal income on stately living, European debts, and his interest in royal monopoly companies like the Royal African Company, which dealt in slaves James was anxious to introduce into his new colonies. As a result, Nicolls, when he resigned in fury, had no other way back to England than as a passenger on a Dutch East India Company ship, a humiliating reminder of England's tenuous hold on the Americas. Nicolls died in 1672 fighting a sea battle against the Dutch, hit by a cannonball while standing next to James on the quarterdeck.

The division of New Jersey grants to Carteret and Berkeley roughly corresponded to Nicolls' two groups of settlers, the Quakers in the west, who settled in agricultural villages, and the Calvinist New Englanders in the eastern port towns.

Predictably, these dual authorities of proprietor and governor, as well as the two proprietors' subsequent sales of the grants, created chaos. Carteret dispatched his nephew Philip Carteret as governor and allowed an assembly of 12 men to establish laws and authorize taxation. This concession alone drew colonists disgusted with the royal government of

New York and refugees from the forced union of New Haven with Connecticut. However, the assembly met once in 1668, and Carteret failed to call them again for 7 years, while tensions built up among settlers about "quitrents" paid in lieu of feudal duties to the proprietors. In 1672, Sir George's bastard son James arrived in New Jersey en route to South Carolina, attracted the attention of frustrated dissidents, and convinced them to name him "president" of an illegal government in defiance of Philip, who fled rather than confront the rebels.

When news of the fracas reached the Duke of York, he was furious. He struck back, using his powers as the ultimate proprietor of the entire region, and threatened to revoke all land titles that did not originate from his hands—a measure that allowed Philip Carteret and his council to reestablish authority and overthrow James Carteret. The trouble, however, convinced Lord John Berkeley to sell his share of the colony for a very cheap £1,000 to a consortium of Quakers, led by Major John Fenwick and Edward Byllynge. This formally separated the colony into East and West Jersey on a diagonal line from 41°40' on the Delaware River to Little Egg Harbor. While West Jersey became progressively more Quaker, especially in a code of law that rejected capital punishment, and tied to Pennsylvania, the East evolved into a more absolutist administration by Carteret.

Trouble erupted again in 1681 when Sir Edmund Andros, the Duke of York's governor of New York, attempted to curtail smuggling from New Jersey to New York, and to collect customs revenue under the duke's umbrella authority. This devolved into an incident where Andros arrested Philip Carteret but was censured by a New York jury for it. The duke was forced to submit the situation to arbitration by English jurists, who found in Carteret's favor. Meanwhile, Carteret died in 1680, and his widow sold her shares in the colony to another consortium of 12 investors, one of whom immediately sold half of his one-twelfth to another. East and West Jersey now had large numbers of proprietors, a dangerous enemy in New York, and an unpopular and unstable divided government with two capitals at Burlington (west) and Perth Amboy (east). In actual history, this early political division of the colony had a long-range cultural impact because East Jersey (now known as North Jersey) became a suburban region centered on New York City, whereas West Jersey (now known as South Jersey) became a set of suburbs and rural areas largely centered on Philadelphia.

The Duke of York's poor leadership was evident in Britain as well. In 1672, he revealed his conversion to Roman Catholicism, shocking the English people and causing a major crisis in government as fears rose that the French would back a Catholic plot to assassinate Charles II and install James as an absolutist king. Although no plot ever materialized, the hysteria unleashed powerful anti-Catholic bigotry, resulting in a political attempt to exclude James from the throne. A political party, the Whigs, formed around exclusion and Protestant toleration, while Charles II supported the creation of an opposite party, the Tories to support the crown.

Gaining the upper hand in 1680, Charles II was able to exile Whig leader Anthony Ashley Cooper, the earl of Shaftesbury, some of whose followers emigrated to East New Jersey for refuge. In the colonies, Charles II allowed James to consolidate his possessions, as well as other colonies under the Dominion of New England, an entity formed by revoking the charters of Massachusetts, Rhode Island, Connecticut, Plymouth, and New Hampshire

KEY CONCEPT   Erie Canal, Transport, and Industry

As a consequence of its limitation to one port and not containing a rich agricultural hinterland such as available in New Jersey, in actual history, New York remained a second-class city through the colonial period, outstripped in importance by Philadelphia. New York did in fact not become a major metropolis until after the opening of the Erie Canal in the 1820s when it became the port of transfer for trade, immigration, and commerce with the upper Midwest via the Hudson River and the Erie Canal.

In the 1820s, in the alternate history, the Erie Canal would have been constructed, opening the inland regions of the Ohio Valley to water transport through New York–New Jersey. With New Jersey representing "downstate New York" much as Albany, Rochester, and Buffalo represented "upstate New York," the New Jersey region benefited as part of the Great Empire State of New York and New Jersey. The "Empire State" that opened the inland Empire via the canal would emerge as the dominant political and economic influence in British North America. With the Albanian Assembly based in New York City, the Empire State, including the downstate counties of the New Jersey region, would continue to be

In both actual and alternate histories, the Erie Canal was a major component of the development of the New York–New Jersey region. (Library of Congress)

KEY CONCEPT   *Erie Canal, Transport, and Industry (Continued)*

a mecca for European immigrants through the following decades. The continuing diversity of religious climate, particularly in the downstate counties, would draw from every new sect that emerged in Europe over the following decades.

In both the actual history and the alternate history, New Jersey was the location of the first regularly scheduled railroad in the Western Hemisphere, connecting New York and Philadelphia by way of Amboy in New Jersey, first to Burlington on the Delaware River and later to Camden, New Jersey, directly across from Philadelphia. This railway link, in both the Actual History and the Alternate here, assisted in the growth of New York City as a major business and commercial center.

Colonial industries in New Jersey included the first major glass industry, lumber industry, and iron

foundries. Early in the 19th century, New Jersey saw the opening of silk and other textile factories in North Jersey. Early-20th-century industries included electrical equipment, embroidery and lace work, optical glass works, and oil refineries, supplied with crude oil by tanker and barge in both North Jersey and along the Delaware River in South Jersey. In addition, New Jersey drew considerable revenue from a thriving tourist industry as visitors from both New York City and Philadelphia regions flocked to seacoast resorts from Cape May at the southern tip to Atlantic City and other beach towns. These transportation and industrial developments would probably have taken place whether New Jersey remained united with New York or was independent, and represented underlying economic forces.

The Atlantic City, New Jersey boardwalk in 1911. (Library of Congress)

and ending the short-lived assembly he had been forced to grant to New Yorkers. Both New Jerseys were added after negotiations with the large group of proprietors ended with their surrender of their grants to James.

Things changed dramatically when, on June 10, 1688, James II's young second wife, the Italian Catholic Maria Beatrice of Modena, gave birth to a son, James Francis Stuart. Whigs, and even more moderate Englishmen, now saw a dynasty of Catholic Stuarts stretching on into an oppressive future.

Their reaction was to invite William of Orange to invade England and unseat his own father-in-law, a task William agreed to in order to gain advantages from England in his wars with Louis XIV's France. Landing at Torbay in the south of England, aided by a "Protestant wind" that kept the French navy and James II's supporters becalmed in port, William had quickly been aided by the Church of England and the majority of the British military establishment, all of whom abandoned James. In return, James abandoned England, fleeing to France. Although the legal niceties were debatable—had James been overthrown? or did he abdicate by fleeing?—leading politicians acted to summon a "Convention Parliament" that offered the throne jointly to William III and Mary. This was an extraordinary move, establishing a constitutional monarchy in Britain in which the monarchs were contractually limited in their powers. This was formally written up in the 1689 Bill of Rights, which ended the divine right of kings and required the monarchy to be bound by laws made by Parliament and to summon regular parliaments, and it protected subjects from arbitrary arrests, court proceedings, quartering of troops, and taxation without parliamentary consent.

The Revolution of 1688 spilled over into the colonies when word arrived in April 1689. In Massachusetts, where Andros headquartered the

The British Parliament offers the crown to William and Mary. (James Northcote/Library of Congress)

Dominion of New England, Boston militia seized him and declared a return to their old charter. In New York, a Dutch faction led by Jacob Leisler turned out the lieutenant governor Francis Nicholson, but quickly became an unpopular dictatorship over the English population because Leisler declared military rule in order to stave off Catholic invasion. In Maryland, the Protestant majority of the colonists turned on Lord Baltimore, their Catholic proprietor and his administration of relatives and co-religionists to establish a government that remained in place with royal support until 1714, when Lord Baltimore's heir converted from Catholicism to the Church of England.

This reaction in the colonies was motivated by both a hatred of the absolutist policies imposed by the Dominion as well as a deep suspicion of a Catholic conspiracy tied to France and reinforced by a 1690 invasion of New England by Governor Frontenac of New France to sack Schenectady, New York. In Britain, the Revolution segued into a European war between William III's League of Augsburg and France, including a French-backed invasion of Ireland by James II and fighting in the Netherlands and German palatinate.

James II was defeated at the Battle of the Boyne in 1690, leading to harsh political restrictions against Catholics in Ireland and the establishment of a minority Protestant ascendancy there. In England and Scotland, the political backlash established the Whigs as the favored party of the Protestant Succession, and William organized British resources to provide maximum contributions to his wars, including setting up the Bank of England in 1694.

Politically, the threat of a foreign-backed James II or his descendants made it possible for the Whigs to dominate British politics from 1714 until 1760, passing harsh law codes against property crimes and using those convictions as leverage to transport thousands of petty criminals to the colonies. Without an opposition party, members of parliament had little reason to consider the colonies, and they engaged in mercantile policies that antagonized American producers and merchants through enforcement of the Navigation Acts and taxation.

Colonists realized that, although the British Isles had negotiated a dramatic shift toward limited monarchy and the rights of individual subjects, these liberties did not apply to colonials. Suspicion in London of any extraparliamentary authority as a venue by which foreign powers or religious extremists might influence the American colonies scotched talks of a colonial assembly as suggested by the Albany Conference in 1754.

These frustrations, that Americans were not given the proudly held rights of Englishmen, that administration centered in London was not responsive to colonial realities, that the Whigs were able to dominate British politics to the exclusion of opposition that might have integrated the colonies better, and that an ongoing war with France ended with the spectacularly expensive Seven Years' War, were all factors leading to the American Revolution. Conspiracy theories, while still sometimes Catholic-centered and fed by British policy like the Quebec Act, had morphed into a more general sense that the British state was obtusely and deliberately blind to American concerns and participating in a plot to oppress them and hinder their economic and political development. Thus the seeds for the American Revolution and the rise of an independent United States were firmly planted by the central fact that James had lived until 1701, long after he had proclaimed his adherence to the Catholic faith in 1671.

KEY CONCEPT   Migration and Immigration

Many would use the Erie Canal and, later, railroad links to the West to facilitate settlement of the Midwest and far West. Britain would support the addition of California to the American Union after the discovery of gold there in 1848, quickly suppressing Spanish-Mexican efforts to retain the region.

As European states underwent a series of revolutions from the 1840s through the midcentury, and later, as depressed agricultural prices drove European farmers from rural districts and then into cities, millions would emigrate to the religiously tolerant and welcoming American Union. Often, their first entry point would be New York City, and from there they would move into the growing industrial towns of upstate and downstate Greater New York and New Jersey, further fueling the cultural and ethnic diversity of the region. Like Canada, Australia, and New Zealand, the British American Union, stretching from Greater New York–New Jersey to the Pacific Coast, would become a modern and flourishing parliamentary democracy that thrived on the arrival of new citizens from Europe, and later from Africa and Asia.

ALTERNATE HISTORY

James, Duke of York, would have died of the plague in this alternate history in 1664, before announcing his Catholic faith. His elder brother, King Charles II, would have immediately taken custody of James's property and his two infant daughters. Unlike James, the king insisted that they be educated as future sovereigns rather than just English gentlewomen—Charles II's own politically savvy Queen Catherine of Braganza oversaw their reading program, hiring an impressive young political theorist, John Locke, who had impressed her with a poem written to celebrate her marriage to Charles II.

In this alternate scenario, Charles II transferred proprietorship of "New York and New Jersey" to his cousin, Rupert of the Rhine, an interested investor in colonial ventures. Rupert allowed Nicolls to continue with his policies, and did not split New Jersey from the New York colony. Rupert was able to spend the rest of his life improving New York, which, because it now included New Jersey, had an Atlantic coastline for the whaling industry, good soil for farmers, and a political system that, as Nicolls promised, allowed town meetings and a type of religious toleration. However, without the development of the proprietorship, the wide variety of religious localism promoted by Nicolls would continue to dominate the New Jersey, "Albanian region" of New York. In 1672, with a third Dutch War on the horizon, Rupert authorized a colonial assembly that won the loyalty of the colony's inhabitants. They successfully defended New York against a Dutch reconquest in 1674. Richard Nicolls died heroically during the fighting when a Dutch cannonball cut him in half on the fortifications of lower Manhattan. Although dominated by the established Dutch landowners, the assembly also contained Quaker and Calvinist members representing the southern part of the colony. It even included a Portuguese Jewish physician, a fact that greatly amused

Queen Catherine, herself from Portugal. The continued connection of New Jersey with New York in the colonial period would have deep and lasting effects on the region into the future developed under this alternate history.

This blended assembly would have wrestled with the task of providing a law code for the colony that took the best parts of the Dutch patroon tradition, the New England town meeting, and the Quaker insistence on a humane system of criminal law. Greater New York and New Jersey would become world renowned for its religious variations and local autonomy. Rupert, a naval expert, sent retired naval officers like Robert Holmes to his colony, where they insisted on better port facilities, a New York merchant fleet, and a crackdown on smuggling and piracy that made the coastal area safe for honest travel and trade. Because of the general prosperity, Greater New York–New Jersey was also able to fortify its northern frontier, a fact that impressed the Mohawk, allowed greater settlement into the area around Albany, and provided a strong deterrent to French and pro-French native raids.

Without Catholicism or Jacobitism as a dangerous "other," British politics would have been far better able to deal with Ireland and Scotland, negotiating generous unions with them. Ireland's Catholics were willing to exchange their loyalty to the Vatican in exchange for seats in the Dublin parliament and an Irish Catholic Church modeled on the Gallican Catholic Church of France. With Irish and Scottish troops fighting alongside their English colleagues, and no diversionary Jacobite invasions backed by foreign enemies, Great Britain fought effectively against France in the War of the Spanish Succession.

In this alternate history, both Anne and Mary III had been educated by Locke to believe in a monarchy very different from their uncle Charles II's reign. Both queens increasingly shifted power to the House of Commons, choosing their ministers from the dominant parties of coalitions formed after every election. A true constitutional monarchy, however, might not have emerged until 1714, when Anne died without a direct heir. The next in line for the throne was George I, the elector of Hanover. The House of Commons balked at acclaiming his accession until George volunteered to enter into a constitutional relationship with Parliament, adapted from the 1628 Petition of Right, limiting the sovereign from quartering troops on a civilian population, levying taxes without Commons' approval, or arresting a subject without cause. Thus some of the changes that came about in actual history in the Revolution of 1688 would have been delayed in this scenario until 1714. George, however, might have retained the right to call and postpone parliament, a tactic he could use cleverly to aid the Whigs, his favored party. Also, he retained command of the British military.

However, without the one-party dominance experienced in the real timeline by the Whigs, each party would have had to cultivate a constituency that included imperial policy. The Tories became the party of England's empire and had strong connections to the British East India Company and the wealthiest of the sugar planters in the Caribbean, as well as some of the traditional Anglican and Catholic landholders of Virginia and Maryland (and the favor of the inherited French in

Acadia). The Whigs cultivated popularity among the growing "middling" colonists, whose livelihoods were made more difficult by the monopolies of the British East India Company and the Navigation Acts. Using their wealth and the "rotten borough" system, both parties arranged for Americans to be elected to seats in the House of Commons and to get appointments to the Board of Trade and Plantations, which assessed taxation and colonial policy. Such an ameliorative and balanced parliament would have been able to prevent the excesses that led, in actual history, to the causes of the American Revolution, and thus, New York–New Jersey, along with the other colonies, would have remained part of the expanding British Empire in the 19th century.

Emigration to the colonies would have remained popular, especially because the poor and landless took advantage of generous grants from philanthropic organizations to make the Atlantic crossing and arrive as free people rather than indentured servants. Self-help banks organized by Quakers and "low-church" Anglicans like John Wesley aided emigrants by making small loans for travel and small business investments upon arrival. Without a pool of freed indentured people anxious to differentiate themselves from racially based slavery, southern colonies might never have implemented the harsh Black Codes of the actual history timeline that led to the differentiation between black slaves and white indentured servants, and instead exploited a constant turnover of cheap free laborers of both races, who generally fled to a city as soon as possible for industry or commercial jobs when they were available. Others would work their way to freedom and become yeoman farmers, again of both races.

Some areas, like the rice- and sugar-growing regions of Carolina and the British Caribbean islands, would have maintained a slave economy, but it would be tempered by the high cost of slaves smuggled from Cuba after the British declared the slave trade a vital economic target during the 1754–1758 war with France. Unthreatened by the increasingly weak French, the British Whigs pushed for more industry in the colonies, leading to the establishment of textile mills, iron foundries and a boom in infrastructure building.

Because there would have been no negative lingering fear of extralegal bodies, savvy politicians in the House of Commons negotiated with their parties' American members of parliament about the establishment of a colonial legislature to deal with American issues of frontier settlement, colonial boundaries, and American defense against the Spanish in Florida and the French in the southern Mississippi Valley. In 1754, with Britain on the brink of war with France and Austria in Europe, the Albanian Assembly was created, with its meeting house, designed in beautiful neoclassical style by Robert Adam, located in New York City, in the heart of Greater New York–New Jersey.

The Assembly was bound to consider bills sent down from London but was not required to assent without a majority approval. However, the British became adept at using subsidies and internal improvement projects to win over recalcitrant delegates. The British cabinet created a new position, secretary of state for America, who liaised with the monarchy. The New York–New Jersey delegates marveled at the religious insularity of the Massachusetts Congregationalists, whose insistence on religious exclusivity had driven settlers into the prosperous and more religiously tolerant New York–New Jersey coastal region.

The Board of Trade and Plantations listened carefully to the testimony of British Native Agents, representing the concerns of the increasingly anglicized tribes, and worked with the Albanian Assembly to police westward expansion. In this alternate timeline, the 1754–1758 European war had ended with France signing over the lower Mississippi in lieu of punitive fines after the British army occupied the Seine Valley and threatened to take Paris. The threat of Highlander regiments loose at Versailles might have moved Louis XV to sign over the last of the French North American properties quickly. The British, anxious to do well by their military veterans, sent out advance men into the unsettled territories to establish relationships with the tribes and negotiate acceptable areas for British movement and land settlement. Even so, the British army had to be called to intervene after aggressive Americans violated treaties with the Cherokee in the lower south, and their leader, the charismatic and unruly lawyer Andrew Jackson, was killed by a British dragoon at the Battle of Tuscaloosa in August 1796.

A few ethnic groups unhappy with British restrictions on their rule, and insistence on colonial religious tolerance in New York–New Jersey and Pennsylvania, and restrictions on westward movement, formed protest organizations like the Loyal Prussians and the Fighting French-Canadians but received little aid from European nations.

In 1839, on the accession of Queen Victoria, the Albanian Assembly petitioned the new monarch for formal independence within the British Empire. Pleased by the example of the 1812 union of Acadia, Quebec, and Iroquoia into the Imperial Canadian Union, as well as the thriving newer colonies of Australia and Victoria on the west coast of Canada, the queen recommended that Parliament agree, on the condition that slavery formally ended in America as it was ending in Britain's Caribbean colonies, and that the two nations remain as political and military allies. Tensions rose several times during the 19th century, as the British Empire's American Union pushed the Spanish frontiers of Mexico and contested British control of the Oregon territory, also claimed by Victoria. In both cases, the British defused the situation by allowing plebiscite votes and stationing the Royal Navy to enforce the decisions reached. Victoria joined the Imperial Canadian Union. Americans concentrated on settling the central plains.

The death of James, Duke of York, in 1664 could have created a world without the American Revolution, the French Revolution, or Napoleon, and therefore without the wave of nationalism inspired by the French Revolution. Confident in the good relationship with the American and Canadian Unions, the seeds of British Commonwealth states in the 20th century, Britain might have become more amenable to developing parliaments in its Indian and African colonies as well, encouraging a slow process of independence without the catastrophic and Cold War–fueled tragedies of the modern Third World.

Margaret Sankey

Discussion Questions

1. If James had died before announcing he was a Catholic, the history of Britain would have been very different than it was in fact. What are the most important ways that it would have been different?

2. If Nicolls's original plan for a single, locally chosen, tax-supported church in every community had become even more fixed in New Jersey culture and heritage, what would have been the consequences for ethnic and religious diversity in the region?

3. If New Jersey had remained connected to New York, how would the combined colony (later state or province) have been more powerful than the two as separated?

4. If England had a politics in which Whigs and Tories were balanced during the 18th century, the American Revolution might not have happened. Why not?

5. How would the opening of the Erie Canal have benefited the combined New York–New Jersey region?

6. How would Quaker values from the southern (western) counties of New Jersey have changed the politics and culture of New York if the two regions had been represented in a single colonial or state assembly?

7. If New Jersey had not been temporarily divided into the east and west proprietorships but had remained united with New York, would the New Jersey region have been a greater or a smaller influence on later events?

Bibliography and Further Reading

Callow, John. *The Making of James II: The Formative Years of a Fallen King.* Gloucestershire, UK: Sutton, 2000.

Craven, Wesley Frank. *New Jersey and the English Colonization of North America.* Hoboken, NJ: Van Nostrand, 1964.

Fleming, Thomas. *New Jersey.* New York: W.W. Norton, 1977.

Leiby, Adrian. *Early Dutch and Swedish Settlers of New Jersey.* Hoboken, NJ: Van Nostrand, 1964.

Lovejoy, David S. *The Glorious Revolution in America.* New York: Harper and Row, 1972.

Pomfret, John E. *The Province of East New Jersey, 1609–1702.* Princeton: Princeton University Press, 1962.

Pomfret, John E. *The Province of West New Jersey, 1609–1702.* Princeton: Princeton University Press, 1956.

Ritchie, R.C. "The Duke of York's Commission of Revenue," *New York Historical Society Quarterly* 58 (1974).

Sosin, Jack. *English America and the Restoration Monarchy.* Lincoln: University of Nebraska Press, 1980.

Webb, Stephen Saunders. *The Governors-General.* Chapel Hill: University of North Carolina Press, 1979.

 **TURNING POINT**

William Penn was given the colony of Pennsylvania in 1681, and encouraged German religious settlement. What if Pennsylvania became a German province?

INTRODUCTION

The history of the colony of Pennsylvania begins in 17th-century England, with the growth of the Religious Society of Friends, or Quakers. Prior to the Toleration Act of 1689, it was illegal to practice any kind of religion in England other than that sanctioned and governed by the crown. This meant that anyone who worshipped outside of the Church of England was subject to persecution by the crown. Despite these laws making non-Anglican worship illegal, numerous Protestant sects proliferated in 17th-century England. Although many of the groups were short-lived, the Quakers were successful in becoming a vibrant alternative to the established church.

George Fox founded the Quaker sect in 1647. Fox believed that there was no need for clergy, churches, or theology and that individuals could follow the teachings of Jesus Christ by listening to their own conscience. He called this the inner light. By 1658, he had converted at least 30,000 people to his movement. Fox also urged his followers to embrace a simple lifestyle and reject aristocratic pretensions. Ironically, one of the most prominent early converts to Quakerism was a young English nobleman by the name of William Penn.

Penn had always rebelled against authority, and, as a young man at Oxford University, he refused to attend Anglican religious services. At this time he first came into contact with the Society of Friends and began to explore their beliefs. By 1667 he had fully embraced the Society and was arrested for attending a Quaker meeting. In response to his arrest, he defended himself in court and began to write pamphlets that defended freedom of conscience. After this experience, he became an active Quaker as well as a vocal defender of the liberty of conscience. For the next 10 years, he engaged in a number of public debates with Puritans and Anglicans about the true nature of Christianity and traveled to speak with Quakers in Holland and Germany. However, by the end of the 1670s, intolerance of Quakers and other dissenting sects was still

William Penn, founder of Pennsylvania, was an early convert to Quakerism. (Kneller/Library of Congress)

oppressive, and Penn applied to the crown for a grant of land in America, where he hoped to set up a colony where all religious groups would be accepted.

Penn received the grant for the colony of Pennsylvania for two reasons, notwithstanding his professed Quakerism. The first was his friendship with the Duke of York, a close friend of King James II. The Duke lobbied the king and his advisers on Penn's behalf. The second and more important reason: the English government owed William Penn £16,000. In the 1660s, when Charles II had been king, Penn's father, a navy admiral, had lent the king this amount. Because Penn's father had died in 1670, the crown now owed young William the money. Instead of repaying the money in kind, James II granted Penn the rights to a colony in North America to be called Pennsylvania in honor of William Penn's father.

Penn originally created the government of the colony of Pennsylvania to conform to his ideas about good government and freedom of conscience. He did not believe that any one religious creed should be imposed on people by the state. Although his belief paralleled modern beliefs about the separation of church and state, Penn continued to believe that government was firmly rooted in a divine plan for humanity, and he excluded atheists from the protections of Pennsylvania's government. Penn also believed that good government had room for a head of state or proprietor who did not govern by the consent of the people. Despite these differences with modern concepts of democracy, the government of colonial Pennsylvania worked to protect the well-being and promote the happiness of most of its inhabitants. Penn worked hard to create a colony whose government conformed to Quaker principals, including an equilibrium between people's rights to property, political control, and equality of treatment. Although he had difficulty in achieving a perfect balance, Pennsylvania was the first British colony to attempt to protect its inhabitants against the arbitrary will of government officials, such as cruel and unusual punishments for crimes. As proprietor, however, Penn could still institute measures unchallenged, for he was technically, according to the crown charter, the only ruler of the colony. Believing, however, that people should take part, to some extent, in their own government, Penn began formulating constitutions to facilitate more popular involvement in the colony's government.

In the first two frames of government for Pennsylvania, in 1682 and 1683, Penn tried to put these basic beliefs into action. By the time that the second constitution, or frame of government, had been finished in 1683, Pennsylvania had a constitution with two representative bodies. The council (along with Penn, who would act as proprietor and governor) would write bills, and the assembly would either approve or veto bills written and passed by the council and governor. Pennsylvania's

KEY CONCEPT   The English Reformation

The English Reformation officially began when King Henry VIII broke with the Pope in 1533 over his divorce of Katharine of Aragon and remarriage to Anne Boleyn. Although Henry's break with Rome was not driven by deeply religious reasons, it allowed people within England who were already in favor of religious reforms to come forward without fear of punishment. Led by men like Thomas Cromwell, these reformers worked to create a reformed English church called the Church of England or Anglican Church. Later, English Protestants, known as Puritans, however, did not feel that the efforts of these original reformers and their followers had really purified the church. The official church and government persecuted those who practiced this ultrareformed version of English Protestantism. Puritans gained control of the English government during the 1650s and attempted to impose their own version of religion on the country, but the Reformation had already generated dozens of splinter groups that each claimed to have the true path to God. By 1660, the Puritan experiment in government, known as the Commonwealth Period (because there was no king or queen during these years) failed, and parliament restored the monarchy. It was during this period of turmoil, a result of the more than a century-long reaction to the original English Reformation, that the Quakers became a vibrant alternative to the Anglican establishment.

residents had some say about who would serve as members of both the council and the assembly. All freemen who owned 50 acres of land or had £50 of property were eligible to vote. This is how the government stood when Penn returned to England in 1684. In 1696, however, the assembly drafted a new constitution called Markham's Frame, which made the assembly a legislative body with the right to initiate legislation. When Penn returned to the colony in 1699 he had to adjust to

William Penn and colonists trading with Native Americans. (Darley/Library of Congress)

these changes and, on October 28, 1701, he reluctantly signed the Charter of Privileges, which allowed for an annually elected assembly that would become the sole lawmaking body of Pennsylvania. The council lost all legislative powers and became a body of eight men appointed by the governor as advisers. The proprietor and crown retained the right to veto laws passed by the assembly and approved by the council and governor.

By the time that William Penn died in 1718, at the age of 74, Pennsylvania had taken his ideas about rights, happiness, and self-government beyond his original wishes and created a modern form of government with clear executive, legislative, and judicial branches to protect and provide for Pennsylvania's inhabitants. It was upon this basis that Pennsylvania would become the most diverse and tolerant of all England's North American colonies in the 18th century.

TURNING POINT

Penn's belief in giving people some say in their own government led to a much more participatory and democratic colony than he had originally envisioned. The majority of the colonists were Quakers, and until the second half of the 18th century, they dominated Pennsylvania politics. But other groups of Protestants had also been among the first settlers in Penn's "holy experiment." In particular, Penn had advertised his colony widely in the German-speaking areas of central Europe, hoping to lure persecuted pietists to Pennsylvania. Many of them took Penn's promises of toleration seriously and embarked for the New World.

Between 1683 and 1709, however, only a few hundred German immigrants came to Pennsylvania. Men like Francis Daniel Pastorius, a German lawyer and radical pietist from Krefeld in southern Germany, led these first immigrants. On one of his trips through Germany, Penn convinced Pastorius to take a chance on Pennsylvania. Pastorius came to the colony in 1683 and founded Germantown, the first German settlement in Pennsylvania. He eventually became its leader and lawmaker and later converted to Quakerism. Despite his conversion, he remained a member of the German immigrant community, although he also developed close ties with English Quakers, including William Penn himself.

The German immigrants who arrived between 1683 and 1709 were similar to Pastorius. They came mostly from southern Germany and Switzerland, where religious wars were ravaging the region and local officials routinely persecuted radical sects. Life in Germany and Switzerland was difficult for these groups because the government and official church tried to prevent them from practicing their religion. Pennsylvania held the promise of freedom of religion and escape from the cycle of violence that ravaged the region in the late 17th century. When the first ship of German Mennonites, a radical pietist sect from central Europe, arrived in Philadelphia, both Pastorius and Penn welcomed them to their new home. They helped the Mennonites settle about 2 hours upriver from Philadelphia.

KEY CONCEPT   Radical Pietism

Radical pietists were small groups of Protestants in the 17th-century German principalities who dissented from the established Lutheran Church because decades of religious warfare in central Europe had destroyed their faith in existing religious institutions. During the 17th century, these groups proliferated throughout central and western Germany and in many parts of Switzerland. Toward the end of the century, some immigrated to Pennsylvania at the suggestion of William Penn. In many ways the radical pietists of Germany fit in well with Pennsylvania's English Quakers because they also emphasized pacifism, kind treatment of those who did not share their beliefs, and the role of the inner light in bringing individuals into a relationship with God. There were also members of the Lutheran Church who promoted many of the same ideals of personal devotion and religious toleration as the radical groups.

Unlike these church pietists, however, the radical pietists believed that they could find purity of faith and perfection in life only by breaking from the established church and totally separating themselves from existing worldly institutions. These beliefs often led to cases of extremism, such as the members of the Ephrata Cloister in Pennsylvania and the Rosicrucians, who promoted the complete celibacy of all their members. Despite these excesses, radical pietist groups such as the Amish, Moravians, Mennonites, and Dunkers were members of a tolerant faith that promoted sympathy for those who disagreed with their religious beliefs. They were, in many ways, the perfect settlers for William Penn's holy experiment.

A Mennonite child, descendent of the original German settlers of Pennsylvania. (FSA/Library of Congress)

Another of the original German immigrants to Pennsylvania was a man named Johannes Kelpius, who led a group of radical pietists called Rosicrucians to the colony in 1694. Rosicrucians, like Quakers, believed in an inner light that they called the inner fountain, although they renounced worldly goods and pursuits to an even great degree. Kelpius's Rosicrucians were men who hoped to live a celibate life devoted to God. Forty of them eventually settled on a ridge outside Germantown and became known as the Monks of the Ridge. The Rosicrucians and Mennonites were among many small groups of radical pietists who made Pennsylvania their home at this time. Many other pietist groups followed them to Pennsylvania both before and after 1709, including a large number of Moravians and a smaller number of Amish.

By 1709, however, a more secular group of German immigrants began coming to Britain's North American colonies. These immigrants came for economic rather than religious reasons. This second wave of immigration occurred between 1709 and 1714. During this period, thousands of German and Swiss immigrants flowed into America's ports to make their way in the New World. Pushed by poor economic conditions in Europe and pulled by the promise of employment and a free passage to America paid for by the English government (which hoped to employ them in the colonial shipyards), these immigrants flowed into Pennsylvania, New York, and North Carolina.

However, it was not until 1717 that Pennsylvania became the colony of choice for German immigrants. Between 1717 and 1775, more than 80,000 German immigrants came to Pennsylvania. They were much like the few thousand who came to the colonies between 1709 and 1714, and radically different from the pietists who had originally staked their claim in Pennsylvania. These immigrants fled declining economic conditions and oppressive control by local feudal lords because, in the 17th and 18th centuries, Germany was not yet a united country but a group of small, independent principalities that spoke the same language. Residents of these German-speaking areas, more easily referred to as Germans, hoped to become landowners and to find independent economic success in Pennsylvania. Although these immigrants were members of nonpietist churches like the Lutheran or Reformed Churches, they were able to meld easily into the colony because of Penn's views on religious toleration and the existence of the small but successful German community that had been established by the radical pietists in the late 17th century.

William Penn had set the stage for this first major immigration of a non–Anglo Saxon immigrant group to what was to become the United States by recruiting radical German and Swiss pietists for his colony. He welcomed them to the colony and believed that they would contribute to

Amish farmers today continue with many of the traditions practiced by the original German settlers in Pennsylvania. (Loretta Carlisle)

its growth, prosperity, and utopian vision. Because they had similar beliefs to Quakers and most of them embraced pacifism, they seemed to be a perfect fit for the holy experiment. Penn allowed them to buy tracts of land in his colony and to become independent, prosperous, and equal members of society. This group was so small as to be nonthreatening, but what if the newer immigrants of the 18th century had overwhelmed the English settlers? How would this have changed the course of Pennsylvania and American history?

Penn might have ended up regretting his decision to invite persecuted German pietists to Pennsylvania if the large numbers of later immigrants had made a successful political move to take over the government of Pennsylvania. Germans might have more openly protested the severe abuses that many began to face upon arrival in the colony. And if immigration had remained unregulated, as it did until 1729, German immigrants may very well have come in large enough numbers to gain the political advantage necessary to control Pennsylvania politically, instead of having to choose sides in the debates controlled by Penn and the English colonists. Thus, through their economic success and the political power granted to all property-owning freemen, they might have made a successful play to gain control of the colony's government and usurp Penn's charter.

ACTUAL HISTORY

In actuality, Penn did not have to regret the welcome he gave to the original radical pietists. They created a small but thriving German community in Pennsylvania that was able to absorb, welcome, and help later immigrants assimilate into a primarily British colony. The thousands of Germans who came to Pennsylvania between 1717 and 1776 became active and full participants in the political, social, and cultural life of the colony. These immigrants also helped to make Pennsylvania one of the most ethnically and religiously diverse colonies in North America and prefigured the ethnic, religious, and racial diversity that would come to define America in the 19th and 20th centuries.

The major German immigration of the 18th century drew from the towns of southwest Germany. The people who chose to leave their villages did so for a variety of reasons. They did not leave for religious reasons or in huge organized ventures, but in small groups with members of their families and towns. These immigrants left subsistence agrarian villages, where church and town officials were becoming stronger, not weaker. Serfdom still existed in Germany in the 18th century, and under this feudal system, peasants owed allegiance to the person who owned the land that they farmed, a person they called their lord or noble. Nobles and church officials wanted to keep serfs tied to the land to protect their own power and economic interests in a Europe where local officials were beginning to lose their power to new nation-states. Legally, in order to immigrate, serfs had to be freed and receive permission to leave their village. Finally, the lords required them to pay dues as compensation for their lost labor. Many young Germans wanted to

Pennsbury Manor, William Penn's country home in Bucks County, Pennsylvania. (Loretta Carlisle)

escape this system and left without paying the dues and without permission. Thousands of them moved to Pennsylvania where there was abundant land and personal freedom.

Upon arriving in Pennsylvania, these Germans integrated themselves into existing communities such as Germantown and built new Lutheran and Reformed churches to accommodate their religious practices. These communities were important resources for the many immigrants who had trouble adjusting to conditions in Pennsylvania. Many arrived with no money and in ill health, but the German community was often able to help them succeed by providing short-term loans to pay off their debts, helping them to find a place to settle, and giving them the time and space to recover their health after the long journey. By 1764 German immigrants had formed the German Society of Pennsylvania to pressure the government to correct abuses that immigrants faced upon arriving in America and to provide assistance to Germans in need.

German communities in Pennsylvania remained, for the most part, divided from English towns and cities. Despite the religious differences with the German communities, most German immigrants preferred to live with those who shared their language and culture. Many radical pietists, however, continued to maintain their own separate religious communities. Once immigrants arrived and settled in Pennsylvania, they tended to put down roots quickly. These communities, however, were different from the ones they left behind in Germany. Instead of heavily settled towns and villages, the landscape of Pennsylvania was diffuse. People lived fairly far apart, and the nearest church, doctor, or school could be miles away. Despite these obstacles, the German immigrants did establish schools, churches, and necessary services. By the 1720s Germantown was home to a German-language press, and in the 1740s and 1750s, Christopher Saur, a printer, began to sell advice books for new immigrants.

Once settled, these immigrants quickly integrated themselves into the political life of the colony and became naturalized citizens of the British Empire, which allowed them to vote, and, therefore, gave them an ability to acquire, pay for, and protect their land. Their vote for members of the assembly and council, as regulated by the Charter of Liberties, gave them a powerful voice in Pennsylvania politics, and the German community became a strong force in favor of protecting the colony during the French and Indian War. They were also major advocates of American independence from Great Britain. Because the majority of the 18th-century German immigrants to Pennsylvania came to escape the control of oppressive feudal lords and to achieve economic success, these issues dominated German involvement in Pennsylvania politics, and they mounted the first major challenge to Quaker control of the government.

When these larger waves of German immigrants began to arrive, however, they aroused some opposition within the colony. Many English-speaking colonists feared the arrival of large numbers of men and women who did not speak English or follow English customs. As early as 1717, they began to speak against selling the immigrants more land. In response, several German immigrants petitioned the government for land, emphasizing their honesty and conscientiousness. Many of the English, however, began to fear that their colony would become a German one, especially as poorer immigrants began to arrive in Philadelphia. In 1730, after attempting to pass laws that would effectively prevent all German immigration, the assembly passed a law that prevented the immigration of convicts by placing a duty of £5 pounds on their head. Additionally, to prevent the arrival of poor people who might become a burden to the colony, the assembly enacted a law stating that each shipmaster must either transport such people back to their place of origin or cover the costs of settling them in the colony. These measures effectively kept out poor German immigrants while still allowing those with sufficient funds to make their way in Pennsylvania.

By the time of the French and Indian War in the 1750s, however, German settlers in Pennsylvania had become numerous and successful enough to have a voice in colonial politics and to shape the history of the colony and state of Pennsylvania. Their voices became particularly loud and persuasive in 1732 when Thomas Penn, William Penn's son, came to Pennsylvania to reorganize the land system. Having a charter from the crown for a proprietorship, Thomas retained control of all Pennsylvania's lands, much as the feudal lords in Germany did. Penn's first actions were to set up a land office and extend his "manor system" so that he kept one-tenth of each new tract of land, raised the price of 100 acres of new land by £5, and raised taxes on all land in the colony. His scheme, however, did not work. In such a sparsely settled Pennsylvania, there was little government power to enforce the new laws, and the Quakers who ran the assembly were against Penn's new land policy. Most of the German immigrants just ignored the new laws. Frustrated, Thomas Penn tried to use the increasing number of naturalized Germans to his advantage by recruiting them to his side of Pennsylvania politics, called the Proprietary

---

IN CONTEXT   The French and Indian War

The French and Indian War occurred between 1754 and 1763. Europeans referred to it as the Seven Years' War. During this war, the English and French, who were fighting in Europe, continued their battles on North American soil. It is termed the French and Indian War in the United States because it featured battles between the British, French, and each side's native allies. The American name highlights the presence of Native Americans in the conflict, probably because the French and their allied natives made so many attacks on frontier settlements in Britain's American colonies. Many colonists, including many Pennsylvania Germans, truly lived in fear of French–native attacks on their homes. In reality, these attacks were only part of a larger imperial war between France and England. The French astutely used the British colonists' fears of native attacks to further their military goals. In the end however, the British won when General James Wolfe defeated General Louis-Joseph de Montcalm to capture Quebec City, the capital of New France in September of 1759.

By 1763, the French had completely lost their foothold in North America and signed the Treaty of Paris giving the British all their lands, with the exception of a few small islands. Britain and Spain became the last remaining imperial powers in North America. The French and Indian War is also notable for helping to create many of the conditions that led to the American Revolution, including the need of the British government to raise money through taxes to pay for the expensive military campaigns to protect their North American colonies. The American colonists, however, reacted unfavorably to British attempts to impose these taxes, which included the Stamp Act (1765) as well as the Townshend Acts (1767) that taxed common imported goods like tea. The American colonists' anger at these laws led to the formation of a unified resistance that emerged in the 1770s as the full-blown war for independence that we now call the American Revolution.

(as opposed to the Quaker Party), but the Germans refused to support him because of his coercive land policies. Penn had failed to recruit the Germans to his side, but he had succeeded in making them important actors in Pennsylvania politics. For most of the century, the majority of the German community voted for the Quaker Party.

During the French and Indian War, however, the Germans split with the Quakers over the defense issue. Although the original pietist Germans were, like the Quakers, pacifists, the newer German immigrants, who made up the majority of the community, supported actively defending the colony from French attack. As more and more Germans moved further to the west in search of land, the defense issue became more important. Western settlers wanted protection from both the French and the natives on the frontier. In November 1755, a group of Germans from the western part of the colony went so far as to march into Philadelphia carrying several corpses mutilated by natives. They demanded that their families and communities be protected from native attacks, many of which were supported by the French. The Quaker assembly finally acceded to their demands and approved £60,000 for the colony's defense.

Although the Quaker Party reluctantly agreed to raise money for frontier defense, the increasing violence on the frontier led to splits in the German vote in the 1760s. German immigrants and their children were increasingly frustrated with the Quaker Party's foot-dragging on the defense issue, especially as violence began to escalate during the 1760s. At the same time, Thomas Penn instituted land reforms that brought many of the Pennsylvania Germans to his side. By the summer of 1765 he had lowered land prices, recognized improvements that people made to their land, and gave squatters the first chance to purchase tracts at reduced rates even while he doubled taxes on land. In this way, he was able to undercut speculators and bring the Germans, always ready to protect their property, to his side. The plan also worked for Thomas Penn, whose income increased due to his new financial policies and the new bureaucracy he established to enforce them. He found that German immigrants were willing to pay higher taxes if they could buy land at a cheaper price. Thus, on the eve of American independence, the German community had shifted its allegiance to an English lord.

Yet, when the time came to declare their allegiances, most Germans in Pennsylvania sided with the struggling colonies. By the time of the American Revolution, the British government's unwillingness to open western lands to settlement, and promulgation of the onerous Stamp Tax, led many Germans to believe that British rule was becoming an obstacle to their success. Thus the vast majority of Germans supported the American War of Independence. Their support was manifested in the German-language publication of Thomas Paine's *Common Sense*. The most popular pamphlet of its day, *Common Sense* eloquently articulated the cause of independence from Great Britain. The lay councils of the German Reformed and Lutheran churches in Pennsylvania signed their names to a printed letter in support of the revolutionary effort that was to be circulated among Germans in New York and North Carolina. While supporting the effort, Pennsylvania's Germans also petitioned the Continental Congress and won concessions that would make them full citizens of the new nation.

By the time the United States became a nation, Pennsylvania's German immigrants had established themselves as full, if not dominant, members of the new nation. Their communities survive to this day in central and eastern Pennsylvania and they are often known as Pennsylvania Dutch (a misapplication of the German word Deutsch). Many members of the Pennsylvania Dutch communities are the descendents of the earliest German immigrants to America. When another wave of Germans immigrated to the United States in the 1840s, they came to a nation already somewhat familiar with German immigrants and their experiences. Thus, although the United States became a country based on the English customs, law, and language, the German immigrant experience in Pennsylvania in the 18th century proved to foreshadow the multicultural nation that the United States became in the 19th and 20th centuries, as waves of immigrants came from every continent.

ALTERNATE HISTORY

A few minor changes in the history of Pennsylvania might have resulted in the colony becoming a German province instead of the center of much revolutionary activity in the English colonists' fight for independence. First, had Penn been more successful in recruiting German settlers for the colony in the 17th century, perhaps spending more time traveling and speaking with those considering the New

World option, the earliest German communities might have been larger and more influential in the earliest days of the colony. The Moravians, in particular, might have had a larger impact on the course of Pennsylvania history had they arrived in larger numbers before the middle of the 18th century.

Had the Moravians, a highly centralized and fervent pietist sect, entered Pennsylvania in large numbers in the late 17th as opposed to the 18th century, they could have developed enough political power to lay the groundwork for an even larger German immigration in the first half of the 18th century. In actuality, the Moravians did not begin coming to Pennsylvania until the 1740s, but they had been in existence in central Europe since the 15th century. Their move to Pennsylvania in the 1740s resulted from a renewed energy and expansionist impulse provided, beginning in 1727, by a new leader, Count Zinzendorf. Had Zinzendorf been born half a century earlier he would already have been a community leader when William Penn swept through the German provinces in the late 17th century looking for settlers for his new colony. Thus Zinzendorf and his Moravians might have provided the largest number of German settlers to the new colony. Despite their zealousness, the Moravians were ecumenical and cosmopolitan and would have provided a strong force in the early colony for uniting all German cultural groups into a strong, centralized community. As a result of these differences in the pattern of early German immigration, later waves of immigrants would have had an easier time integrating themselves into the political, social, and cultural life of colonial Pennsylvania. Instead of finding themselves in diffuse communities spread across an English-dominated landscape, they might have found larger and more urban German communities originally established by the early settlers who had enthusiastically embraced William Penn's offer of asylum.

In the alternate history, the later influx of immigrants, who came for primarily economic reasons, might have banded together with these earlier groups, under the influence of the Moravians, and changed the course of Pennsylvania's history. Had Penn been more successful in his recruitment of German settlers and had the Moravians entered their expansionist phase earlier, the German population may have been large enough in 1730 to prevent the passage of laws restricting German immigration. If they had been able to prevent this, the influx of poorer immigrants would have continued unabated, and by midcentury, English fears that the colony was becoming German might have become reality. Therefore, while in actual history, Germans made up over 70 percent of the population in several Pennsylvania counties and totaled somewhat less than 40 percent of the total population by the end of the 18th century, if the restrictions of the 1720s and 1730s had not been passed, Germans may easily have made up over 50 percent of the colony before the end of the century.

In actual history, Pennsylvania's German community initially became an important political voice in the colony. However, in alternate history their numbers would have been large enough to block the restrictive immigration policies of the Quaker assembly, and by the late 1730s, they might have become a major party of their own. If this had happened, they would not have needed to support the Quaker Party's politics, but could have made their own stand within the assembly when Penn began to institute his medieval land policies.

By the middle of the 1740s, with the absence of the immigration restrictions, Germans would have had enough votes to control the assembly and render Penn's desires powerless. Harkening back to the early years of the colony when the Quaker settlers battled with Thomas's father, William Penn, over the shape of the government, the newly empowered German immigrants could easily have changed the face of Pennsylvania's government and separated themselves from the British government even before the French and Indian War, although it is unlikely that this would have happened. With a strong foothold in the assembly, including the power to block anti-German laws and prevent Penn from instituting his land policy, they would have had no particular quarrel with the Quaker members of the government. In particular, the radical pietists within the German community would have continued to feel a certain spiritual bond with their Quaker neighbors.

However, in the alternate history, the French and Indian War would have been a major turning point in the history of colonial Pennsylvania, possibly making Pennsylvania the first independent nation in North America. The larger numbers of German settlers would have faced an even more heightened state of violence on the colony's western frontier as these landless peasants sought to push farther west in search of arable land on which to establish their families. As they pushed to the farthest reaches of Pennsylvania's hinterlands, they would have encountered the same attacks by natives that sent a group of Germans marching into Philadelphia with dead corpses in 1755. There would have been more frontier settlers, more dead bodies, and a more sympathetic assembly.

In this case, the height of the French and Indian War in the late 1750s might have marked the end of Pennsylvania as an English colony. By this time, German immigrants might have controlled the assembly with their numbers and could have voted for defense appropriations without the support of the Quaker Party. Still despising Penn and his land policies, they might have seen this as their chance to declare themselves independent of Penn, and by association, Great Britain's rule as well. The German Party in the assembly would have had plenty of advantage in making this decision because it would have taken them out of the direct crossfire of the French and Indian War, making attacks on German settlers on the western edges of Pennsylvania less likely. Thus, by declaring Pennsylvania to be free of the proprietary rule of Thomas Penn and overwhelming the Quaker Party, the German community of colonial Pennsylvania would have established the first independent state in North America.

The likely leaders of this push and heroes of the new independent Pennsylvania would likely have been Heinrich Melchior Muhlenberg and Conrad Weiser. Muhlenberg was known as the "patriarch" of the Lutheran church in North America and was the de facto leader of the largest segment of the German community in Pennsylvania, the church Germans. Although he remained a Lutheran all his life, Muhlenberg a native of the Halle region of Germany, where pietism was extremely popular, subscribed to many ideas associated with the radical pietists and advocated a more pietistic religion than could be found in most of Europe's Lutheran congregations.

More prominent than Muhlenberg, however, was his father-in-law, Conrad Weiser, known to many as "the interpreter" because of his knowledge of native languages. Weiser was most famous, however, for his skills in negotiating with the colony's native tribes and helping to maintain peaceful relations between them and the colony's government. He knew the Native Americans of the region better, perhaps, than any other white settler, and his prominence as a negotiator would have made him a likely candidate to lead the German Party. Additionally, his pietist-leaning Lutheranism would have made him sympathetic to radical pietist and Quaker pacifism in crafting a defensive plan for the colony that used the establishment of good relations with Pennsylvania's internal native inhabitants to defend against attacks by French-allied natives from the Ohio Valley.

It is unlikely that the new state, led by men like Weiser and Muhlenberg, would have instituted a monarchy, considering the German community's poor experiences with feudal lords in Europe and America and the possibilities that Pennsylvania's democratic system had provided them. The face of America's earliest democracy might very well have been German. But what would the future of what we know as the United States of America have looked like without Pennsylvania as the site of the First Continental Congress, the approval of the Declaration of Independence, or the adoption of the Constitution? How would Pennsylvania have fared when Great Britain's remaining English colonies decided to break their relationship?

The existence of the German example in Pennsylvania may have inspired the supporters of American independence, showing them that a democratic and independent nation could exist outside the bounds of imperial control on the North American continent. It is almost certain that the residents of German Pennsylvania would have supported the efforts of the surrounding colonies to become independent of colonial rule. After all, in alternate history, they had managed to successfully break the bonds of feudal slavery and assert their rights to self-defense 2 decades earlier. The English colonies of North America would have bound themselves, if not in government, then in friendship with German Pennsylvania. In fact, they might have won their independence earlier and more easily because of the existence of an independent Pennsylvania.

In the first case, a smaller number of colonies would have had to bear the weight of British taxes to pay for the French and Indian War. The Stamp Tax as well as the taxes on imported goods may have fallen more heavily on the residents of the remaining colonies, creating even more anger toward Britain's postwar imperial policies. Also, King George III, then ruler of the British Empire, and the British Parliament, would have found it more difficult to call in Hessian (German) mercenary troops to fight against the colonists. With the presence of a large, free German population supporting the colonists these troops may have found sanctuary in Pennsylvania and found it difficult to fight against a cause that their fellows in language and culture supported.

If Pennsylvania had continued to exist as a separate nation in North America throughout the 19th century, the primary locus of its conflicts with its English-speaking neighbors would likely have been in westward expansion, although its friendly disposition toward the colonies during the American Revolution would probably have led to the new American government giving special consideration to Pennsylvanians looking to move westward in the late 18th century. However, because Pennsylvania would have been surrounded by a strong and growing United States that continued to expand westward, and due to its strong English minority population, there may have been a push to integrate independent Pennsylvania into the new nation. In many ways, this would not have changed 19th-century U.S. history much because Pennsylvania, as a nonslaveholding state, would have supported the Union side during the Civil War as it did in actual history. Pennsylvania's German history, however, may have led to an even larger influx of German immigrants into the United States in the mid- to late-19th century, creating a larger German community with a more vocal presence due to its successful and initially independent history on the continent. Socially and politically, the United States might have become a bilingual and bicultural nation, constantly balancing English and German social, cultural, and political heritages.

These developments, however, might have changed the course of U.S. history drastically during the 20th century, when the United States went to war twice against Germany. The heavily German population of Pennsylvania would no doubt have supported the German state in World War I, or at least supported U.S. neutrality, and German communities in other states would no doubt have followed suit. Woodrow Wilson and Congress may have, therefore, had no choice but to stay neutral during the war due to the important votes of the German population. Neutrality in World War I could have set the stage for a tradition of isolationism, the idea that the United States should stay out of internal European affairs. The peaceful ideology of German pietism might have contributed to such a viewpoint by encouraging Americans to hearken back to the earliest German settlers' dreams of peace and intergroup unity. In actual history, isolationism was a prominent ideology, but eventually succumbed to the wishes of the larger American public to enter World War I.

In alternate history, however, during World War II, this dominant isolationism as well as the strong political voice of the German American community could very well have prevented the United States from joining the fight against fascism in Europe, leaving Great Britain, France, and the Soviet Union to fight German Nazism without the help of the United States. In particular, because the British circulated so many untrue rumors about German atrocities during World War I, many German Americans might not have believed the stories about Adolf Hitler's concentration camps and, therefore, would not have believed it necessary to get involved in the European conflict. When the United States declared war on Japan after Pearl Harbor, Hitler and Nazi

Germany, Japan's ally, may very well have refrained from declaring war against the United States because of its significant German population. The United States would have remained neutral in the war in Europe. The face of the United States today might, therefore be that of an isolated North American nation unwilling to get involved in foreign affairs and tainted by its unwillingness to fight fascism in the 1940s.

Instead of celebrating the American worldwide economic, military, and cultural dominance entering the 21st century, Americans might instead be looking back at a proud history of independence from the world and its affairs. In the early years of the 21st century, instead of fighting wars in Afghanistan and Iraq and facing the brunt of international terrorism, the United States, although a geographically large nation, might be an isolated one, refusing to get involved in affairs outside North America. Most Americans would probably be bilingual in English and German, and, alongside the history of the Pilgrims landing at Plymouth Rock, American school children would also learn about the early Moravians who brought a cosmopolitan, ecumenical, and peaceful worldview to early Pennsylvania that planted the seeds for a largely neutral United States in the 21st century.

Alexis A. Antracoli

Discussion Questions

1. What other aspects of American life, in addition to language, might also be different had Pennsylvania become an independent nation under the leadership of a majority German population?

2. Considering that the origins of a German Pennsylvania would probably have been democratic, do you think that it would have been possible for Americans to side with the Nazis in World War II, even if Americans of German ancestry had made up half or more of the nation's citizens in 1940?

3. Why did William Penn and the Quakers seek to establish a holy experiment in the New World? Why was their similarity and openness to radical pietists an important part of the Pennsylvania settlement experience?

4. Do you notice any other points in the history of colonial Pennsylvania that might have been turning points? What are they? Why do you think they are turning points, and what are the other possible outcomes?

5. How did Thomas Penn, William Penn's son, shape the history of colonial Pennsylvania? Why were his attempts to gain the support of the German inhabitants of the colony important to its actual history?

Bibliography and Further Reading

Anderson, Fred. *Crucible of War: The Seven Years' War and the Fate of Empire in British North America, 1754–1766.* New York: Alfred A. Knopf, 2000.

Andrew, Charles McLean. *The Colonial Period of American History*. New Haven: Yale University Press, 1964.

Atwood, Craig D. *Community of the Cross: Moravian Piety in Colonial Bethlehem*. University Park: Pennsylvania State University Press, 2004.

Bittinger, Lucy Forney. *The Germans in Colonial Times*. Westminster, MD: Heritage Books, 1968.

Collinson, Patrick. *The Reformation: A History*. New York: Modern Library, 2004.

Ephrata Cloister, "History of the Ephrata Cloister," www.ephratacloister.org (accessed March 2005).

Evans, Richard J. *The Coming of the Third Reich*. New York: Penguin, 2004.

Fogleman, Aaron. *Hopeful Journeys: German Immigration, Settlement, and Political Culture in Colonial America, 1717–1775*. University Park: University of Pennsylvania Press, 1996.

Holian, Timothy J. *The German Americans and World War II: An Ethnic Experience*. Bern: Peter Lang, 1996.

Klein, Philip S. and Ari Hoogenboom. *A History of Pennsylvania*. University Park: Pennsylvania State University Press, 1980.

Longnecker, Stephen L. *Piety and Tolerance: Pennsylvania German Religion, 1700–1850*. Lanham, MD: Scarecrow Press, 1994.

Merrell, James H. *Into the American Woods: Negotiators on the Pennsylvania Frontier*. New York: W.W. Norton, 1999.

Reichmann, Eberhard, Lavern J. Rippley, and Jorg Nagler. *Emigration and Settlement Patterns of German Communities in North America*. Indianapolis: Max Kade German-American Center, 1995.

Roeber, A.G. *Palatines, Liberty, and Property: German Lutherans in Colonial British America*. Baltimore: Johns Hopkins University Press, 1993.

Schwartz, Sally. *A Mixed Multitude: The Struggle for Toleration in Colonial Pennsylvania*. New York: New York University Press, 1987.

TURNING POINT

Jamestown, Virginia, settled in 1607, was at first unsuccessful. What if the settlers had better relations with Native Americans and had survived?

INTRODUCTION

In the early 17th century, England was a prosperous island off the coast of Europe and had yet to establish colonies overseas or to adopt military methods common in Europe. Although English privateers preyed on Spanish commerce around the globe and the English Navy had won a great victory over imperial Spain in 1588, those naval successes did not translate into an ability to project power across the ocean and establish colonies in North America by force. In 1585, the English adventurer Sir Walter Raleigh attempted to establish a colony in Virginia at Roanoke, but the entire population of the settlement vanished before the end of the decade.

The 17th century saw the culmination of a series of trends in warfare known as the Military Revolution. Collectively, this refers to the transition of European armies from human-powered weapons such as bows and swords to the dominance of gunpowder weapons on the battlefield, and to the development of tactics and forces best able to exploit the advantages of new technology. Large, linear troop formations were developed to exploit these new weapons, formations that allowed one rank of soldiers to fire, while other ranks were reloading their weapons, allowing the formation as a whole to maintain a steady volume of fire. Whereas older types of weapons required years of training and experience if they were to be used properly, firearms offered a great deal of power, without requiring such extensive training. Although firearms could have a devastating terminal effect when their projectiles struck home, they were also notoriously quick to foul, slow to load, inaccurate, and vulnerable to dampness. In Colonial America, such problems were magnified, but such weapons still proved an essential element in the European conquest of the Native American peoples.

Large military forces, however, were not common in the colonies until the 18th century. In the 17th century, Virginia's most effective military force was the militia, a system in which men of military age were expected to bear arms if called upon to defend their colony. All too often in Colonial America, standing armies were seen as anathema to liberty.

KEY CONCEPT   Firearm Revolution

Even though historians in Europe have tended to believe that gunpowder used in weapons was invented by Europeans, there is solid evidence that the Chinese used gunpowder in small, hand-held cannons as early as 1290 or 1300. Roger Bacon described a Chinese formula for making gunpowder in 1242, but there is no evidence that Europeans were using gunpowder in weapons before about 1327.

Europeans began to develop cannons and handheld tubular weapons such as the matchlock, flintlock, and musket over the period from the 1300s through the 1600s, bringing about a revolution in warfare. Although the weapons were often almost as dangerous for the user as for the targeted enemy, they were easier to master and required less training than longbows and crossbows. Furthermore, when used against an enemy without firearms, they were intimidating. Between the psychological effect and the occasional shot that hit home, armies equipped with such weapons soon became a regular feature of European warfare.

A key technical problem in early firearm design was the issue of exactly how to ignite the powder. A Spanish arquebus required that the soldier carry a burning or smoldering match to set off the powder. The matchlock, introduced in the 15th century, employed an **S**-shaped clamp known as a serpentine that held the burning wick or slow-burning match. Squeezing a trigger lowered the serpentine and the smoldering match into a pan of priming powder on the side of the gun barrel. If the weapon failed to fire, all that would happen would be a "flash in the pan." However, if successful, the flame would get through a tiny hole in the breech, firing off the powder packed inside the gun barrel. This system allowed the soldier to steady the weapon

Although British troops were not seen in Virginia in large numbers until the 18th century, when they did arrive, they were a great source of friction between the British government and the colonists.

Military change was not the only type of change taking place in 17th-century Europe that would affect America. The Protestant Reformation sparked by Martin Luther swept over Europe, spawning centuries of conflict between Protestants and Catholics and keeping European nations locked in struggles with each other that would bleed over into the New World. Vast conflicts such as the Thirty Years' War nominally pitted Protestant and Catholic countries against each other and descended into an orgy of cruelty and death. Conflicts such as the English Civil War saw members of the same faith fighting to see which particular interpretation of their creed would come to dominate a particular country. English attempts to colonize Virginia were played out against this backdrop of military change and religious strife.

By 1606, the Virgin Queen, Elizabeth I, for whom Virginia was named, was dead. King James of Scotland succeeded her and it was he who issued a charter to the Virginia Company of London on April 10, 1606. The company sought to establish a foothold in Virginia, which could later be expanded into a profitable colony. Three Virginia Company ships, the *Discovery*, *Godspeed*, and *Susan Constant*, commanded by Captain Christopher Newport, arrived in what is now the James River on May 14, 1607. The ships transported just over 100 colonists, who carried with them the hopes and expectations of their king, their country, and their company, as well as their own aspirations. They disembarked onto Virginia's shore expecting to create a successful colony with great ease. They could not have been more wrong.

KEY CONCEPT   *Firearm Revolution (Continued)*

with both hands, rather than using one hand to bring a burning match to the priming powder.

Matchlock weapons included the arquebus and the musket. The musket, introduced in the early 1500s, fired a large shot through a plain tube barrel that was not rifled, or lined with twisted grooves to impart spin. For this reason, the musket was notoriously inaccurate but extremely effective at fairly close range if several muskets were fired at the same targets at the same time. The best way to employ muskets was to get a whole troop of soldiers to load, aim, and fire simultaneously, at close quarters, on the enemy. The blast of shot, while not precisely targeted, could wipe out opposing massed troops. Such tactics explain the practice of lining up forces that would march in ranks and fire on each other.

Another early form of musket used a trigger to snap down a piece of flint that would send a spark into the priming powder. The problem with such a flintlock gun was that it would jerk as the flint struck the spark, often ruining the aim. On the other hand, the matchlock musket had the disadvantage of giving away its position at night because of the glowing ember, so there were advantages and disadvantages to both types. For some 200 years, beginning in the 1620s, most musket weapons were fired with one or another type of flintlock. Early in the 19th century, flintlocks were superceded by weapons that used a percussion cap to set off the gunpowder. Similar to the paper caps used in modern children's capguns, these small charges would ignite when struck by a hammer, setting off the main gunpowder charge.

Even with the improvement of percussion caps and the introduction of rifled gun barrels in the 19th century, soldiers continued to use smoothbore muskets up through the American Civil War of the 1860s.

TURNING POINT

Virginia's turning point came early in the colony's history. The early years of the Jamestown settlement were marked with privation, death, and conflict with the natives, and the colony survived only by the narrowest of margins. Had the colony been more stable from the beginning, history might have turned out differently.

Unlike the Puritans who settled New England to practice the Protestant faith according to their own specific beliefs, Virginia's early settlers ventured to the New World in search of a fortune. These were not the hardy frontiersmen of popular imagination, but city dwellers, often unaccustomed to agricultural labor. All were unaccustomed to the climate of Virginia, which, although far milder than other parts of what is now the southern United States, was far hotter and more humid than that of England. Becoming accustomed to the new colonial climate was a process known as seasoning. That process, by which men and women from northern Europe adjusted to the climate and diseases of the American South, took a heavy toll in human life. Anyone who has ventured to Virginia knows of the debilitating heat and humidity of a summer there, even in the 21st century with the presence of amenities such as ice, air conditioning, and indoor plumbing.

English settlers established a small village, which they named Jamestown, roughly 60 miles from the mouth of the James River, in 1607. Jamestown was located on an island in the James River, a situation that offered a measure of security against an attack from the mainland, along with relatively easy access to the ships that were the colonists' lifeline to England. Both were important considerations. A poorly defended colony might simply vanish, as had Sir Walter Raleigh's Roanoke colony, founded in 1580s and gone within a few years. In an age before well-made roads, water was the easiest way to travel and transport goods and was also the only highway to England. Proximity to water deep enough to accommodate oceangoing vessels was, therefore, a crucial element in the life of any colony in America. Jamestown's earliest occupants could not hope to make their fortune without being able to ship their treasures back to England, and to return to England to enjoy their wealth.

Unfortunately, Jamestown's island location had two severe drawbacks. First, the island lacked natural springs that could provide fresh water, and the water of the James River proved too brackish for human consumption. Second, the swamps and marshes of the Virginia tidewater bred mosquitoes at an alarming rate. Mosquitoes carried the tropical diseases that felled colonists with fever and dysentery. The latter could lead to an especially gruesome death from dehydration due to severe vomiting and diarrhea. With antibiotics and intravenous fluids still centuries away, only those colonists who had both sturdy constitutions and good luck would survive.

Poor nutrition also proved a major problem because most early Virginians failed to devote enough time to growing their own food. Early in the life of the colony, Jamestown's settlers all too often went hungry because of their own greed and because many of those from the larger English cities were unaccustomed to the agricultural year and the need to husband food to get through it. Also, many who were gentlemen in England believed that it was beneath them to perform manual labor. Even in later years, many settlers preferred to plant tobacco rather than food. Failing to grow their own food, early Virginians all too often hoped to purchase, steal, or extort food from the Powhatans, a decision that would lead them into perpetual conflict with the Native Americans.

Unlike the colonists who settled New England, those in Virginia enjoyed poor relations with Native Americans from very early in the life of the colony. Small-scale raids and attacks took place throughout the early years of the settlement, culminating in the large-scale attack staged by the Powhatans in 1622 that devastated the colony.

Rather than enjoying a period of stability in which to get their colony started, the settlers at Jamestown endured years of failure and death. By building Jamestown in the middle of a pestilential swamp, refusing to grow enough food for their own needs, and constantly fighting with the natives, the early colonists of Virginia consigned themselves to begin their colony under circumstances that almost doomed it to failure. Only luck, stubbornness, a constant influx of new settlers, and hard fighting allowed the Virginia colony to survive its first years of existence.

ACTUAL HISTORY

Virginia is, arguably, the most important of the 13 colonies that declared their independence from Great Britain in 1776. It provided the world with vast amounts of tobacco, and America with an odd combination of liberty and slavery. Virginians commanded the Continental Army and wrote the Declaration of Independence. The climactic victory of the Revolutionary

War was won at Yorktown, Virginia, in October 1781. Colonial Virginia also produced many of the leaders of the United States; of America's first five presidents, four, George Washington, Thomas Jefferson, James Madison, and James Monroe were born and reared in Colonial Virginia.

Yet, although Virginia eventually became a successful and powerful colony that produced some of America's greatest leaders, the colony almost failed in its early years. The Virginia that emerged at the end of the colonial period came as the product of a very difficult founding. Following the establishment of the settlement at Jamestown in 1607, the colony almost collapsed from starvation, illness, mismanagement, and sustained combat with the Native Americans. Virginians made almost every conceivable mistake that could be made by those wanting to establish a colony in a hostile wilderness an ocean away from home.

The first settlers of Virginia arrived not as representatives of the English government but as members of the Virginia Company, a joint-stock company designed to generate revenue for investors back in England. This arrangement would last until 1624, when the Crown seized control and made Virginia a royal colony.

One man, more than any other, helped ensure that the colony at Jamestown survived its early years: John Smith. In his mid-20s by the

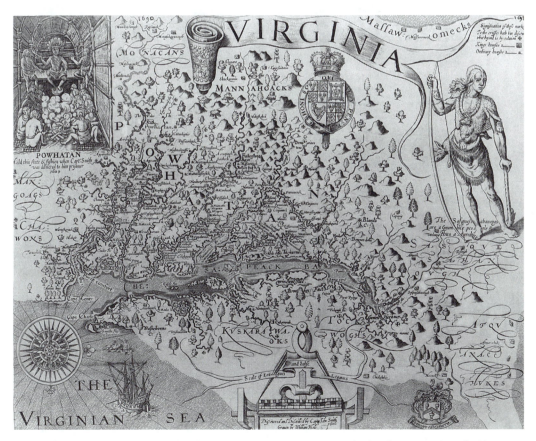

A map of Virginia in 1606 showing the Chesapeake Bay, Potomac River, and other features as described by Captain John Smith. (Library of Congress)

Captain John Smith rescued by Pocahontas from capture by Native Americans. (Library of Congress)

time he arrived in Jamestown, Smith had spent years fighting in the Low Countries and Hungary. Because of his capacity for decisive, violent action, Smith pursued courses of action that often led him into conflict with his own settlers and with the Native Americans. Attempting to impose military-style discipline upon his fellow colonists, Smith bred discontent in Jamestown. When dealing with the Native Americans, Smith was equally confrontational, and although his encounters with them often resulted in deaths, those encounters also often provided the settlers with much needed corn for food.

Native Americans clashed with the English settlers from the earliest days of the colony, yet they took a long time before organizing a broad campaign to destroy the colony of Virginia. In 1622, Native Americans of the Powhatan tribe struck the English settlements in Virginia and dealt them a heavy blow. Almost 350 settlers would die in the attacks. One of the worst attacks hit the English colony of Martin's Hundred, southeast of Jamestown. On Friday, March 22, 1622, the Powhatans visited Wolstenholme Town, the main settlement of the colony, in peace, sitting down to dine with the colonists, trading with them, and doing nothing to rouse suspicion. Then, without warning, the Powhatans attacked. Out of about 140 inhabitants of Wolstenholme Town, 58 were massacred, and another 20 taken prisoner. Those civilians were neither the first nor the last murdered in the wars that raged between Native Americans and European settlers.

ANOTHER VIEW   Martin's Hundred

The settlement known as Martin's Hundred was overrun by a Powhatan raid in 1622. There were about 140 settlers when the community was attacked. Twenty of the settlers were taken as captives by the Powhatans and 58 were killed. When settlers returned after the attack, they came well-armed for defense, bringing with them a large number of firearms, including a cannon, 26 matchlock guns, some 91 pounds of gunpowder, and about 360 pounds of shot. Eventually the Wolstenholme Town site was abandoned, and the community moved inland a bit to a site near the present Carter's Grove Mansion. The parish identified as Martin's Hundred eventually merged into York-Hampton Parish early in the 18th century.

The community has been studied, not only because of the Powhatan massacre and the spiriting away of 20 captive women, but because of the severe reprisals that the English settlers took on the native peoples the next year. In May 1623 the colonists set up a meeting, supposedly to discuss peace with the Powhatan chief, Opechancanough, but with the real purpose of springing a reprisal trap. On May 22, Captain William Tucker and his men, armed with muskets, met with Opechancanough and other prominent Powhatans on a neutral spot on the Potomac River. The Powhatan contingent had come to negotiate the release of some of their captives, but Tucker planned the slaughter of Powhatan leaders. After the captain and the Native Americans had made a number of speeches, Tucker supplied the natives with poisoned wine prepared by the colony's resident medic, Dr. John Pott. Many Powhatans fell sick or dropped dead, and then Tucker's musketeers shot and killed another 50 or so. Opechancanough got away, and the Powhatans kept the surviving captured women for a while longer. Finally, at the end of 1623, Dr. Pott ransomed the remaining captives. However, they were not welcomed into the colonists' community, and at least one woman complained that they were treated as slaves by Pott after they returned.

Despite the heavy losses sustained in 1622, Virginia endured. The colonists responded with a methodical campaign to kill Native American warriors and to destroy their crops and homes as well. European warfare in the colonies targeted both Native American fighters and their ability to wage war. If colonists could not kill their opponents in battle, they would destroy their homes and food and let starvation and exposure to the elements take their heavy toll.

In Virginia, though, tobacco cultivation and daily survival remained at the forefront of daily life. It was John Rolfe who first planted tobacco in the colony. The first shipment of tobacco left Virginia for England in 1617. Thereafter, tobacco would play a significant role in the life of the colony as its most lucrative cash crop. Tobacco proved difficult to grow, for it demanded constant attention from a farmer, and luck to survive the harsh weather conditions of the American South. Even if a crop could be raised successfully, it still needed to survive the trip to England, where it could then be marketed. Tobacco prices remained high until the second half of the 17th century, after which prices would stagnate.

The colony had far more land available for farming than could be worked by the colonists, so colonists looked to import laborers. For a long time, the colony relied on what was called indentured servitude. Persons in England would sell their labor for a term of years in exchange for passage to Virginia. Although this did somewhat mitigate the problem, servants imported from England still had to survive the harsh conditions

The wedding of John Rolfe and Native American Pocahontas. (Library of Congress)

of Virginia for their full term for the investment to pay off. Also, young men released from their servitude, but with few prospects, became a source of discontent for the colony. In addition, as people in Virginia began to live longer lives, they looked for ways to secure forced labor for longer terms, such as those offered by human slavery. For the Virginia planter, especially later in the 17th century when both masters and slaves possessed greater longevity, the purchase of African slaves became an economically viable option. African slaves had been brought to Jamestown in the early years of the life of the colony, but they were brought to Virginia in far greater numbers in the latter decades of the 17th century.

A series of events in 1676 helped drive Virginia to embrace more thoroughly the concept of African slavery. Nathaniel Bacon led a rebellion of restless young men, servants, and slaves against the ruling elite of Virginia. Although a dramatic disturbance, the rebellion eventually fizzled out, causing more damage to property than to life. The long-term consequence of the rebellion was that Virginia gradually embraced a slave system of labor, rather than one of servants who would eventually be free and restless. Slavery rested on brutal violence designed to keep slaves in bondage; Virginia laws gave masters the power to torture and kill their slaves. Slavery was introduced into a system of labor based on servitude, and the transition from one form of labor to another was aided by the racist contempt that Englishmen exhibited toward African slaves.

The Virginia that emerged from those early years of struggle and agony eventually achieved some stability. Unfortunately, it further plunged into a morass of suffering and cruelty by embracing African slavery as a system of labor. Ironically, slavery grew in Virginia alongside a political

The governor's palace in Williamsburg, Virginia. (National Archives)

culture that extolled liberty and freedom. The slave economy that was established in Virginia in the 17th century would spread throughout the South in various forms, only to be abolished in 1865 after 4 years of devastating civil war.

Virginia's political culture in the 18th century developed in light of this shift to a slave-based economy. With the African labor force powerless and enslaved, Virginians developed a view in which all white men were seen as equals. The larger, wealthier planters of Virginia achieved a kind of solidarity with the smaller landowners: they all shared in the fact that they were free and white.

Near the turn of the 17th century, Virginia shifted its capital from Jamestown to Williamsburg. Centrally located on the peninsula between the York River and the James River, Williamsburg would serve as Virginia's capital until the Revolutionary War, when it was moved further inland to Richmond so that it might be less vulnerable to British raids from the sea. Williamsburg was the site of Virginia's oldest institution of higher learning, the College of William and Mary. The college attracted many scholars who would play a role in American history. George Wythe, signer of the Declaration of Independence served as law professor there starting in 1779, and afterward he counted among his pupils James Monroe, John Marshall, and Henry Clay. In the 20th century much of Williamsburg,

Williamsburg's colonial appearance has been restored and converted into America's largest living history museum. (National Archives)

which had been left as a historical backwater, was restored to its colonial appearance and converted into America's largest living history museum.

In the late 17th century and throughout the 18th century, Britain and France fought a series of wars that would increasingly be fought in the American colonies. The largest and most significant of these was known in Europe as the Seven Years' War and in America as the French and Indian War, and was waged from 1756 to 1763. During that conflict, Britain destroyed French power in North America, but at an enormous financial cost. In the years after the war, the British government tried various schemes such as the Stamp Act and the Townshend Duties to try to raise revenue to pay off the debt incurred during the war.

Virginia played a major role in opposing such measures. In 1765 and 1766, Virginia saw widespread resistance to the Stamp Act, including the formation of groups known as the Sons of Liberty, to intimidate those who sought to carry out the act. Later measures triggered Virginia boycotts of English goods and caused men such as George Washington to support the development of manufacturing within the colony so that it would not need to import so many goods from Great Britain.

By 1775, Britain and America were headed toward armed conflict. In Virginia, the royal governor, Lord Dunmore, attempted to forestall rebellion by seizing the powder magazine at Williamsburg. Dunmore later fled Williamsburg, clashed with rebels at the battle of the Great Bridge, and issued a proclamation offering slaves their freedom if they would fight on behalf of the British. As war broke out in the colonies, Virginia supplied the rebellion with political leaders such as Thomas Jefferson, Patrick Henry, and Richard Henry Lee, and with the military leader who proved essential to an American victory: George Washington.

The War for American Independence came to Virginia most vividly in 1780 and 1781. During that period British troops raided Virginia, causing devastating property damage in parts of the state. Yet, on October 19, 1781, a combined Franco-American force compelled the British army at Yorktown to surrender. The penultimate battle of the war was fought on Virginia soil, with a Virginian in command of Allied forces, just across the York–James Peninsula from Jamestown, where the English began the colonization of Virginia.

In the late 18th and early 19th centuries, Virginia provided the new republic with crucial leadership. Washington, who had provided America with necessary leadership during the war for independence, also helped to start the impetus for a new constitutional convention that was called in 1787. James Madison played a major role at the constitutional convention and also in the ratification process where he wrote justly famous essays contained in the *Federalist*.

Slavery continued to be a major presence and source of conflict in Antebellum Virginia. Nat Turner's slave rebellion in 1831 rocked the colony and resulted in more severe laws governing the lives of slaves. Twenty-eight years later, John Brown's failed insurrection at Harper's Ferry, Virginia, helped ignite the Civil War.

The state that played a crucial role in forming the Union would also play a major role in the drama of its potential dissolution. In 1861, Virginia did not secede from the Union until after Fort Sumter had been fired upon, but once it seceded, the state played a leading role. Also, while Virginia seceded from the Union, the western part of the state broke away from Virginia and formed the new state of West Virginia. Much of the fighting in the eastern theater of the war took place in Virginia, which also provided the Southern Confederacy with two of its most successful generals: Robert E. Lee and Thomas J. "Stonewall" Jackson. Lee's eventual surrender at Appomattox heralded the end of the Confederacy and of the Civil War. Virginia was readmitted to the Union far more quickly than were other states during Reconstruction. In the years following the war, Virginia suffered from the loss of so many lives of its citizens, and the ravages committed on the land during 4 years of fighting.

In the 20th century, northern Virginia in particular saw a return of a strong federal presence, but this time in the form of sprawl from Washington, D.C., as offices and federal employees spread out south of the Potomac River. Northern Virginia hosts two buildings that were crucial to the exercise of American power during the second half of the 20th century and that remain symbols of American power into the 21st century: the headquarters of the Central Intelligence Agency and the Pentagon. Indeed the Pentagon, located in Arlington, Virginia, is such a symbol of American power, that it was attacked by terrorists on September 11, 2001.

ALTERNATE HISTORY

Here is how history might have been: Early in Virginia's history, leaders of the Jamestown settlement recognized that they and their colonists lacked both the military might to destroy the Native American tribes nearby and the agricultural skills necessary to grow enough food to survive without their aid. They wisely pursued, therefore, a policy of accommodation, trading with the natives for food, and offering them compensation for the land that the English settlers appropriated for their own use. With the ability to purchase food from the natives and without the need to devote so much time and energy to the defense of the colony, Jamestown would have prospered.

By 1640, Virginia would have grown into the most prosperous colony in America. Early cooperation with the natives would allow settlers to establish a colony far enough inland to avoid the mosquito-ridden swamps of the James River coast, although Jamestown would serve as a port for the ships sailing to and from England. In addition, colonists would have turned first to developing food crops, tobacco later. Carefully husbanding their resources, Virginia's colonists would have developed a thriving colony that was largely self-sufficient and that generated substantial profit from tobacco. Virginia's plantations and farms would have produced their own food and as many of the essentials of daily life as could be produced in America. Ships from England could provide luxuries from England, and treats, such as sugar from the West Indies.

Migration to Virginia would have continued to increase throughout the first half of the 17th century. As a thriving and relatively stable colony, Virginia also would have attracted a small amount of English elites, drawing enough men who won favor at court to give the colony a distinctly Royalist and Laudite character. Virginians idolized life in the Old Country, even as they made fortunes in the New World and might have developed a peculiar attachment to the Stuart monarchy. While Puritans fled England for the "Shining Citie on a Hill" in Massachusetts, those who settled in Virginia sought to make a fortune in agriculture and to acquire large estates no longer available in the mother country. Virginia colonists, indeed, would have seen the Puritans as more foreign than the Native Americans they lived among on a daily basis. Although Native Americans and Virginians might work side by side to grow staples and tobacco, the Puritan faith and ideology would have been perceived as a threat to both a political and a divine order.

Nevertheless, Virginia might have proved slow to respond to the outbreak of the English Civil War. Virginians had little contact with the Puritans, Separatists, and other Protestant sects, preferring, instead, a conservative, high-church Anglicanism. They enjoyed their church services, which were as elaborate and ostentatious as they could be in Colonial America, and had little first-hand contact with the sorts of agitators who caused so much trouble in England. Besides, Virginians took their religion rather lightly by 17th-century standards, preferring dancing, foxhunting, and whiskey to theological debate.

As the war in England turned against King Charles I, a steady tide of refugees would have begun to arrive in Virginia. They would come with stories of Roundhead depredations, of the Puritan faith crammed down the throats of the people, and with the despair of those who gave everything to a cause, and lost. After the Royalist defeat at Naseby in 1645, King Charles I himself might have numbered among their refugees. Rather than surrender, Charles would have donned a disguise and made his way to the coast and a ship for America. He would direct that as many of his loyal followers as could do so accompany him to Virginia to carry on the struggle.

With the possible escape of Charles and just over 1,000 of his army to Virginia, the Puritan tide would have begun to ebb. The Puritan army, led by Oliver Cromwell and other extremists, turned to deal with more pressing matters in Scotland and Ireland, and the Spanish Navy remained enough of a threat to England to prevent Cromwell from launching a naval expedition to the New World to finish off Charles. Although the Royalist cause had failed in England, Royalist power in America might never have been stronger.

The English Civil War, for so long fought only in the home islands, would have come to America. Charles and his followers might have arrived in Jamestown in the fall of 1645 and set about refitting their forces to continue the fight. Free from an immediate threat, Charles and Prince Rupert of Bavaria would have retrained the Royalist army, substantially augmented by Virginians, in the manner of Cromwell's New Model Army. The newly trained Royalist army would achieve a level of discipline and training that would have made it competitive on any battlefield on the continent of Europe. Against colonial militias, the power of Charles's army would be overwhelming.

By the following spring, Charles and his reformed army would have been ready for battle. Their target would have not been England, but Boston. England lay too far away and Cromwell's forces were too formidable for Charles to mount a transatlantic expedition, but Boston lay within his grasp. As the center of Puritanism in the New World and a rich seafaring city, Boston offered a tempting target.

The verdant forests of Virginia provided the Royalists with their requirements for timber to build a fleet of transport ships sufficient to carry their forces north. In May 1646, Charles and his army would have sailed northward. Seven hundred veterans of the English Civil War might have sailed forth, along with 3,000 Virginians, and 200 Native Americans. Native Americans had fared well with the Virginians and, although they suffered heavily from European diseases, they knew well the price of a Puritan victory. They knew all too well how the men of New England had annihilated the Pequot several years earlier.

The voyage may have passed without incident, and on June 14, 1646, the Royalist fleet would have arrived off Boston and begun to disembark. Action would have followed swiftly as the Boston militia poured out of the city to give battle. According to prearranged signal, the Royalist center initially would give way, luring the militiamen into a trap. As the Bostonians charged forward, gleeful in battle, certain that the god of Calvin and Luther brought them victory once again, they failed to notice Prince Rupert's cavalry troop swinging around to their rear until it was too late to save themselves. Those not killed in the fighting would have surrendered and begged for their lives.

They would have kept their lives, most of them, but not their freedom. The Puritan leaders would have been hanged, drawn, and quartered. King Charles then would give the citizens of Boston a choice: embrace the true faith of the Church of England and take an oath of loyalty to the king or submit to the king's judgment. Two-thirds might have refused the oath. They would have been put in chains and they and their descendants consigned to work in the tobacco fields of the Virginians and to wear red leggings as a sign of their condition. Those who proclaimed their loyalty to the king would have vanished into history, for the Virginians viewed them with suspicion, and the other colonists of New England saw them as traitors.

Charles would have had the Puritan churches razed and then given the city of Boston to his army as a reward. Soldiers could choose a bride from the Boston women and a home from those vacant in Boston, on the condition that they would support the king and rally to his banner if needed. In effect, this would have established a new feudalism in Massachusetts. The Virginians who did not choose to be so rewarded would have received payment in the form of their new white slaves, the stores from the wharves of Boston, and a share of a monopoly of the lucrative fishing business. Charles would have returned to Jamestown in triumph.

With Charles's victory in Boston and the influx of new forced laborers into the Virginia economy, Virginia would have become more prosperous and prestigious than ever before. Yet beneath the glittering facade lay the grim reality of the system of "confessional slavery" that would have forced many to endure a lifetime of bondage because of their faith, or the faith of their ancestors. While religious conflict in Europe would cool to a mild simmer after the conclusion of the Treaty of Westphalia ending the Thirty Years' War in 1648, it would have continued to boil in Virginia. The Anglican elite set themselves apart from their Puritan slaves by worshipping in a manner even more elaborate than some Catholic churches and by treating their slaves as brutally as possible. Frequent rebellions would leave the colony unstable.

Rather than embracing African slavery, which Virginians found to be an expensive way to import a labor force, they would have relied instead on confessional slavery. The Puritans who were defeated by Royalist forces would have been enslaved and forced to wear distinctive garments to set themselves apart from the rest of the population. They and their descendants would be condemned to perpetual bondage. The ruling class of Virginia might also have taken the drastic step of legally preventing Puritan slaves and their descendants from converting to another faith. Such a step would be necessary, lest the Puritans simply convert themselves out of bondage, leaving Virginia without a source of forced labor.

This version of America's "peculiar institution" would have separated Virginia from both the mother country and the other American colonies. To Britons, especially after the Restoration, Virginia would have appeared a barbarous anomaly, a relic of a vicious civil war that most wanted desperately to forget. While Britain gradually crept toward religious toleration, Virginia would have clung to a vicious, vestigial form of the Church of England. Other American colonies also would have viewed Virginia with suspicion. Northern colonies failed to adopt a slave system on a large scale. Other Southern colonies embraced African slavery as a means to solve the perpetual problem of having more land available than could be worked by the available English colonists. Yet this too would have become a cause for conflict with the Virginians because Virginians sought to recover Puritan slaves who fled into other colonies in which they could gain their freedom. This would have led to small-scale, internecine conflicts, especially on the Virginia–North Carolina border, which, although not leading to open warfare between the colonies, would have resulted in a constant string of vendettas and reprisals.

By the 1760s, Britain had driven France from North America by winning the Seven Years' War, known in America as the French and Indian War. With that threat removed, the colonies no longer faced a threat that required the British army for defense. The continued presence of the British army in the American colonies, and the measures that the British government instituted to try to raise money to pay for the cost of the war helped bring the American colonies to the brink of revolution. Except Virginia. Obstinately devoted to the crown and to its own reactionary version of the Church of England, Virginia would have remained loyal to Britain during what would be an abortive war for American independence. With a strong colony dividing the Carolinas and Georgia from New England and the Middle Colonies, and providing a secure base of operations, the British would have turned on their divided rebelling colonies and defeated them in detail. Once again, Virginia would have proved to be an essential support to the power of the British crown. It would have remained the jewel in the crown of Britain's North American empire.

Throughout the 19th century Virginia would have continued as part of the British Empire, yet it would come under increasing attack for its continued brutality toward the Puritan slaves. Successive British governments would have attempted to compel Virginia to abolish slavery, but to no avail. The breach with England eventually would have come during World War I. The German invasion of France would have been met with enthusiastic volunteers to join the British army from across the British Empire. Unfortunately, the call for soldiers and weapons to fight the Germans in Europe would have left the American colonies vulnerable. Mexico, aided by German military advisers and armed with German weapons, might have sent an invasion force across the Mississippi River to attack the virtually undefended British colonies in North America. The British government would have refused to redeploy colonial forces to America, sparking mutinies among the Virginia colonial forces fighting in France. The British high command would have reacted harshly and put down the Virginia mutinies with enormous brutality and loss of life.

That action would have prompted Virginia to secede from the British Empire. Faced with mutiny among its troops in France and imperial conflict in America, Britain might have made a separate peace with Germany, and shifted its attention to Virginia. In Europe, that would allow imperial Germany to retain the gains made at the Treaty of Brest-Litovsk, and to compel France to cede more territory to Germany. In America, the British army, after much hard fighting, would have succeeded in regaining control over Virginia, driving out the Mexican Army, and in abolishing Puritan slavery in North America. Britain then would have installed a military government that would hold power until the middle years of the 20th century, when Britain began to draw down its imperial commitments abroad. With the Soviet Union and imperial Germany locked in a continental cold war, Britain would have needed all of its troops and resources in the home islands.

After decolonization, Virginia would have begun to establish itself as an independent nation. Centuries of religious hatred would have left the new nation subject to bouts of internal violence. Late-20th-century Virginia would have struggled to assert a new national identity and to find a unifying factor to replace the intense Royalist sentiment that collapsed when Britain attacked and conquered its own colony. It would remain to be seen how a country so steeped in the past would make its own way in the future.

Mitchell McNaylor

Discussion Questions

1. How did the Protestant Reformation in Europe, sparked by Martin Luther, affect colonial development in America?

2. By building Jamestown in the middle of a pestilential swamp, refusing to grow enough food for the settlement's own needs, and constantly fighting with the natives, the early colonists of Virginia consigned themselves to begin their colony under circumstances that almost doomed it to failure. Why had the colony not been better planned?

3. What role did Virginia play in actual history in the Revolutionary War and Civil War? Why was Virginia the home of many of the key figures during these crucial periods in American history?

4. What do you think of the author's idea in the alternate history that Virginia might have created a slave population not of African Americans but from the ranks of Puritans in the northeast?

5. Do you agree that it is plausible that King Charles I might have become a refugee in Virginia? What other alternate historical outcomes might have come about with a British king in exile in the American colonies?

6. In actual history, African American indentured servants in Virginia became lifetime slaves, with the status passed to their children, during the mid-1600s. In the alternate history presented in this chapter, white Puritans from Massachusetts become enslaved as well. What factors would make such a status more difficult to impose on whites than on African Americans?

7. What aspects of the culture and economy of colonial Virginia made landowners seek to establish slavery?

8. What factors in actual history tended to work against the sort of war between the colonies outlined in the alternative history presented in this chapter?

9. What factors besides religion contributed to tensions between the colonies that tended to work in favor of armed conflict between the colonies?

10. In the 18th century, when France, England, and other European countries were influenced by the ideas of the Enlightenment, how would Enlightenment thinkers have viewed the persistence of slavery of whites in Virginia? What factors limited the impact of such views on the persistence of the enslavement of African Americans in actual history?

Bibliography and Further Reading

Billings, Warren M., John E. Selby, and Thad W. Tate. *Colonial Virginia: A History*. White Plains, NY: KTO Press, 1986.

Billings, Warren M., *The Old Dominion in the Seventeenth Century: A Documentary History of Virginia, 1606–1689*. Chapel Hill: Published for the Institute of Early American History and Culture, Williamsburg, VA, by the University of North Carolina Press, 1975.

Bridenbaugh, Carl. *Jamestown, 1544–1699*. New York: Oxford University Press, 1980.

Carlton, Charles. *Going to the Wars: The Experience of the British Civil Wars, 1638–1651*. New York: Routledge, 1992.

Flexner, James Thomas. *Washington: The Indispensable Man*. Boston: Little, Brown, 1974.

Hume, Ivor Noël. *Martin's Hundred*. New York: Alfred A. Knopf, 1982.

Isaac, Rhys. *Landon Carter's Uneasy Kingdom: Revolution and Rebellion on a Virginia Plantation*. New York: Oxford University Press, 2004.

Isaac, Rhys. *The Transformation of Virginia, 1740–1790*. Chapel Hill: Published for the Institute of Early American History and Culture, Williamsburg, VA, by the University of North Carolina Press, 1982.

Morgan, Edmund Sears. *American Slavery, American Freedom: The Ordeal of Colonial Virginia*. New York: W.W. Norton, 1975.

Parker, Geoffrey. *The Military Revolution: Military Innovation and the Rise of the West, 1500–1800*. Cambridge: Cambridge University Press, 1988.

Price, David. *Love and Hate in Jamestown: John Smith, Pocahontas, and the Heart of a New Nation*. New York: Alfred A. Knopf, 2003.

Royster, Charles. *The Fabulous History of the Dismal Swamp Company: A Story of George Washington's Times*. New York: Alfred A. Knopf, 1999.

Trevelyan, Raleigh. *Sir Walter Raleigh*. New York: Henry Holt and Company, 2002.

Wertenbaker, Thomas Jefferson. *Virginia under the Stuarts, 1607–1688*. Princeton: Princeton University Press, 1914.

TURNING POINT

The charter for the Maryland colony was granted in 1632. What if Catholic and Protestant conflict in England had made Maryland a permanent religious haven for Catholics?

INTRODUCTION

The founding of the colony of Maryland has its origins in two specific historical developments: the English Reformation and the emergence of the proprietary system of colonial settlement. The former was critical because it meant that Protestantism became the official religion of England in 1533, and the government outlawed the practice of Roman Catholicism, except for during the brief reign of the Catholic Queen Mary Tudor from 1553 to 1558. As such, Catholics in England had been severely persecuted and unable to openly practice their religion or hold public office since 1558. The second historical development to shape Maryland's founding was the emergence of the proprietary system, in which the King of England granted land and a charter to one English lord who then held supreme feudal power over the land and government granted to him. This system had been used in England in medieval times to protect against attacks on the Scottish and Welsh borders and was revived in the early 17th century by English noblemen who had lost much of their power in the 16th century and were eager to expand their holdings, investments, and power abroad.

These two historical developments came together in the person of George Calvert, first Baron Baltimore. Calvert, a product of Elizabethan England, played the most important role in the founding of Maryland. Raised as a Protestant by a Yorkshire family, he graduated from Oxford University and began his career in government by holding several minor posts. By 1608 he was clerk of the Privy Council, a member of Parliament, and special emissary abroad of King James I. In 1617 King James I knighted him and he became secretary of state. It was through these government posts and experiences abroad that Calvert developed an interest in overseas ventures. He began by investing in the East India Company and the Virginia Company, but feeling that these companies returned very little to their investors, in 1620 he began a colony of his own in Newfoundland. In 1622, Calvert spent £25,000 of his own money to outfit the initial expedition.

However, his career would change dramatically in 1625 when he declared his conversion to the Roman Catholic faith. He was immediately

Catholic Queen Mary I of Great Britain. (National Archives)

Allegorical scene of Lord Calvert showing the document establishing civil and religious liberty in Maryland in 1649. (Library of Congress)

barred from holding public office and had to resign his position as secretary of state. It was at this time that King James I gave him the title Baron Baltimore. From this time forward, Calvert would focus exclusively on his private interests, including two visits to his Newfoundland colony. During those visits he found the climate too harsh to sustain a successful colony and decided to instead pursue the founding of a colony in the Chesapeake region.

At first, his request to the crown was met with disdain, and he was told to abandon his plans. Calvert would not quit. He visited Virginia to scout the land, and continued to request a portion of the Chesapeake as his own proprietary colony. Despite all the obstacles to achieving his request, Calvert's request for a charter received preliminary approval on April 15, 1632, several days before his death. Eventually, the charter was granted on June 20, 1632, by Charles I, to his son Cecilius Calvert, second Baron Baltimore. Cecilius Calvert went about establishing the colony of Maryland, named for England's last Catholic monarch, Queen Mary.

Cecilius Calvert set about exploring his new colony immediately. At a cost of £40,000, he sent 300 laboring men, about 20 gentlemen, and his two younger brothers on the ships *Ark* and *Dove*. None of the 300 new colonists were Catholics, although the expedition did stop to pick up several Catholic laymen and two Jesuit priests at the Isle of Wight before departing for North America. Calvert understood that, in order to be successful, the colony needed to be profitable, and thus was not concerned that all his initial colonists be Catholic. He did however, ensure that Catholics who settled in Maryland would not face the same discrimination that they did in England and would be free to hold public office and practice their religion.

Leonard Calvert, one of Cecilius's younger brothers, was a practical governor who set the men and women of the expedition to work without delay upon arrival, while he visited Native American tribes and concluded peace agreements and land transactions. By arriving in the summer, the colonists were able to raise enough food for a surplus and to avoid the starvations that had plagued the early Virginia colony, and their friendly relations with local natives spared them from violence. Despite these good fortunes the colony did not grow and prosper at as rapid a rate as initially hoped for by Cecilius Calvert.

IN CONTEXT   The Virginia Colony

Maryland's closest neighbor was Virginia, founded in 1607 with the settlement of Jamestown. The original colony numbered only 105 people, all men. Over the first winter half of the settlers starved to death, leaving only 50 to carry on. With the majority of the colonists bickering and unwilling to work, having hoped to find gold in the New World, the colony seemed on the brink of collapse. The Virginia Company in London, which had invested in the colony, was not, however, ready to give up, and in 1609 they were able to send 500 men and 100 women through their 7-year joint-stock option program. At the end of 7 years of service to the colony, each would receive 1,000 acres of land.

These colonists, however, faced even harsher conditions than the first, with only 60 survivors remaining in the spring of 1610. Only the resupply of the colony with 300 new inhabitants kept these

60 from giving up. It was not until John Rolfe brought tobacco to Virginia from Bermuda that Virginians would find their first staple crop that would produce revenue for the stockholders and the colonists alike. By 1626, Virginia was producing 1,500,000 pounds of tobacco a year for export. It was in this context that George Calvert, first Baron Baltimore, set about establishing the Maryland colony, which would also become primarily dependent on tobacco for its commercial success. Virginia, however, was founded exclusively as a commercial enterprise, with no religious motivation, and the Protestant Church of England was the officially established religion from the beginning. No religious differences would plague Virginia's colonists as they would in Maryland, but the economies of the two colonies would remain closely tied because of tobacco.

During the 1650s, Calvert briefly lost his proprietorship when the Puritans, led by Oliver Cromwell, took over the English government. During this period the Toleration Act of 1649, which assured that Protestants in Maryland would not be discriminated against by a Catholic proprietor and that Catholics would remain free to practice their religion and participate in public life, was ignored. The assembly of 1654 in England excluded Catholics from voting and ignored proprietary authority. It would not be until the restoration of Charles II in 1660 that the second Baron Baltimore would fully recover his rights as Lord Proprietor of Maryland.

After several years of neglect because of English political troubles, Cecilius sent his eldest son Charles to Maryland to attempt to increase settlement, encourage trade, and stabilize tobacco prices. By the 1660s, Maryland remained a pioneer colony with a population of about 8,000 people scattered over six counties. Charles tried a variety of methods to encourage trade and settlement, but most of them failed. Only Cecilius's promotion of heavy English immigration was moderately successful, and by 1688 the colony's population had increased to 32,000, mostly Protestant, settlers.

TURNING POINT

By the 1680s, the number of Protestants in Maryland far outnumbered the Catholics, and some of them began to attack the Catholic leadership of the colony. Baron Baltimore's political opponents began to assert their displeasure in 1669 by claiming that he exercised absolute and arbitrary power and that the Privy Council was composed mostly of Papists. At the time, Reverend Charles Nicholette, a Presbyterian minister, also preached a sermon urging the lower house of the Maryland assembly to resist the

Privy Council and the proprietor. He was forced to apologize for his subversive comments, but the injury to Baltimore's power was already done.

Fearing a revolt of Protestants in Maryland against the Catholic minority, Cecilius Calvert limited voting only to men with an estate of £40 or a minimum of a 50-acre freehold. He also reduced the number of delegates representing each county in the assembly from four to two. At the same time, Lord Baltimore distributed government offices in an impolitic way, giving the most lucrative and powerful posts almost exclusively to Roman Catholics. This policy served to deepen the divide between the majority of the colony's residents and the Catholic elite who governed the colony. At a time when Europeans were still vitally conscious of religious differences between Catholics and Protestants, such a move only served to strengthen the resolve of Cecilius Calvert's Protestant opponents in the assembly.

When Cecilius died in 1675, his son Charles, the third Baron Baltimore became the first resident proprietor of Maryland, but he was even more unsuccessful than his father had been. He continued to give prominent positions to Catholics, he did nothing to strengthen the role of the Protestant Church of England in the colony, and, perhaps most importantly, he constantly interfered with royal customs officials. In 1681 the colony experienced an actual revolt when two men, John Coode, a clergyman and planter, and Josias Fendall, a former governor, began to protest Charles's rule. Residing in Charles County, they worked for several years to agitate the planters. This unrest, however, proved to be more than the work of two malcontents, because Charles County planters feared native attacks and a Roman Catholic conspiracy to keep the colony's Protestants in submissive roles throughout the 1680s. In some cases, they believed the Catholics were trying to use the natives to kill the colony's Protestants.

Both Fendall and Coode were eventually tried and convicted of sedition and conspiracy, but by the end of the decade, their position would eventually win when the colony came under royal control. In 1684, Charles Calvert went to England to try to defend his proprietorship and prevent the colony from falling into the hands of the crown because of the recent unrest. While in England, Charles spent most of his time unsuccessfully defending his control of the government in Maryland. Still in England in 1688, he sent William Joseph to the colony to attempt to maintain his proprietary control. Joseph was a staunch Catholic and defender of divine right. He set an authoritarian tone with his first speech, which accused the provincials of sinfulness and threatened royal wrath for disobedience to his governmental authority. Despite the resistance of the colonists, he continued to assert his and the third Baron Baltimore's authority, but by the early months of 1689, firm news of the revolution in England had arrived, and the proprietary government of Maryland fell quickly and easily.

To assure a Protestant succession to the crown, fearing that the Catholic wife of James II would raise her son as a Catholic, Parliament facilitated a settlement that bloodlessly brought William of Orange and his English wife Mary, James II's daughter, to the throne. Called the Glorious Revolution, this change in the English government had far-reaching implications for colonial governments. In Maryland, the news of the Glorious Revolution caused the Protestant faction in the Maryland assembly to coalesce around about half a dozen leaders, including John Coode. Led by Coode, a group of armed men gathered to announce the new king and queen and to protect the colony from natives and Papists.

KEY CONCEPT   The Glorious Revolution

The Glorious Revolution occurred in 1689 when William of Orange and his wife Mary became the king and queen of England in a bloodless coup by Parliament. When the Stuart monarchy was restored to the throne following the English Civil War, many in England feared that Charles II had Catholic leanings. However, their fears would begin to be realized in earnest when his brother James II became king in 1685. A proclaimed Catholic with a Catholic wife and heir, his rule threatened to return England to Catholicism. This fear united Englishmen of all political leanings and resulted in what has become known as the Glorious Revolution in 1689. Seven leaders in Parliament sent a letter to William of Orange in Holland to invite him and his wife, Mary, the Protestant daughter of James II, to ascend to the throne of England. William gathered an army and landed in Devonshire in 1688. James II, whose Protestant forces deserted him, fled to France. Parliament treated James's flight as an abdication of the throne and William and Mary accepted the invitation of Parliament to be England's reigning monarchs. At the same time, Parliament passed a Bill of Rights that reduced the power of the monarch, prevented a Catholic from ever succeeding to the throne, forbade the monarch from levying taxes without Parliament's consent, and ended the royal power to suspend and dispense law.

This was the beginning of the modern English democratic system in which Parliament governs the country and the monarch rules as a symbolic head of state. It also marked a period when the English Parliament began to assert more direct control over its overseas colonies. At this time, some colonies, like Maryland, became royal colonies, and other colonies, like Massachusetts, received new charters and were forced to accept royal governors. It changed the governments of almost all the colonies and created systems in which royal governors were often at odds with the representative assemblies in their dominions.

Coode, a resident of Charles County, aligned himself with Kenelm Cheseldyn and Nehemiah Blakiston from St. Mary's County and Henry Jowles of Calvert County. Along with several other leaders from around the colony, these men, all outside the proprietary circle, were prosperous planters and prominent colonial men. On July 25, this group, known as the Protestant Association, issued a declaration in which they summarized their complaints against the Catholic lord proprietor. They then proclaimed their intention to defend the Protestant religion in the province and their allegiance to King William and Queen Mary. The declaration was successful in drawing hundreds of men to Coode's side as he marched to St. Mary's City. Once the Protestant Association arrived in St. Mary's City in July, William Digges, a kinsman of Charles Calvert, surrendered to Coode's forces. The last pocket of proprietary resistance surrendered on August 1, when 160 men loyal to Baron Baltimore yielded to the Protestant forces. They were taken safely to their homes and promised their rights and privileges would be protected, but from the time of the Glorious Revolution until the American Revolution, Catholics were forbidden from occupying any civil or military offices in the colony.

Once they had subdued the proprietary forces, the Protestant Association moved quickly to summon the Assembly and hold elections by the end of August. Once each county had elected and sent its delegates they went about the business of formally petitioning the crown for the appointment of a Protestant government. The establishment of a royal governor, however, would take time, and the ordinance passed on the last day of the session gave Maryland its government for the next 2½ years. They appointed officials to local posts such as sheriff and justice of the peace, but left colony offices open for royal appointment. Thus Maryland was governed by local officials until 1692.

ACTUAL HISTORY

In 1690 the Protestant Association received a letter from the crown allowing it to continue as the legitimate government of Maryland. Still, the government remained fractured and no offices were filled above the county level. Meanwhile, in England, Charles Calvert continued to try to save his proprietorship, but with the growing English hostility to Catholicism provoked by the Glorious Revolution and the increasing desire of the crown to assert its direct control over colonial governments, Calvert's attempt to reassert his authority was unsuccessful. Although his charter could not be revoked without judicial action, the crown suspended his charter and left legal proceedings against him incomplete. Thus Maryland became a royal colony by the end of 1691.

The royal government began by appointing a governor for the colony, Lionel Copley. Copley was a loyal Protestant with a history of anti-Catholicism who had recently played an important role in helping the new king, William of Orange, secure Kingston-upon-Hull. Copley left England for Maryland in September of 1691. The crown also appointed Sir Thomas Lawrence to the powerful position of secretary. The governor's council was another matter, and its composition would be fraught with more difficulty.

Originally John Coode, now in England to protect the Protestant Association's gains, suggested a list of his allies for the council. This list did not stand, however, because John Hammond, a Maryland merchant, arrived in England in the fall of 1691, asserting that new nominees be put forward reflecting the changes in the power structure of the colony since Coode had been in England. Baron Baltimore, lacking his original power to approve all council appointments, also attempted to nominate council members. Finally, the lords of trade, responsible for royal colonies, decided on a council from the lists submitted by Copley, the newly appointed governor, Baltimore, and the merchants represented by Hammond. In the end, Henry Jowles, Nehemiah Blakiston, Nicholas Greenberry, Charles Hutchins, George Robotham, David Brown, John Addison, John Courts, James Frisby, and Thomas Brooke became the members of Maryland's governor's council. These men represented the crown's desire for a Protestant government, with 10 of the 12 of them having been members of the Protestant Association, and the last two being Protestants who were loyal to Baltimore during the rebellion. When Governor Copley and Sir Thomas Lawrence finally arrived in Maryland in May 1692, with the power to govern, the people of Maryland greeted their arrival with great relief.

Maryland would continue as a royal colony until 1715. During this period it had several governors, and even a period in which it had to exist without a governor. Copley died on September 9, 1693, only a little over a year after his arrival in the colony. He was immediately replaced by

Francis Nicholson, who arrived in 1694 and was the first governor of the colony to be a dominant enough figure to put an end to petty politics and focus on the larger concerns of the colony.

Nicholson, suspicious of Coode and his faction, began his tenure as governor by demanding reports from officers and accurate record keeping in the future from all government officials. Nicholson also began to travel around the colony, especially to the upper counties, where he had direct contact with officials and common people who never traveled to the capital. Nicholson was even known to dismiss an entire panel of local justices for irregularities or violating their commissions. For the first time in its history, Maryland had a governor who expected the colony's officials, both local and provincial, to obey the laws. While Nicholson's visits to various parts of the colony helped him control local officials, they also allowed him to assess the major needs of the colony, which he concluded were the relocation of the capital, the establishment of public schools, and the appointment of more competent officials to local positions of authority.

The new capital was established at Arundell Towne, renamed Annapolis in 1695, and provided a more convenient and central location for the provincial government. Personally designed by Nicholson, the new capital followed the latest English architectural trends and forbade noisome trades from being situated within the city. Thus Nicholson succeeded in creating a small and pleasant metropolitan center as the colony's capital by the end of the 17th century. Nicholson also convinced the Assembly to establish a "free schoole" as a way of providing for the education of colonists as clerks, to propagate the Protestant religion among youth, and to help provide the colony with more competent officials.

Nicholson's prosperous and peaceful term as governor, however, was upset when the attorney general discovered in the Act of 1692, which established the Anglican Church in the province, language asserting that when the laws of Maryland were silent, the laws of England would prevail. Such language was dangerous because it threatened the royal prerogative to manage the colonies. Nicholson's support of the crown in this matter, against the rights of the colonists, put him in a dangerous position because his reform-minded policies had upset many of the colony's inhabitants. The Assembly refused to pass new laws that would leave out the offending clause, and he was ousted from his position as royal governor on January 2, 1699.

Nicholson's successor was John Seymour, who assumed the post in 1704, after 5 years of the colony existing without a governor. Seymour immediately began persecuting Catholics in the colony, banning all Catholic services, whether public or private. Irish servants brought into the colony were also subjected to an import tax of 20 shillings per person in order to prevent Catholic immigration. The right to hold private Catholic services was eventually restored, but Seymour's initial actions would color his entire term, and his authoritarian approach to government struck colonists as reminiscent of proprietary rule. Seymour's term as governor would thus be fraught with conflict between him and the Assembly, and after his death in 1709 the colony remained without a governor again until Queen Anne appointed John Hart to the post in 1714.

Hart's term, however, saw the revival of proprietary government in Maryland. Although Charles Calvert had lost his government in 1689, he formally retained his property rights because his charter was never revoked, only his political powers were suspended because of his religion. His son, Benedict Leonard Calvert, however, had renounced his Catholic faith and became a member of the Church of England. He also began to raise his children as Protestants. By becoming a Protestant, Benedict Leonard removed the one obstacle to Calvert rule in Maryland, and, when his father died in 1715, the crown restored to the fourth Baron Baltimore his rights of government over Maryland. He allowed John Hart to remain in office as proprietary governor. Benedict Leonard, however, died only 8 weeks after assuming his title of Baron Baltimore, and his son Charles became the fifth Baron Baltimore. However, as a minor, Charles could not assume responsibility for the government of the colony, and his guardian, Lord Guilford, allowed John Hart to serve out his term.

Although Maryland became proprietary in name again in 1715, it remained in most ways a royal province. The Assembly clung to the powers it had established during the rebellion of 1689, and eventually would sustain a half-century of measures for preventing proprietary officials from tampering with their powers. The greater part of 18th-century Maryland politics consisted of battles between the proprietary and antiproprietary factions. The battles between these two factions would foreshadow the conflicts that would arise in the 1770s, as the more democratic antiproprietary faction, known as the Country Party, grew into ardent supporters of the Revolutionary cause.

When a letter reporting on the Boston Tea Party and the subsequent blockade of Boston's port arrived from Massachusetts in 1774, the citizens of Maryland turned their attentions from provincial to imperial politics. Within a day Annapolis residents voted to join in the nonimportation movement. Despite dissent from some of the city's leading citizens, the Country Party carried the day, and fervor for the nonimportation movement spread to more rural areas. Meanwhile, Maryland's Assembly met on June 22, 1774, to officially condemn the British closure of the Boston port and to support the call for a general congress of all the colonies in Philadelphia. The Assembly then chose five delegates to attend the congress in Philadelphia, which would become known as the First Continental Congress.

Conservatives in Maryland dreaded what consequences might come of such actions, but ultimately the Patriot cause would win. During the period after 1776, Maryland set about adopting a new form of provincial government. The new government was structurally very similar to the proprietary one, with a governor and assembly, and limited the vote to men with a 50-acre freehold or personal property worth £30. Officeholding was even more limited, with £500 needed to serve in the lower house, £1000 for the upper house, and an estate of at least £5000 required to be eligible for the governorship. Thus the first government of Maryland, although now run by the antiproprietary Country Party, was not democratic, and functioned to keep local elites in power while severely circumscribing the ability of the common people to participate in their own government.

The history of Maryland in the 19th century was colored mostly by its status as a slave state and later as a border state during the Civil War. Unlike states in the Deep South, however, slavery in Maryland did not experience growth during the early 19th century. Instead, the free black population in Maryland began to grow as the slave population declined.

The Catholic Church continued to maintain a presence in Maryland, and Baltimore was the seat of the first Catholic bishop in the United States. During the 1840s and 1850s, Maryland, like many northern states, experienced an influx of immigrants from Ireland and Germany, although their numbers were comparatively smaller than in New York, Massachusetts, and Illinois. By 1850, these immigrants and the rising tide of sectionalism gave rise to a nativist movement in Maryland that reacted strongly to the presence of increasing numbers of Catholic immigrants from Ireland and Germany. By 1854, nativism had taken hold of Baltimore and the western counties, but it would soon be overshadowed by the specter of the Civil War.

The Civil War threatened Maryland's economic ties with both the North and the South and threatened its precarious position as both a slave state and a site of increasing industrialization. Most Marylanders, however, looked to the South for political inspiration; yet, once Virginia joined the Confederacy, the federal government was forced to prevent Maryland from leaving the Union, lest Washington, D.C., be surrounded by two Confederate states. Thus Maryland remained in the Union throughout the Civil War, although violence and unrest often plagued its communities because the majority of the population resisted Union rule. In particular, the federal government raised the ire of Marylanders when it sent 75,000 Union soldiers through Baltimore on their way to Washington, D.C. State and local authorities could not maintain calm, and on April 19, 1861, when regiments of Massachusetts troops arrived in Baltimore, a mob gathered in Monument Square in Baltimore to protest the move. Before long, rioting ensued as the mob attacked the troops. These events forced the federal government to retain troops in Maryland throughout the war to suppress activities sympathetic to the Confederacy and ensure that Maryland remained in the Union. Throughout the war, many Marylanders remained hostile to the federal government. Because Maryland did not secede, its people experienced an easy transition back to normalcy in the 1870s, and its path followed that of many Northern states as it became more industrialized and, in the 20th century, developed sprawling suburbs that served as suburban communities for Baltimore and Washington, D.C.

ALTERNATE HISTORY

In the alternate history of Maryland, Charles Calvert would never have lost his charter because the Glorious Revolution would not have occurred. King James II would have remained on the throne, married to his Catholic wife, and his son would have been raised as a Catholic. In this case, England may have once again become a Catholic country, or, more probably, Catholicism and Protestantism would have both become acceptable, for most of the country had already become Protestant by 1689. Thus the third Baron Baltimore would never have had to defend his charter in front of King William and Queen Mary, and his rule in Maryland would never have been questioned. The result would have been the safeguarding of Catholic rule over a Protestant majority, and Governor Joseph's rule would have continued until his death.

As a fervent Catholic, Joseph would likely have promoted the Catholic religion in Maryland, probably to the exclusion of all others. With the probability that the English government would remain in Catholic hands, Calvert would have returned to the colony as resident proprietor and assisted Joseph in his rule. Perhaps he would have taken a lesson from William Penn's experiment in Pennsylvania. Penn recruited colonists for Pennsylvania, mostly from Germany, who had similar religious backgrounds to Quakers. Calvert might have made a similar decision to recruit from Catholic areas of Germany and from Ireland. This would have helped to make the colony's religious balance more even and promote the growth of the Catholic religion among Protestants.

In alternate history, this change would not have come without protest from men like John Coode, Kenelm Cheseldyn, and Nehemiah Blakiston, the original founders of the Protestant Association. No doubt they would have tried, probably some time in the 1690s, to resist the rising tide of Catholicism in the colony. With Protestants, at that time, probably still being a majority, they might even have succeeded in controlling the colony for a short period and banning the practice of Catholicism. However, with support from the king, Calvert would have been able to reassert control. He would have had more supporters within the colony because he had the backing of the crown, and the penalty for treason was death. The uprising by Protestants would have convinced Calvert of his need to impose Catholicism more zealously on the population in order to safeguard his investment.

Additionally, Coode, Cheseldyn, and Blakiston, instead of being rewarded for their rebellion with the formation of a Protestant government in Maryland, would have been tried and found guilty of treason against their proprietor and the crown. Instead of trying Baron Baltimore for infractions of his charter and preventing him from exercising his legal and financial rights because of his religion, these three men would have ended up as villains instead of heroes. Other supporters of the Protestant Association would likely have converted to Catholicism, at least in name, to protect themselves from suspicion and improve their chances of success in an increasingly Catholic colony and under a Catholic monarch. Nevertheless, pockets of Protestant resistance would have remained a thorn in the side of the government.

The role of the Assembly would have continued unchanged as a rubber stamp upon the decisions of the governor and council. Governor Nicholson would never have come to the colony, but it is still possible that a forward-thinking Catholic governor might have moved the capital to a more convenient location. Without the impetus to reform the government, however, the capital would have stayed in St. Mary's City, corrupt officials would have dominated local politics, and Calvert would have continued to bestow powerful and lucrative offices exclusively to friends and Catholics. Calvert might have founded a school, as Nicholson did, perhaps a Jesuit seminary to educate priests for the new churches that would have sprung up as a result of an increased

Catholic population. One law that never would have been passed was Governor Seymour's ban on the importation of Irish servants. In the alternate history, such importations would actually have been encouraged in order to increase the Catholic population of the colony. These servants would have eventually become free and contributed to the civic life of the colony, some entering the new seminary and serving as local parish priests.

When Charles Calvert died in 1715, he would have left a colony in his wake that was more Catholic than ever. His son, Benedict Leonard, would never have left the Catholic Church because it would have prevented him from exercising his political and economic rights over the Maryland colony, although when he died later that year, his young son Charles Calvert II would still have had to rule through a guardian because he was a minor. One of the major changes that probably would have occurred in the alternate history is that the proprietary government would have tried to keep the assembly weak. Thus, when the American Revolution arrived, the colony would not have had as strong a history of participatory self-government. However, it is likely that a less empowered, but nonetheless spirited opposition to the Calvert government may have developed.

Thus, despite the domination of Catholics in the alternate history, it is likely that an antiproprietary Country Party would still have been a factor in Maryland history. It would probably not have been as strong, however, because Maryland would not have experienced the period of self-rule between 1689 and 1715 that weakened the governorship and strengthened the Assembly. The proprietary government would still have protected the interests of the landholding elites, whether Catholic or unwavering Protestants, for economic reasons. This would have made it difficult for small and middling landholders to gain a foothold in the government or to push through economic policies that would help them. Thus, whether Catholic or Protestant, they would have banded together to protest proprietary policies. Former Irish servants may have made up a larger percentage of this Country Party because they became freeholders after their terms of service expired. More than long-standing residents, they would have had reason to desire government policies that favored small landholders and artisans.

Thus Maryland would have entered the Revolutionary period with a party of opposition, and the Country Party, though Catholic like the proprietary party, would have supported the Revolutionary cause. Residents of Maryland would have reacted to news of the Boston Tea Party in the same way they did in actual history, supporting it and staking their claim against British and proprietary rule. Marylanders would have had a more difficult time, however, sending representatives to the Continental Congress, because the Country Party would not have been as strong in the Assembly due to strict circumscription of the lower house's powers by the proprietary government. Because the Country Party might have had to declare its own assembly, a rebellion may have occurred. This would probably have been the turning point in the development of Maryland politics because the mass of the smaller landholding Catholics would have had common cause with neighboring colonies to throw off British and proprietary rule. They would have then sent representatives to the Continental Congress and sided with the other 12 colonies in the American Revolution.

Maryland, however, would have been the only state with a Catholic majority, although this probably would not have caused a great deal of conflict because the new nation assured religious freedom to all its inhabitants. The formerly weak Country Party would now run the government and, although it would probably have passed property requirements for voting and holding office, as did other states, it might have lowered requirements, reflecting the economic status of many of the Patriots. Eventually, the members of the new government would have replaced the old proprietary leaders as local elites, perhaps rolling back some of the gains during the Revolutionary period.

In the alternate history, the largest change in Maryland history would probably have come about in the 1840s when the potato famine struck in Ireland and Irish Catholic immigration to the United States began in earnest. In actual history, most of the Irish immigrants of the 19th century went to New York and New England, but in the alternate history, they would have flooded Maryland because of its strong Catholic heritage. It would have been easier to practice Catholicism in Maryland because there were already many Catholic churches and even a seminary. Nativism would not have existed against the Irish or German Catholics who came to Maryland because they would have been joining the already powerful majority. This would, in turn, have changed the social, cultural, and economic makeup of Maryland, setting it on a very different course.

The large numbers of immigrants would have immediately competed for jobs on the docks and in the laboring crafts with the large free black community. This would have created racial tensions of a degree that had previously been unknown in the state. Riots may have ensued. The large numbers of immigrants, welcomed to Maryland because of their religion, would have easily become politically involved and by the time of the Civil War, Maryland laws would probably have been changed to be more hostile to the free black community, encouraging them to leave the state. The influx of immigrants would also have provided a large number of laborers that might have touched off an industrial revolution in the state, making it more like the states to the north than those to the south, for slavery was clearly dying in the upper South by the 1850s.

Despite their hostility to the black community, the influx of Irish immigrants would have caused Maryland to side with the North and perhaps even to abolish slavery in the decade before the Civil War. Although this would seem in opposition to their discrimination against free blacks, it would have made economic sense to the new immigrants. An economy based on slavery would not have provided jobs for a large, free labor force. Thus the federal government would not have had any problems keeping Maryland in the Union during the Civil War and would have been able to use the state for the transport of Northern troops to the South. Instead of riots in Baltimore, there would have been parades encouraging the soldiers. This tide may,

The Potomac River, dividing Maryland and Virginia, was also the division between the North and South during the Civil War. (Library of Congress)

however, have turned as the Civil War dragged on past 1861 and 1862. Marylanders themselves would have been willing to go and fight for the North.

In the aftermath of the Civil War, Maryland's industrialization would have taken off because it had a booming labor force. The success of Catholics in Maryland would also have made Catholic immigrants more welcome in the country. In actual history, only about 8 percent of Maryland's labor force was ever engaged in manufacturing, and most of its industry centered on Baltimore's vibrant merchant community. With the large influx of immigrants and the growth of Maryland cities in alternate history, however, up to 30 or 40 percent of the population may have been involved in manufacturing by the end of the 19th century. Immigrants would have quickly built transportation systems that made the movement of these new manufactured goods possible. Although a small state, Maryland would have become more urban than it is today, with Baltimore and Annapolis becoming booming urban centers on the scale of Boston or even New York. Perhaps New York would not have grown as quickly, because Catholic immigrants from eastern and southern Europe also flocked primarily to a region that was friendlier to their religious culture.

By the middle of the 20th century Maryland would have been a booming state with two urban centers, and perhaps northern Virginia,

Delaware, and southern Pennsylvania would have been providing suburbs to Maryland's booming metropolises. It would be the center of American Catholicism, with its largest churches and finest schools. Maryland would be known as the state that welcomed the Irish and German Catholics and later Italian and eastern European Catholics to the United States, and many Americans would probably trace their ancestry from the shores of Maryland, instead of New York.

Alexis A. Antracoli

Discussion Questions

1. At what other points in Maryland's history might there have been a critical turning point? Why do you think they are turning points, and what might have been other possible outcomes?

2. Considering that the Irish and Germans competed with blacks for jobs when they first arrived in the United States, do you think there is any way that an influx of Irish and German immigrants would have sided with the Confederacy during the Civil War?

3. How did religion shape the history of colonial Maryland? In what ways was it critical to the formation of the colony's government?

4. Why did George Calvert want to establish Maryland? What do you think was more important to him: religion or financial success?

5. Do you think there is any way the Protestant Association might have succeeded even if the Glorious Revolution had not occurred? What obstacles would they have had to overcome?

Bibliography and Further Reading

Andrew, Charles McLean. *The Colonial Period of American History*. New Haven: Yale University Press, 1964.

Burnard, Trevor G. *Creole Gentlemen: The Maryland Elite, 1691–1776*. New York: Routledge, 2002.

Carr, Lois Green and David William Jordan. *Maryland's Revolution of Government, 1689–1692*. Ithaca, NY: Cornell University Press, 1974.

Carr, Lois Green, Philip Morgan, and Jean B. Russo, eds. *Colonial Chesapeake Society*. Chapel Hill: University of North Carolina Press, 1988.

Cottom, Robert I. *Maryland in the Civil War: A House Divided*. Baltimore: Maryland Historical Society, 1997.

Davis, David Brion. *Slavery in the Colonial Chesapeake*. Williamsburg, VA: Colonial Williamsburg Foundation, 1986.

Hall, Clayton Colman. *The Lords Baltimore and the Maryland Palatinate: Six Lectures on Maryland Colonial History*. New York: Nunn & Company, 1902.

Hall, Michael G. *The Glorious Revolution in America*. Chapel Hill: University of North Carolina Press, 1964.

Krugler, John D. *English and Catholic: The Lords Baltimore in the Seventeenth Century*. Baltimore: Johns Hopkins University Press, 2004.

Land, Aubrey C. *Colonial Maryland: A History*. Millwood, NY: KTO Press, 1981.

Main, Gloria L. *Tobacco Colony: Life in Early Maryland, 1650–1720*. Princeton: Princeton University Press, 1982.

Reps, John William. *Tidewater Towns: City Planning in Colonial Virginia and Maryland*. Williamsburg, VA: Colonial Williamsburg Foundation, 1972.

Riordan, Timothy B. *The Plundering Time: Maryland and the English Civil War, 1645–1646*. Baltimore: Maryland Historical Society, 2004.

Vexler, Robert I. and William F. Swindler, eds. *Chronology and Documentary Handbook of the State of Maryland*. Chesapeake, VA: Ocean Publications, 1978.

Walsh, Richard and William Lloyd Fox, eds. *Maryland: A History, 1632–1974*. Baltimore: Maryland Historical Society, 1974.

TURNING POINT

Virginians began to move to North Carolina in the 1650s. What if the British Crown had prevented the Virginian migration, and North Carolina fell under Spanish control?

INTRODUCTION

In 1629, 20 years before his own countrymen executed him, King Charles I of England gave one of his loyal servants, Sir Robert Heath, a massive portion of North American land. It stretched from 31° to 36° latitude. The area was named New Carolina after Charles himself. Heath planned to found a colony there for the dispossessed Huguenots (French Protestants) who were persecuted by their Catholic masters. However, Heath's plan was not successful. For several more decades only the original inhabitants—the Native Americans—populated the Carolinas.

The first region to attract a permanent English settlement was Virginia. Jamestown was founded there in 1607, but early colonists suffered disease, starvation, and attack from the Native Americans. The colony of Virginia overcame its initial problems and flourished by the mid-17th century. Women were attracted to the colony and more equal numbers of men and women lived there. A new generation of settlers was being born in the colony for the first time. Virginia was under British royal control in 1624 and the days of the divisive, faction-ridden government of the Virginia Company were over. Its governor from 1641 to 1677 was Sir William Berkeley. He was a powerful and well-connected man with the lifestyle of a wealthy tobacco planter. He lived at Green Spring, one of the first grand plantation houses of the southern colonies. Berkeley ruled a colony that relied on tobacco as its staple crop. But tobacco quickly exhausted the land, sapping the minerals from the soil in only a few years. Each plot quickly became infertile and useless for years to come. Therefore, Virginia's growing population looked for new land suitable for growing their "noxious weed," as some called tobacco.

In 1648 a group of Virginians led by Henry Plumpton and Thomas Tuke bought land from Robert Heath's successors in what became North Carolina. Their plot of land was situated between the mouths of the Roanoke River and the Weyanoke Creek in a region unexplored by Europeans. Their planned settlement failed but the Virginians' interest in land to the south of their colony was awakened.

KEY CONCEPT   Tobacco Farming

John Rolfe, the famous Englishman who married Pocahontas, started experimenting with tobacco a few years after Jamestown was founded in 1607. He shipped his first cargo to England in 1614 where it found favor. Members of the elite thought the habit of tobacco smoking very fashionable, despite King James I thinking it "loathsome." The local tobacco cultivated for generations by the Virginian Native Americans was of too harsh a flavor for the English. The Caribbean strain grown by Rolfe was much more to their taste. Soon production soared as the planters realized that this was their opportunity to make their fortunes: many did. They became obsessed with the crop, locating their homes in the best growing areas, and using it as currency with all goods priced in amounts of tobacco. In 1637, for example, an ox was worth 600 pounds of tobacco and a pig 120. The Virginia Company tried to encourage the settlers to grow a variety of crops so they could feed themselves and not rely on the unstable tobacco market. However, at the time of the settlement of the Carolinas, Virginia was still primarily known for its tobacco crop.

A few brave men probably explored the southern frontier before 1650, but if so they did not write about their journeys. Edward Bland's book *The Discoverie of New Brittaine*, published in London in 1651, tells the story of his journey south of Fort Henry (present-day Petersburg, Virginia). He went into the uncharted territory, ending up somewhere near what is now Weldon, North Carolina. It was a reconnaissance mission to see whether there was land available for Virginians to settle on. Bland and his party also wanted to trade with the Tuscarora natives. John Bland, Edward's brother, launched a propaganda campaign in England. He tried to convince Oliver Cromwell's Parliament that the group should get a grant for settling this region. Bland's journey did not go according to plan. Fears of conspiracy and attack by hostile natives dogged the expedition.

The landscape was also a disappointment: Bland described in *The Discoverie of New Brittaine* the "rotten marshes and swamps" that the travelers had to cross. Governor Berkeley feared causing trouble with the natives. The Virginians had only recently defeated the Powhatan confederacy in 1646, so he did not encourage explorations in the Carolinas for several years. However, during the 1650s, the inevitable happened: settlers moved southward from Virginia. The colonial and English governments tried to bring order and stability to the area to stop it from becoming a dangerous frontier.

TURNING POINT

In 1653 the general assembly governing Virginia granted portions of land of 10,000 to 11,000 acres each to the first 100 men who settled on the banks of the Roanoke River. We know very little about the people who lived there, but they did provide the information for a map drawn

KEY CONCEPT   Lords Proprietors

Barbadian planters, such as Sir John Colleton, made a lot of money from the sugar trade. They wanted to make even more profit, and for this they had to expand. So Colleton and seven other loyal supporters of Charles II approached the king to ask for a land grant on the North American mainland. However, once the settlement was established, rule by the proprietors caused a great deal of hostility.

They tried to control the native trade and enforce English trade laws known as the Navigation Acts. In the Carolinas as well as in Pennsylvania and New Jersey, settlers fought against proprietary government in the 1690s. For a while they successfully put their own governors into power. Eventually, in 1729, the British government bought out the Carolina proprietors.

by Nicholas Comberford in London in 1657. It shows Carolina with place names in English, not with the usual Native American titles still in use at that time. The Virginians gave the rivers, hills, and woods English names and claimed the area as their own. Comberford's map shows that one of the leaders of the colony was a Mr. Batts. His house was highlighted on the map, illustrating his importance. He was the "governor of Roanoke," although it is not clear whether William Berkeley or the settlers appointed Batts. A little further south, around the Cape Fear River, Puritans from New England and sugar planters from Barbados tried to build colonies. They were not successful, unable to keep the colonies alive for more than a few years. The New England men bought their land directly from the Native Americans. George Durant bought a tract of land on the Roanoke Sound from Kilcocanen, the king of the Yeopim tribe who lived there.

Then, in 1660, the history of England and its colonies took a dramatic turn. The exiled son of Charles I returned to England and took his rightful place on the throne as Charles II. England's experiment of government by Parliament without a king was over. Charles II had many domestic worries to distract him, but he also showed some interest in America. He used land in Carolina to reward some of his supporters. Charles chose four experienced men from the colonies: Sir John Colleton, a Barbadian planter, William Berkeley and John Berkeley of Virginia, and Anthony Ashley Cooper, who had owned a plantation in Barbados but now lived in London, alongside four English aristocrats: Edward Hyde, Earl of Clarendon; George Monck, Duke of Albemarle; the Earl of Craven; and Sir George Carteret. These were the eight lord proprietors of Carolina. They took with them many experienced planters from Barbados who wanted to own more land and slaves and thought Carolina was the place to do this.

In March 1663 Charles granted these men the right to sell and lease land, to create titles and manors, and to make defensive war or impose martial law in Carolina. The land he gave them was extensive. It stretched "from the north end of the island called Luck Island . . . and to the west as far as the South Seas [the Pacific] and southerly as far as the St. Matthais River which bordereth upon the coast of Florida." They divided the land

ANOTHER VIEW Spanish Interests in North America

As well as having a foothold in Florida, the Spanish also had other interests on the North American continent, in regions that had not yet attracted the English settlers. Spanish soldiers and Franciscan missionaries fought the Pueblo Indians in New Mexico and eventually gained the upper hand at the turn of the 17th century. They established a number of forts and missions along the Rio Grande. They settled in small numbers in Texas, although their French neighbors in Louisiana to the east constantly threatened them. The Spanish could not persuade migrants to go to New Mexico and Texas. There was no opportunity to make a fortune there, unlike in Mexico, Peru, and the Caribbean sugar islands. So even by the mid-18th century, there were only a few hundred Spanish settlers in this region. Spain's colonial focus remained on its Caribbean and Central American possessions that provided its wealth.

into two provinces, Albemarle in the north, and Clarendon in the south. These provinces roughly coincide with the territories of North and South Carolina today. These eight men, already very wealthy, could now make vast sums of money for themselves and their families if they encouraged migration. The lord proprietor tried to recruit settlers from other American colonies to save money. They hoped their colonists might avoid the health problems that affected those who moved from England to the warmer southern climate. They wanted experienced planters to protect the area from pirates such as the infamous Captain Teach, otherwise known as Blackbeard. He caused difficulties for English ships in the waters between North America and the Caribbean when the war between the Spanish and the English ended in 1667.

John Colleton and another Barbadian, Sir John Yeamans, led the first voyages of exploration. The lord proprietors found that various groups from Virginia were already there. These Virginians fought for the control of the northern province of Albemarle. One year after the royal grant of Carolina, William Berkeley, governor of Virginia and also one of the lord proprietors, offered land in Albemarle province to Virginians on the same terms as land in Virginia itself. The proprietors thought that too little land was offered to make people come from Virginia and the rent was too high. The best way to attract settlers was to parcel the land into large tracts and sell it to very rich men. They then put a number of tenants on that land. But people did come from Virginia, not in large numbers at first, but they soon established a society that looked very similar to Virginia. They were subsistence farmers who also grew small quantities of tobacco. Soon, they created their own assembly, based on the House of Burgesses in Virginia. They established their own capital at Edenton. However, they worried about security. Attacks from hostile natives were possible, and the Spanish were also a threat before 1667 when they were at war with the English.

Thus the turning point in North Carolina's British history came with the establishment of the lord proprietors and Charles II's encouragement for Virginians to settle south.

ACTUAL HISTORY

For the first 50 years, the colony of North Carolina was little more than a frontier outpost. There was some resentment in Virginia that Albemarle was included in the 1663 Carolina grant. Virginians thought that it belonged to their colony because they had explored and settled there before the lord proprietors had even considered it. Anthony Ashley Cooper, later made Lord Shaftesbury, moved quickly. With the philosopher John Locke, he designed a form of government called the Fundamental Constitutions of Carolina. This radical document defined the powers and rights of the monarch, the proprietors, and the settlers. The colony would be governed by a provincial parliament, which consisted of the proprietors, other members of the colonial nobility, and representatives of every precinct in the province. The Church of England would receive money from public funds, but other sects would be tolerated, even Jews. They defined the landowning structure, which created the lesser nobility in the colony known as the landgraves and the caciques. Its approach to religion and its land distribution system were unique. But North Carolina never agreed to this document and South Carolina did not confirm it until 1698.

The famed philosopher John Locke helped design the first government of the Carolinas. (Library of Congress)

Over the next few decades, tensions rose between different groups of migrants within Carolina. The Barbadian planters were unruly: they did not want to develop the sort of society recommended in the Fundamental Constitutions. Barbados, like many of the sugar islands in the Caribbean, was overcrowded and the land was exhausted by years of sugar planting without allowing the soil to rest. The proprietors wanted Carolina to be divided into large baronies of thousands of acres owned by the landgraves and caciques. But the planters wanted each man to own a successful sugar plantation, as they had done in Barbados. As in early Virginia, the settlers did not bother to establish many towns or villages. Instead they preferred to spread out along the rivers to pick the best land for growing their staple crops. The proprietors wanted the colony to be tolerant of all Christian groups, but the Barbadians were fiercely loyal to the Church of England. Most crucial was the difference regarding slavery: the Caribbean planters used black African labor to farm sugar and saw no reason why they should not do the same in Carolina. The proprietors had hoped to keep slavery out of their colony.

The Barbadians became known as the Goose Creek men. They were powerful and often got their own way, especially in the Goose Creek area around the Charles River, from which they took their name. The proprietors encouraged other migrant groups too, such as Huguenots and English religious dissenters, to counteract the power of the Goose Creek

IN CONTEXT   Slavery in North America

Spanish, Portuguese, and Dutch colonies in the Caribbean devoted to the production of sugar began importing vast numbers of black slaves from Africa in the 16th century. As early as 1619, the first Africans arrived in North America, dropped off by a passing Dutch ship. They were probably slaves seized from the Portuguese somewhere in the Caribbean. In Virginia, at first the slaves were given relative freedom. They were treated in a similar way to the poor white indentured servants who could also be bought and sold by their masters.

By the middle of the 17th century, England had realized how lucrative both the slave trade and sugar

production could be, and in 1640 had converted Barbados into a sugar colony. Within 15 years, there were 20,000 slaves on the island. Many Barbadian planters began to feel it was getting rather over-crowded. Some considered moving to other English island colonies such as Jamaica, recently acquired from the Spanish. Many were keen to move to the mainland and to take their particular form of planta-tion slavery with them.

By the end of the 17th century, the British were playing a central role in the importation of slaves from Africa, and Charleston was the hub of this trade.

African American slaves operating one of the first cotton gins in the Carolinas. (Library of Congress)

men. The proprietors also wanted to control the trade with the Native Americans. This was partly for financial reasons and because they did not want misunderstandings over trade to cause violence with the natives. They knew that the young colony was vulnerable and could be wiped out if the natives attacked. But they had learned the lessons of the Virginia Massacre of 1622 (nearly one-third of the English settlers in Virginia were killed when local tribes led by Opechancanough turned on them) and they discouraged unlicensed trading. It was a criminal offense to be vio-lent toward the natives, although some settlers ignored this and a few even took native slaves.

After early setbacks, the southern settlement flourished, and in 1670 Charles Town (later Charleston) was established. This was important in the development of both North and South Carolina because Charles Town became one of the largest ports in North America. It imported African slaves in vast numbers in return for the rice and tobacco produced by the region's planters. Slaves came directly from Africa, often from the Angola region, rather than via the West Indies. Charleston was soon known as the most important place to buy black artisans, laborers, and fishermen. Foodstuffs and other provisions arrived from England and other colonies, although the English government was unhappy about Carolina trading directly with other colonies. The Committee for Trade and Foreign Plantations, which was made up of important members of the English parliament, wrote to the Council of Albemarle Province to express their displeasure. A few years later, this question sparked the Culpepper Rebellion of 1674. The colonists who led the rebellion had come to Carolina before the era of proprietary government. John Culpepper and his followers, including several of the leading planters, opposed the 1673 Navigation Act. The act prevented colonists trading without a license from the English government. Culpepper's opponents accused him of treason and they tried to steal his land. But Culpepper traveled to England to defend himself in person, and was found to be innocent of the charge of treason. He returned to his plantation a free man.

Just as the southern part of Carolina developed its own identity, so did the northern region: Albemarle Province attracted more settlers, especially nonconformist Christians. A group of Swiss Protestants settled there and named their town New Bern. A contingent of Quakers moved to the Albemarle River from New England where they had suffered extreme persecution, including jail sentences, exile, and even execution. Albemarle took on its own identity, and this was shown in 1712 when it appointed

Tobacco became a staple crop in North Carolina and required the labor of slaves to be farmed profitably. (Library of Congress)

its own governor. This effectively split the region into North and South Carolina. But the proprietors' fears for the security of the region were confirmed. Animal pelts had become an extremely expensive luxury item in Europe, so the settlers could not resist trading for them with the local native tribes. It did not take long for the natives to realize that they were being taken advantage of, and hostility turned to violence. In the south, settlers battled a combined force of Yamassee and Creek tribes, whereas the Cherokees remained loyal to the English settlers. In North Carolina, the traders angered the Tuscarora tribe, usually peaceful allies of the English, and the natives attacked the settlers, killing several hundred of them. The English only finally defeated the Tuscarora with the help of other Englishmen from the neighboring colonies.

When the proprietary government collapsed after a series of policy failures, the English government wanted more white settlers to go to the area. This would balance the large numbers of slaves brought in by the Barbadian planters in the Carolina low country, in the Cape Fear area in North Carolina, and in Charleston itself. The vast majority of settlers lived in the tidewater areas because the rice that they grew with the knowledge and labor of their African slaves did not exhaust the soil as did tobacco and sugar. The differences between the settlers coming from Virginia, settling in the northern parts of the colony, and the southern settlers who had more in common with the slave-holding planters of South Carolina, simmered throughout the 18th century. At first the northern part of the colony around the Albemarle Sound area held the most political power, but soon, in 1734, power shifted to the south. The southern Cape Fear region became more populous, and Gabriel Johnstone, a planter from that area, was appointed governor. Even the colony's capital moved south from Edenton to New Bern.

By 1750, settlers traveled from northern colonies to settle in "backwoods" North Carolina. They came down the Great Philadelphia Wagon Road and along the Appalachian Mountain trails to settle along the Virginia–North Carolina border. These migrants were often extremely poor. As Governor William Tryon said in 1765, they barely had enough money to buy a piece of land to raise a log cabin and plant a crop of corn in the ground. They could not afford to invest in slaves or farming on a larger scale. Tryon claimed that those families in the backcountry who owned slaves had less than 10, whereas on the coastal plantations the masters owned several hundred slaves. These migrants, who were mostly of Ulster (Scots-Irish) and German extraction, brought the two regions of the colony closer together. They had no allegiance to either and so the traditional divisions between north and south within North Carolina itself were broken. One of the groups who came to central North Carolina in the 1750s consisted of members of the Moravian church from eastern Germany. They wanted their settlements to reflect this distinct identity. The group's leaders were also realistic about the survival of their settlements; they would need to welcome outsiders in order to thrive. They set up agricultural villages around a Moravian church, but they combined this traditional lifestyle with a version of the extensive rather than intensive farming practices used by other North Carolinians.

The tumultuous history of North Carolina then took another dramatic turn. Relations between Britain and its American colonies broke down after the end of the French and Indian wars at the Peace of Paris in 1763. North Carolina issued the first official call for a declaration of independence in April 1776. After North Carolina's inauguration as a state in the new nation, new arguments erupted in the United States in the 19th century. The conflicts raged between the pro- and antislavery parties, between Democrat and Whig, between Northerner and Southerner. Reluctantly it seemed, North Carolina did secede from the Union in the spring of 1861, although not until after the first shots of the bloody Civil War had been fired at Fort Sumter. This happened only a few months after an election in which calls for secession had been strongly defeated. That conflict, which scarred America's history forever, took its toll on North Carolina along with all the other states. One hundred and fifty years later, the state of North Carolina has emerged from those days of racism and hatred to take its proud place in a powerful and prosperous United States.

ALTERNATE HISTORY

If the crown had not allowed settlers from Virginia to move into North Carolina, the history of the region would have been very different. Eventually, American settlers would have expanded into those regions whatever the attitude of the British crown. A century later, in 1763, they pushed west against the recommendations of the British government that established the Proclamation Line. This was supposed to prevent colonists migrating into native territory. However, the support of Charles II for those who did want to move into Carolina was significant. Without it, the map of the United States might look very different today. When the province of Carolina had barely seen any white immigration, the lord proprietors and the few pioneers were worried about attacks from the Spanish. The Spanish had held a well-established military base down the coast in Florida at St. Augustine since 1565.

   If the English crown had not moved fast, the Spanish would have built more forts along the coast. These military outposts were very important, especially during conflicts with the French or the English. The Spanish wanted to use them to defend their treasure ships returning from Peru and Mexico, laden with silver and gold. These ships had been the target of pirates from other nations since the mid-16th century. But the Spanish also had another aim. They wanted to convert the Native Americans to Catholicism, so Jesuits and Franciscan friars lived alongside the soldiers. The missionaries needed the soldiers' protection but thought them immoral and uncouth and a bad example for the natives. The intention was to convert the natives to Christianity and to make them live like Spaniards. They were encouraged to abandon their traditional nomadic lifestyles, to settle down and grow crops, to speak Spanish and wear European clothes. By 1620 a missionary station was built as far north as St. Catherine's Island, in present-day Georgia, less than 50 miles south of Savannah.

The Spanish in Florida were actually quite weak. The English under Captain John Davis nearly destroyed the fort at St. Augustine in 1665. However, the Spanish might have gained the upper hand without the crown support for the settlement of Carolina. Although the two countries were supposed to be at peace by 1667, there was still rivalry between the two. Both wanted to control southeast North America. The Spanish had the power of the Catholic Church behind them. They hoped to advance northward from Florida, converting the natives to their religion and their military cause as they went.

In 1686 a force of 150 Spanish, Native Americans, and mulatto slaves prepared to attack the port of Charleston. They had already attacked and looted plantations to the south of Charleston. They only failed to overrun the city because of the brave actions of the local militia and bad weather that hindered their progress. If English Charleston had not been there, this force would have continued northward unhindered. They would have established missionary posts and forts well into Carolina. The English government was most concerned and sent Edward Randolph to report on the possibility of a Spanish attack. The government was aware of the threat in the 1680s and sent out expeditions to destroy the missions in Carolina territory. The English population also grew. This is why the Spanish did not completely take over the region.

What would have happened if the Spanish had controlled Carolina? English settlers, who moved into Carolina from Virginia, would have been in a much weaker position. They would have had no support from the English or the Virginian governments. They would have encountered the hostile Native Americans whose minds were influenced by the Spanish against the "heathen" Protestant English. Spanish soldiers would have easily looted and burned the homes of settlers who did manage to build a home.

By the end of the 17th century, the power of the Spanish was waning in favor of their near-neighbors, the French. In 1701 family ties united the Bourbons—the Spanish and French royal families. This made Spain very weak, and the English in Charleston launched an attack on the Spanish missions in Carolina and Florida. They even ransacked St. Augustine. A few hundred soldiers and friars hung onto their land, but the Spanish enterprise in southeast North America never recovered.

However, other countries might have shown an interest in the Carolinas. France wanted to expand its colonies, especially after Louis XIV came to the throne and made the French nation one of Europe's most powerful countries. From 1682 onward the French struggled to establish a permanent settlement in the Mississippi Valley area. Their main concern was the fur trade. This had brought them wealth in the northern parts of America and they hoped to control it in the south as well. They successfully formed alliances with the Native Americans because they did not demand full conversion to the Catholic faith.

During the last quarter of the 17th century French explorers moved down the Mississippi River. They recorded the best areas to build settlements and forts, and how to protect these areas from

Spanish attack. If the English had not settled in Carolina, the French would still have proceeded in this way. The difference would have come later, once the French became interested in moving into the interior of the Carolinas. They would have done so unimpeded by an English presence. Perhaps they might have clashed with that other great Catholic imperial nation, Spain. The peace between the two nations in 1702 meant that the French could proceed with their ambitions. In 1699, two French aristocrats, Sieur de Bienville and Sieur d'Iberville, led a group of migrants and soldiers into the territory of Louisiana. After a false start at Biloxi, where the settlement failed due to the infertile land surrounding it, the French settled at Mobile. It was only a short distance from the Spanish fort at Pensacola. By 1718 they had chosen the site for their regional capital, which became the great and troubled city of New Orleans.

Although control of the Mississippi was the French aim, the Tennessee River was also important to them. This river led into the interior of the Carolinas. It would have provided another trading zone for the French fur merchants if England had not already sent traders there. By the late 17th century the English were trading with the Cherokee in the upper Tennessee River area. If the settlement of Carolina had not happened, these traders would never have reached the interior. The French would have made the alliance with the powerful Cherokees. In 1690, one of the French explorers, Jean Couture, defected to the English cause and guided the English traders in searching for silver mines. Had the English not settled there, this knowledge may have remained in French hands. The map of the Carolinas would have been peppered with French names for rivers and hills, and with French forts.

The English in Virginia watched the French activity in the Tennessee River area with concern. Governor Francis Nicholson of Virginia encouraged the English traders to negotiate with the natives so they would not become allies of the French. However, Nicholson was too remote from the region to have much effect. Some English fur traders began negotiating with the French. In July 1701, three Frenchmen arrived at Biloxi Bay, having traded with the English in Carolina who sold them a number of animal pelts. The French authorities saw these men as rebels and treated them very harshly. They wanted to prevent English and French traders from working together and sharing the prizes of this lucrative business. In any case, the cooperative spirit only lasted a year or two. Queen Anne's War, also known as the War of Spanish Succession, a conflict between Britain and France, broke out. This led to rivalry between the two nations until peace was declared in 1713. If the French had maintained an even stronger trading presence in Carolina, no access would have been allowed to English trappers and merchants. The French wanted to dominate that trade from Canada in the north to Louisiana in the south.

The settlers in Charleston, seemingly distant from this French activity, were concerned too. Governor Joseph Blake of Carolina had to calm their nerves by sending out a party under the French defector Jean Couture. They claimed the part of the Mississippi River valley as a dependency of the English. The party made liaisons with certain native tribes, enemies of the French allies, and tried to stir up war between the two groups. How much harder their task would have been if the English had not moved into the Carolinas at all. There would have been no base at Charleston from which to send out exploratory expeditions and claim the interior. The peace between Spain and France would have allowed those two nations, especially the more powerful French, to move into the Carolinas from the south and west. They would have brought their Catholicism and imperial ambitions with them. England's land in North America would have seemed a lot smaller and more vulnerable with the French and Spanish and their native allies surrounding the English on three sides.

As it was, the French position in Louisiana was weak. They found it hard to grow the food crops that they were familiar with, and they were very isolated. In fact, the survival of the colony was threatened during Queen Anne's War. When the settlers turned to a slave-based plantation colony, its survival was ensured. Problems with local hostile native tribes dogged the region. They maintained a perilous existence, with the English threatening to encroach on their territory and their trade. It would have been different had the English government not permitted migrants to move into the Carolina region. The wars of the 18th century might have occurred on battlefields in North and South Carolina, rather than in the northern colonies and the Caribbean. If the French and their allies had maintained a strong foothold in the southeast corner of the continent, the history of the United States and the culture and society of the region today would be very different.

The absence of an English presence in Carolina would have changed the history of the Native Americans. The French and Spanish seemed more ready to work with the tribes. They were not intent as the English were on removing the natives from the region entirely. The English policy culminated in the Trail of Tears, the enforced march to the Indian Territory in the 1830s. Tensions still would have been created because the friendly natives agreed to convert to Catholicism while secretly maintaining their traditional religious practices. Among these may have been the Cherokee tribe, who, by the 19th century, in actual history had developed a version of the Bible in their own language. Native groups who resisted the missionary activities might have mounted hostile attacks. They would have incurred the wrath of the soldiers sent to support the friars. Violence would have disrupted trade connections.

Life for the French and Spanish who had moved to the region would have been very challenging because they would not have the strength in numbers provided by the mass migration of the English to the northern colonies. Perhaps the region would have become a haven for the native tribes that were pushed out of the English colonies to the north. The rivalries among the natives would have become worse, resulting in a diminished native population. This sort of upheaval prevented the French from using the natives as a workforce. They would have eventually used the area for plantations as they had done in Louisiana. Slaves would have come to the area via the Caribbean through the port of New Orleans. As the English actually did, the French and Spanish might have experimented with sugar in the Carolinas. Finding it unsuitable, they could well have turned to crops such as rice, indigo, and, eventually, cotton.

The presence of a strong French colony to the south would have meant that Britain's victory in the French and Indian wars of the mid-18th century was less comprehensive. If the French maintained a hold on the Carolina region, the English North American settlements would not have felt secure. Consequently they might not have so hastily separated from the powerful British. But the debates about "no taxation without representation" would have pushed the English colonies to rebel against their British masters eventually, even without an English Carolina. Much of the drive for independence originated in northern colonies. This discontent would have fomented in the towns of Boston, New York, and Philadelphia anyway. In actual history, the colony of North Carolina led the call for a Declaration of Independence. There is no reason to assume that without a North Carolina, another colony would not have taken that role.

The French Carolina territory may have been included for sale in the Louisiana Purchase of 1803 by Napoleon Bonaparte. The higher price he would have asked might have caused difficulties for the eager American buyers. If they could afford the land then, the region would develop a culture similar to that of Louisiana: old European settlers and new American immigrants living side by side in an uneasy peace. However, it is likely that the higher price put on the Carolina–Louisiana Purchase in 1803 would have deterred Thomas Jefferson. Then the history of the United States would have been very different.

The slave states of Virginia and Maryland alone would not have rebelled against the North; they would not have been strong enough. The United States would have continued negotiations with French Carolina to gain access to its ports and rivers. It did so with Louisiana before agreeing to the Purchase. Its industrial development would have been harder. Cotton grown by the French and Spanish planters in the Carolinas would have been harder to acquire. England's Industrial Revolution would also have been affected. Eventually though, the United States would have agreed to the asking price for both Carolina and Louisiana, and westward expansion would have proceeded as it actually did. Perhaps the French would have dropped their price, wanting a quick sale so they could devote their resources to campaigns in Europe.

This late acquisition of territory would have changed the balance of power that led to the American Civil War. If Carolina was bought from the French after 1848, the slaves in that territory would have already been freed. This may have forced outnumbered slaveholders in Virginia and Maryland to bring slavery in their states to a natural end without the bloodshed of a civil war. But this would mean that the abolition movement and the civil rights movement also would be very different. At the end of the 19th century and into the 20th, with no cause to fight for, the position of African Americans within society would have been left in limbo. They would have been seen as second-class citizens, and whites would have taken all steps necessary to separate themselves from black society. This position could have gone unchallenged until the late 20th century, when an international campaign against segregation in the United States would cause the government to give blacks equal rights (much as international pressure negated apartheid in South Africa). Trade sanctions and the fear of becoming an international outcast would persuade the United States to allow blacks to enjoy the rights of full citizenship. Of course, the social problems that separation had caused would not be immediately solved. In many regions of the country, blacks would remain at an economic and political disadvantage, but their position would gradually improve, and racism would become unacceptable, as has happened in actual history.

Carolina would have contained Spanish- and French-speaking enclaves as Florida and Louisiana do today. The power of the English-speaking United States would have dominated the region and gradually homogenized its culture. The Carolinas would always retain a strong Catholic, continental European connection. Carolinians would see themselves as very different from the northern Protestant states. Even without the horrific slaughter of the American Civil War in this counterfactual story, there would be a very different north–south divide in its place.

Catherine Armstrong

Discussion Questions

1. Why did the English want to settle the Carolinas?
2. Would the history of slavery in North America have been different if the English had not settled there?
3. What would the Southeastern region of the United States be like today if Spain or France had settled there in the 18th century?
4. Would the Native American tribes have maintained a stronger presence on the east coast if England had not claimed the Carolinas?
5. What cultural aspects, such as food and language, of North Carolina might be different today if the state had been more settled by the French or Spanish?
6. If there had been no Civil War in the United States, how would the U.S. government have evolved differently than it did?
7. If there had been no slavery in states south of Virginia, when do you believe Virginia, Maryland, and Delaware would have followed New Jersey and New York in abolishing slavery? How would they have done it?
8. If all the states in the United States had abolished slavery by 1840 or 1850, what other issues do you think might have led to sectionalism in the nation? Could such issues have so divided the nation that it would lead to attempts at secession by some of the states?

Bibliography and Further Reading

Bannon, J.F. The *Spanish Borderlands Frontier 1513–1821*. New York: Harcourt College, 1970.

Crane, Vernon. "The Tennessee River as the Road to Carolina," *Mississippi Valley Historical Review* 3 (1916).

Cumming, W.P. "The Earliest Permanent Settlement in Carolina," *American Historical Review* 45 (1939): 82–89.

Edgar, Walter. *South Carolina: A History*. Columbia: University of South Carolina Press, 1998.

Johnson, Paul. *A History of the American People*. London: HarperCollins, 1997.

Middleton, Richard. *Colonial America: A History*. Oxford: Blackwell, 1992.

Rosen, Robert. *A Short History of Charleston*. Charleston: University of South Carolina Press, 1982.

Saunders, William. *Colonial Records of North Carolina*. Raleigh, NC: Broadfoot Publishing, 1886.

Waterhouse, Richard. "England, the Caribbean and the Settlement of Carolina," *Journal of American Studies* 9 (1975): 259–281.

Wright, J. Leitch, Jr. *Anglo-Spanish Rivalry in North America*. Athens: University of Georgia Press, 1971.

TURNING POINT

Carolina was founded in 1670 and developed slavery with the rice plantation system. What if the rice crops did not develop and slavery did not spread?

INTRODUCTION

There was something different about the English settlers who founded the colony of South Carolina. Unlike other British mainland colonists, many Carolina settlers did not come straight from Great Britain but instead came from the British West Indies. Between 1670, when South Carolina was founded, and 1690, roughly 54 percent of white colonists were from the sugar-growing island of Barbados. Although originally from England, they were now seasoned travelers who understood the difficulties of settling unfamiliar regions. They also brought with them a readymade workforce: African slaves. South Carolina was the only mainland colony to have African slaves from the very beginning.

The island of Barbados is small, roughly 21 miles long and 14 miles wide, but the soil and climate are ideal for sugar production. African slaves planted, harvested, and processed the sugar while their masters grew rich from the sale of sugar to English merchants. Barbados planters knew very little about the Carolina climate or geography, but they understood how to run large-scale plantations. A plantation is a very large farm concentrating on the production of a single crop, usually for export. Plantation crops were labor intensive, meaning planters needed more than just wage labor or family members to work the fields. Although they did not have a clearly developed plan, many of these early settlers hoped to establish plantations in Carolina and re-create the financial success they had enjoyed before leaving Barbados.

Unfortunately for the newly relocated colonists, things did not go as smoothly as they had hoped. There was no simple, obvious way to re-create another plantation economy in South Carolina. Sugar would grow in the region, but West Indies planters already controlled the sugar market. Similarly, South Carolina was well suited for tobacco production, but planters in Virginia and Maryland were already well-established tobacco producers and South Carolina planters could not successfully compete with them. Although they were experienced planters and businessmen and they had more than enough laborers, early Carolina settlers struggled to find their economic footing.

Between 1670 and 1700, Carolina colonists experimented with a number of possible crops, hoping to find one that would bring them commercial success. Because the colony was at about the same latitude as southern Europe, residents thought Carolina climate might support the same kind of plants. Residents tried growing olives, grapes for wine, orange and lemon trees, silkworms, and indigo but had little success. The grapes and orange trees were killed by sudden frosts. The silkworms were eaten by ants. Indigo, a plant that produces a deep blue dye, was native to the region, but converting the plant into dye is a complex process, and settlers quickly abandoned their efforts.

Carolinians had better luck with their other ventures: trade with neighboring Native Americans. First, it was deerskin, as the colonists tapped into existing trade networks established by the Creek, Yamassee, and other local natives. In exchange for cloth, guns, powder, rum, or other English goods, the natives would supply skins to be shipped to overseas markets. Soon, however, Carolinians asked their Native American allies to supply them with another export: native slaves. Native trade partners were encouraged to raid other villages and sell the captives to Charlestown (later Charleston) merchants. The combination of deerskins and native slaves made up much of the economy in early Carolina.

From the growing port city of Charlestown, colonists also exported corn, peas, pork, beef, and lumber, much of it going to feed and supply planters and slaves still living in Barbados. Pitch, tar, and turpentine were also exported. In all, the economy was stable but not at all what the early settlers had anticipated. By 1700, about one-fourth of the total population of 6,000 was slaves. They were not, however, working on plantations or producing anything as lucrative as sugar or tobacco.

South Carolina slaves were involved in a range of occupations. Slaves helped to clear the land, cutting trees, pulling stumps, and burning brush. They helped construct houses, barns, and other outbuildings. Slaves traveled into the forests to collect pine tar and pitch. They worked on the Charlestown docks, loading and unloading ships. Slaves planted and harvested crops for local consumption and surplus crops for export. They were involved in all aspects of raising livestock, building cowpens, marking cattle, rounding up strays, butchering cattle and hogs, salting and packing the meat for export. In fact, tending cattle became the most common occupation for slaves. By 1708, there were 1,800 adult male slaves in the colony; roughly 1,000 of them were "cattlehunters."

By itself, this range of slave activity is not especially unusual. In most plantation societies, slaves performed a variety of duties and held a number of different occupations. Most plantation slaves worked as field hands, but others worked to support the plantation economy. South Carolina in the late 1600s, however, was *not* a plantation society. Although many early settlers came from a plantation environment in Barbados and hoped to re-create that situation in their new homeland, without a staple crop that could be planted on a large scale, like sugar or tobacco, South Carolina's economy remained mixed. The colony had the slaves to support plantation

Ships in the harbor at Charleston, South Carolina, with a distant view of the city in the background. (Library of Congress)

agriculture, but most of those slaves were working, instead, in nonagricultural activities.

As long as South Carolina's economy remained diverse, there was no need to import more slaves. It was not economically efficient to feed, clothe, and house a slave year-round in exchange for only occasional labor. Wage workers or indentured servants could tend cattle, cut trees, or harvest grain. Large slave populations only made economic sense when they worked in labor-intensive environments like plantations. By the end of the 17th century, the expansion of slavery in South Carolina seemed unlikely.

TURNING POINT

Rice was one of the many crops tried during the early years of settlement, but it was not until the 1690s that it became a viable option for South Carolina planters. The first recorded shipment of rice was in 1695, when 1¼ barrels were shipped to Jamaica, another British colony in the West Indies. By 1699, roughly 2,200 barrels of rice were exported from South Carolina. The amount of rice grown and exported from the colony continued to increase until, by the 1720s, it became the leading Carolina export.

KEY CONCEPT   Coastal Rice

The cultivation of rice with the tidal-flow method transformed the coastal southeastern United States between 1783 and the early 19th century. This highly productive method was practical only on the lower stretches of a few rivers from the Cape Fear in North Carolina to the St. Johns in north Florida. The creation of a tidal-rice plantation required a substantial capital investment and a tremendous amount of back-breaking labor. Slaves under planter direction cleared riverside swamps of timber and undergrowth, surrounded them with earthen levees, and then constructed an intricate system of dams, dikes, floodgates, ditches, and drains. The planters relied on the rise and fall of the tide to irrigate their fields several times during the growing season to encourage rice growth and control weeds and pests.

The entire hydraulic apparatus of a rice plantation required constant maintenance by skilled slaves. Today, Hofwyl-Broadfield Plantation on the Georgia coast offers the rare opportunity to enter the world of a rice plantation. The Civil War and Reconstruction seriously affected rice culture. No longer able to compel work in the harsh environment of the rice fields, planters faced chronic labor shortages. Finally, a series of devastating hurricanes in the 1890s ruined the rice fields and put an end to commercial rice growing in the Southeast.

Rice is a plantation crop that requires year-round attention. The method of production changed over time, but by the mid-1700s, it involved several stages, including the construction of dikes and dams to control water, and the labor of many slaves. First, the swampy coastland was drained and prepared for planting. After the rice was planted by slaves in April and May, the fields were flooded periodically to kill off weeds. In May and June, slaves stood knee-deep in water to hoe the plants, removing pests or persistent weeds that might destroy the crop. In September, slaves would cut and stack the rice, then begin the process of threshing and winnowing. Threshing separated the grain from the husk, winnowing blew away the husk, leaving only the cleaned rice kernels. In November, the rice was packed into barrels, transported to Charlestown, then shipped to overseas markets. In January, slaves prepared the fields for a new crop; in February and March they made repairs to trenches, ditches, or irrigation equipment. In April, slaves planted new seeds, and the annual cycle began again.

The success of rice transformed the colony in a number of ways. First, it influenced settlement patterns. Rice grew best in the black, muddy soil found along the Carolina coast. But it also needed fresh water for irrigation. The population, therefore, tended to settle in a strip north and south along the coast, where the soil was muddy, and concentrated on the banks for the rivers that empty into the Atlantic Ocean. Population did gradually move west into the backcountry, but those who could afford it bought "rice land" along the coast. Moreover, rice fields also took up a great deal of room, so settlement was more rural, with neighbors spread out rather than crowded together in villages or towns.

The focus of the economy narrowed, and people turned away from the production of other commodities to grow rice instead. Those who could afford it shifted their efforts away from other economic pursuits and began producing rice for export. Whenever possible, new settlers bought land in rice-growing areas, preferring rice over less lucrative economic activities.

Hoeing rice in South Carolina in the early 1900s. (Library of Congress)

Over time, more planters cultivated more land, producing more rice. Although the volume of rice exported varied from year to year, it tended to increase throughout the 18th century. In 1700, for example, South Carolina exported slightly less than 400,000 pounds of rice. In 1730, the colony exported over 18 million pounds, and in 1770 the amount increased to almost 84 million pounds. Greater rice production also meant more wealth for the colony. By the 1760s, rice brought more wealth to the colony than any other export.

Even more importantly, rice production changed the nature of the Carolina population and the occupations of African slaves. More slaves were needed to keep up with the growing demand for labor. By 1720, the black population had surpassed the white population; 10 years later there were twice as many blacks as whites. This ratio remained relatively consistent for the rest of the colonial period.

Population and Pounds of Rice Exported, South Carolina, 1670–1770

Year	Pounds of rice exported	White population	Black population	Native slaves	Total population
1670		170	30		200
1680		1,000	200		1,200
1690		2,400	1,500	100	4,000
1700	394,130	3,300	2,400	200	5,900
1710	1,600,983	4,200	4,300	1,500	10,000
1720	6,485,662	6,500	9,900	2,000	18,400
1730	18,774,900	10,000	20,000	500	30,500
1740	48,326,000	15,000	39,200		54,200
1750	27,372,500	25,000	40,000		65,000
1760	35,327,250	37,100	57,000		94,100
1770	83,708,625	42,200	82,000		124,200

Source: U.S. Census Bureau (Public Domain)

These slaves did not work at a variety of occupations; most of them worked on rice plantations as field slaves. Gone were the chances for autonomy or variety; slave opportunities disappeared as most were funneled into the regulated plantation work. Rice created a need for more slaves and rice dictated the nature of slave work. Rice swamps were "the gold mines of Carolina," transforming a diverse economy into a plantation environment and locking slaves into the narrow path of agricultural labor.

ACTUAL HISTORY

South Carolina's plantation economy got a boost in the 1740s, when a second staple crop was introduced. Indigo production was reintroduced to the region in 1747 and, together with rice, anchored slavery even more securely. Indigo could be grown on land not suited for rice, thus many planters could grow both crops. Moreover, indigo could be grown in the South Carolina backcountry, so as the population spread inland, so did slavery. With two growing plantation industries, planters and farmers needed more slaves, and they continued to import slaves from both Africa and the West Indies.

The growing number of slaves presented white colonists with an unusual paradox. On the one hand, planters and farmers wanted and needed the labor provided by slaves, but as whites became the minority population, they also feared for their lives. Blacks resisted and rebelled against the bonds of slavery, and white settlers began to look for ways to control and manage the enslaved labor force. The Stono Rebellion and aftermath reflect these growing tensions.

Five generations of a slave family in Beaufort, South Carolina, 1862. (Library of Congress)

In 1739, some 20 runaway slaves attacked and killed storekeepers in Stono, South Carolina, about 15 miles southwest of Charlestown. They seized guns, ammunition, and other supplies, and then headed south toward Spanish Florida. As they traveled, they were joined by more runaway slaves, until they totaled from 60 to 100 strong. They did not get very far, however. Local militia forces caught up with them and a battle ensued.

The Stono Rebellion was the largest slave rebellion in mainland British America. It reflected the anger and frustration of an enslaved population, forced to work in harsh, brutal conditions. The response by white settlers in South Carolina was quick and extreme. Rather than loosening the bonds of slavery or shifting to a system of free labor, white colonists enacted strict, harsh slave codes to more tightly control and manage the slave population.

The Slave Code of 1740 outlined the limitations and restrictions placed on slaves. Slaves were required to have a pass if they were off the

KEY CONCEPT   Stono Rebellion

Early on the morning of Sunday, September 9, 1739, 20 black slaves met in secret near the Stono River in South Carolina to plan their escape to freedom. Minutes later, they burst into Hutcheson's store at Stono bridge, killed the two storekeepers, and stole the guns and powder inside.

The group of slaves grew in number as they headed south. Stono Rebellion, the largest slave uprising in the colonies prior to the American Revolution, was under way.

When the slave owners caught up with the rebels from Stono River, they engaged the 60 to 100 slaves in a battle. More than 20 white Carolinians, and nearly twice as many black Carolinians, were killed. As a result, South Carolina's lawmakers enacted a harsher slave code. This new code severely limited the privileges of slaves. They were no longer allowed to grow their own food, assemble in groups, earn their own money, or learn to read. Some of these restrictions were already in place, but they had not been strictly enforced.

Stono Rebellion was only one among the 250 rebellions documented in the colonies and later in the southern United States. In 1822, a conspiracy to incite 9,000 slaves became known as Vesey's Rebellion. After Nat Turner's Rebellion in 1831, where nearly 60 white people were killed, Turner was executed.

plantation. Because owners were afraid of another uprising, no slave could be taught to read or write, and slave quarters could be searched without warning. Slaves found in violation of any ordinance could be whipped. Parts of the new slave code outlined the master's responsibility to his slaves. Owners were required to feed and clothe their slaves. Field slaves were not to work more than 15 hours per day, and never on Sundays. Anyone who killed or maimed a slave was required to pay a fine.

Overall, the Slave Code systematically stripped blacks of their civil rights, marginalizing them as a permanent underclass. The code dehumanized blacks, making them property rather than humans, it encouraged racism, and it institutionalized slavery. While not the first or the only slave codes in colonial America, they became the harshest and most rigorously enforced. Moreover, they provided the legal framework of slavery until the Civil War.

By the time of the American Revolution, thanks to rice and indigo, slavery was deeply entrenched in South Carolina. After the colonies won independence from England, many northern states wrote state constitutions abolishing slavery. Maryland and Virginia wrote constitutions making it legal to free slaves. South Carolina, however, had grown rich on the labor of slaves. Moreover, slaves were considered property and much of South Carolina's wealth was tied up in this type of "property." After the Revolution, South Carolina remained one of only a few states that held tightly to the institution of slavery.

During the constitutional convention, when delegates were designing the government for the new United States, South Carolina's commitment to slavery helped to influence the final draft of the Constitution. Southern delegates insisted that slaves be counted as part of the population when determining representation. A compromise that counted slaves as "three-fifths" of a person finally settled the issue. In addition, Southern states fought to delay the end of the foreign slave trade and to ensure that the new government legitimize the return of runaway slaves from free states.

While South Carolina delegates negotiated post-Revolutionary political changes, other Carolinians fought to rebuild the state's economy. The state suffered a great deal during the war: plantations were burned, slaves ran off, and British markets disappeared. Southern politicians were fighting to protect slavery, but it was not clear exactly how to employ those slaves.

During the 1780s, planters began to rebuild the rice and indigo industries, but by the 1790s they turned their attention to a new plantation crop: cotton. The Industrial Revolution in England created a huge demand for cotton, and Carolina planters saw a great opportunity to meet that demand. Short-staple cotton grew in the South Carolina backcountry, but there was a catch: numerous, sticky seeds that were difficult to remove. With the invention of the cotton gin in 1793, these seeds could be removed more efficiently, and South Carolina planters were on the verge of an economic rebirth.

Cotton breathed new life into an old economic pattern. While Northern states were moving into a new age of industry, commerce, and transportation, South Carolina remained rooted in an economic pattern that resembled an earlier colonial time: plantation agriculture, slave labor, and the export trade. While Northern states abolished slavery, moving instead to wage labor, the cotton South remained committed to the protection of slavery. By the mid-1800s, plantation agriculture and slavery were entrenched in the South, creating a Southern society that was very different from its Northern counterpart.

U.S. Census Bureau data offer a glimpse into the ways that cotton and slavery transformed South Carolina. In 1790, before cotton revitalized the institution of slavery, whites outnumbered blacks, 140,178 to 108,895. By 1820, blacks outnumbered whites 265,301 to 237,400, and by 1850 South Carolina's population was 58.9 percent black.

This pattern quickly spread west, bringing plantation agriculture and slave labor to other Southern states. By 1860, intense cotton production could be found across the Deep South. The distribution of slaves followed a similar pattern. In 1790, slaves were a significant part of the population only along the South Carolina and Georgia coast. By 1860, however, slaves represented a major part of the population all across the South. It is clear that by 1860 the South had followed the same pattern that had been established earlier by South Carolina.

As the South grew ever more dependent on cotton and slaves, it became more committed to protecting the plantation system. While some Northern politicians lobbied for an end to slavery and the promotion of free labor, Southerners saw things differently. Southerners argued that slaves were property, and they expected the federal government to respect and protect that property. Tensions escalated as the population moved west of the Mississippi River and new states entered the Union. Each new state forced the issue of slavery to the forefront. Who decided whether the state would be free or slave? Did Congress have the constitutional

KEY CONCEPT Civil Rights Acts

Between 1866 and 1875, Congress passed several civil rights acts to enforce the Thirteenth, Fourteenth, and Fifteenth Amendments, allowing the federal government to impose heavy penalties for violations.

The Civil Rights Act of 1866: This act granted black citizens equal rights to contract, to sue and be sued, to marry, travel, and own property. It made all citizens subject to "like punishment, pains and penalties." Any person guilty of depriving citizens of their stated rights because of race, color, or previous condition of servitude could be fined, imprisoned, or both.

The Reconstruction Act of 1867: This act allowed former slaves to participate fully in the political arena. As a result, African Americans sat in constitutional conventions, helped draft state constitutions, and supported new comprehensive programs for state education in the South.

The Enforcement Act of 1870: This act stated that all citizens otherwise qualified to vote in any election should not be denied the vote because of race. States could set up prerequisites for voting, but all persons were to have equal access to the vote.

The Civil Rights Act of 1871: This act set up a system of federal supervision of elections within the states in order to stop illegal voter registration practices.

The Ku Klux Klan Act of 1871: This act was intended to protect black citizens against intimidation by illegal action, such as by the KKK, in cases where states could not, or would not, provide protection.

The Civil Rights Act of 1875: This act entitled all persons the "full and equal enjoyment" of public accommodations, such as hotels, transportation, or theaters. It granted blacks the right to sue for personal damages and allowed any qualified person to serve as a juror. This was the last piece of civil rights legislation passed by the United States Congress until 1957. (National Civil Rights Museum, Memphis, TN civilrightsmuseum.org)

power to restrict slavery? If slaves were indeed property, did not the Constitution protect an individual's right to life, liberty, and property? Did Congress have the power to force Southern states to conform to Northern values and beliefs? By 1860, these tensions reached a breaking point. Abraham Lincoln was elected president and the nation erupted in the Civil War.

The Civil War was a defining moment in American history. Slavery had divided the North and South for decades, creating different views on labor, government, and organization of the west. The Civil War would decide if the two disparate regions would go their separate ways or, if they remained a nation, which vision would prevail. More than three million Americans fought and over 600,000 died. In the end, the North was victorious, and one by one, Southern states returned to the Union. The institution of slavery, however, did not return.

In 1865, Congress passed the Thirteenth Amendment, ending slavery in the United States. In order to return to the Union, each Southern state had to write a new state constitution that ratified the Thirteenth Amendment. Congress also passed the Fourteenth and Fifteenth Amendments, granting citizenship for all blacks and voting rights for African American males. The federal government also protected African Americans in other ways: establishing the Freedman's Bureau, the 1866 Civil Rights Act, and the Reconstruction Acts that promised to establish new social, economic, and political opportunities for former slaves.

Although Congress successfully abolished the institution of slavery, the racial prejudice that drove the system was not as easily erased. Many Southerners resisted the changes proscribed by Congress and sought ways to resist the pressures to conform. Several Southern states passed "Black Codes" that restricted the freedoms of African Americans. Modeled after the pre–Civil War slave codes, these codes prevented former slaves from serving on juries or testifying against whites. In South Carolina, the codes required that blacks get a special license if they wished to work at anything but agricultural labor. In Mississippi, the codes made it illegal for blacks to buy or rent farmland.

In many Southern states, a number of local organizations formed to protest the changes being forced upon the South. The most famous of these groups, the Ku Klux Klan, began in 1866 in Tennessee. The Klan, and other groups like it, harassed Northerners who attempted to help former slaves in the South and intimidated African Americans who tried to exercise their right to vote. Although the institution of slavery was a thing of the past, the abuse and disenfranchisement of African Americans continued long after the Civil War.

The legacy of slavery continued to shape the nation throughout the 20th century. Many Southern states continued to codify racist ideology, passing discriminatory legislation commonly referred to as Jim Crow laws. These laws further marginalized African Americans, requiring them to use separate facilities and schools, and forcing blacks to sit in separate sections on trains, buses, and in theaters. The Supreme Court upheld many of these laws. Although slavery was formally abolished, a government endorsed system of discrimination and segregation continued to limit freedoms for African Americans in the South.

By the 1950s, tensions over race issues came to a head as many blacks refused to conform to these racist regulations. Challenges to the status quo came in a variety of forms. In the 1954 case, *Brown v. Board of Education*, the Supreme Court ruled that segregated schools were inherently "unequal." In 1955, African Americans in Montgomery, Alabama, organized a bus boycott to protest segregated seating. In 1960, four African Americans sat at a "Whites-Only" lunch counter, demanding to be served. Leaders like Martin Luther King Jr., Medgar Evers, and Malcolm X organized rallies, addressed the media, and challenged the social, economic, and legal disenfranchisement of blacks in America.

The Civil Rights Movement of the 1950s and 1960s overturned much of the institutionalized racism that continued after the Civil War. However, the fight is ongoing, as African Americans continue to struggle for social and economic parity.

The introduction of rice in colonial South Carolina was not solely to blame for the racial divide in America, but it was clearly a moment that changed the course of history. Rice established a plantation system and created an experienced, wealthy planter class dependent on slave labor and committed to the protection of their property. Cotton would not have been a viable option in South Carolina without the well-established slave system that existed in the 18th century. Without cotton, plantation agriculture, slave labor, and the export trade would not have spread through the South. Rice set in motion all the variables necessary for the creation of a cotton South, an American Civil War, and the legacy of slavery.

ALTERNATE HISTORY

Without the introduction of rice, the history of South Carolina and the nation would be very different. The diverse economy that existed in the colony in the 1690s may well have continued into the 18th century. Carolinians would continue to ship lumber, corn, peas, beef, and pork to their neighbors in Barbados and export tar, pitch, turpentine, and skins to merchants in England. Employment opportunities for slaves would also be different. Slaves would continue to assist their masters in a number of ways: as blacksmiths, carpenters, dockworkers, shop assistants, and farm laborers.

With no plantation staple, white settlers in South Carolina would have little reason to import slaves. Without rice, there was limited demand for labor, and that demand could be filled by hiring from the local population. Slavery would still exist in the American colonies but the characteristics and pattern of distribution would be very different.

The Lower South (South Carolina and Georgia) would no longer have a black majority by 1740. Without rice, South Carolina would no longer be dominated by blacks. Instead, the Upper South (Virginia, Maryland, and North Carolina) would be the region with the largest slave population. Between 1700 and 1770 roughly 80,000 Africans were imported to that region. By 1770, more than a quarter million slaves labored in the Upper South, most in the tobacco fields. This would give the Chesapeake region the largest slave population in mainland British America.

Northern colonies also employed slaves, but the numbers were small and the occupations varied. Slaves worked on farms, on docks, in shops, and as domestic laborers in households. There were even communities of free blacks in the North. By 1770, for example, free blacks made up 15 to 20 percent of the population in the cities of New York and Philadelphia. Without rice, South Carolina's slave population would have resembled that of the Northern colonies rather than the Upper South. This would change the course of history in a number of ways.

First, without a large slave population, the cultural makeup of the Lower South and the nation in general would be very different. Many of South Carolina's slaves came directly from West Africa, in particular the regions of Gambia, Sierra Leone, Angola, and the Guinea Coast. Once in Carolina, many lived in separate, close quarters, far removed from the white population. In these conditions, slaves retained much of their West African culture and, in many cases, cultural practices were absorbed by the white, mainstream population.

West African slaves working in kitchens introduced new recipes and spices into American diets. African folk medicines found their way into mainstream practice, African prints and patterns were used on fabrics in the American South, African architectural styles could be seen on plantations and in towns, and southern music and dance were influenced by West African instruments and rhythms. Without a large South Carolina slave population, American culture would be without the varied influences of West African society.

The 13 colonies would have declared independence in 1776 but the shape of the new nation would have changed considerably without rice and slaves in South Carolina. The state of South Carolina might have joined with the northern colonies and abolished slavery. This would mean slavery was legal only in the tobacco colonies, and even there the institution was in decline. Tobacco prices were falling and the Chesapeake soil was exhausted from years of overplanting. Farmers and planters were beginning to shift their attention to other crops. Many grew wheat, a crop that could be grown without slave labor. By 1790, it is possible only a small pocket of slavery would have remained in the country, along the Virginia and Maryland coast.

England's Industrial Revolution would still require cotton for its textile operations, but America's method of supplying cotton would have been very different. There would be no slave population to assume the burden of planting, harvesting, and processing the cotton. The cotton gin would still make large-scale cotton production viable, but the labor would have been done by wage employees. To meet the demand for cotton, the South might have developed large-scale commercial operations, supported by wage labor. Like in the North, these agricultural businesses might have been linked together by railroads, canals, and roadways and subsidized by government funds. Rather than developing in opposition to the North, the South would mirror its northern neighbors.

The demographic makeup of the United States would be noticeably different. The country would still consist of Anglo-Americans, Native Americans, and immigrants from around the world, but the African American population would be a fraction of what it became in the 19th century. Between 1790 and 1860, the slave population of the South grew from roughly 700,000 to over four million. If commercial farms and wage labor had replaced plantations employing slave labor, that increase would not have occurred. The population of African Americans in this country would have increased, but not at that rate.

Without a slave South, there would be little to strain at the fabric of American society. Certainly there would be social, economic, and political differences, but there would be nothing as extreme as the fight over slavery. As the population moved west, there would be no quarrel over the inclusion of slave or free states. There would be no social or political divide, and there would be no Civil War.

The South would be spared the vast destruction of fields, homes, and communities. Young men would not lose limbs, young women would not lose husbands, and the nation would not lose over 600,000 lives in four short years. It is possible that slavery would continue to exist on Virginia tobacco plantations, or perhaps it would die off as other commodities replaced tobacco. In any case, slavery would not have been at the center of a war that tore apart a nation.

Without the Civil War, the political and constitutional history of this nation would also change. There would be no Thirteenth, Fourteenth, or Fifteenth Amendments. The Declaration of Independence would still read "All men are created equal," but without slaves there would be no driving force to question that phrase. Women and other disenfranchised people might eventually have called into question their unequal treatment, but without a large black population to point out the hypocrisy of slavery in a democratic, "free" nation, the fight for women's rights would have been slowed.

As the 20th century unfolded, there would be no Jim Crow laws, no court cases, and no civil rights movement. Prejudice and discrimination would still exist, for people tend to be biased against each other and ideas that are different, but racism may not have evolved in the same way. Racist ideology, the idea that race determined an individual's traits and abilities, evolved to justify and rationalize the institution of slavery. Planters argued that African Americans, by virtue of their race, were not capable of caring for themselves or their families; slavery, they argued, provided blacks with food, clothing, a place to live, and a job. Slave owners were, according to their own definition, benevolent caretakers. Without a large Southern slave population, prejudice would have continued, but racism and the legal structures that supported it might not have evolved.

The new century might still have seen the rise of strong, outspoken leaders like W.E.B. DuBois, Marcus Garvey, Malcolm X, or Martin Luther King Jr., but their agendas would have been different. Without the Fourteenth and Fifteenth Amendments, African Americans would not be citizens and would not be allowed to vote. The civil rights movement that emerged in the 20th century might have been focused on issues of citizenship first, then voting rights. Women did not get the vote until 1920; Native Americans were not legally declared citizens until 1924. It is possible that African Americans would also be fighting for these rights well into the 1920s.

The baby boom generation that came along after World War II would still have come of age in the 1950s and 1960s, questioning the status quo and creating a rich and varied counterculture. But without a legacy of slavery, the social, cultural, and political landscape would be very different. It is quite possible that there would be racial prejudice and discrimination, but the protests organized in response to these injustices would be less extreme. The struggle for equality would continue, but the Freedom Rides in Mississippi; the federal troops sent into Little Rock, Arkansas; the Watts riots in Los Angeles; and the black power movement would not have electrified a nation and the world.

The introduction of rice into the South Carolina economy in the 1690s was clearly a turning point in American history. It transformed a small, diverse slave population into the largest plantation economy in the mainland colonies. It created an insatiable need for labor that was filled with slaves from West Africa. As historian Ira Berlin explains, "Rice bankrolled the expansion of plantation society."

America in the 21st century would be a very different place. The legacy of slavery and racism would not continue to influence the cultural, economic, and political structure of the nation. But without the influx of West Africans and the creation of a large African American population, the country would not boast the same rich cultural landscape. Perhaps the greatest irony is that slavery and racism gave rise to the voices that demanded freedom and equality. Without slavery, the words "All men are created equal" would not have been put to the test; the phrase might not have seemed so hypocritical. If the generation of men who wrote those words had no slaves, the meaning of the words might have seemed less significant to later generations.

KEY CONCEPT The Cotton Gin

After the invention of the cotton gin in 1793 by Eli Whitney, the yield of raw cotton doubled each decade after 1800. Demand was fueled by other inventions of the Industrial Revolution, such as the machines to spin and weave it and the steamboat to transport it. By midcentury, America was growing three-quarters of the world's supply of cotton, most of it shipped to England or New England, where it was manufactured into cloth. During this time tobacco fell in value, rice exports at best stayed steady, and sugar began to thrive, but only in Louisiana. At midcentury the South provided three-fifths of America's exports—most of it in cotton.

However, like many inventors, Whitney (who died in 1825) could not have foreseen the ways in which his invention would change society for the worse. The most significant of these was the growth of slavery. Although it was true that the cotton gin reduced the labor of removing seeds, it did not reduce the need for slaves to grow and pick the cotton. In fact, the opposite occurred. Cotton growing became so profitable for the planters that it greatly increased their demand for both land and slave labor. In 1790 there were six slave states; in 1860 there were 15. From 1790 until Congress banned the importation of slaves from Africa in 1808, Southerners imported 80,000 Africans. By 1860 approximately one in three Southerners was a slave.

Because of the cotton gin, slaves now labored on ever-larger plantations where work was more regimented and relentless. As large plantations spread into the Southwest, the price of slaves and land inhibited the growth of cities and industries. In the 1850s seven-eighths of all immigrants settled in the North, where they found 72 percent of the nation's manufacturing capacity. The growth of the "peculiar institution" (slavery) was affecting many aspects of Southern life.

Virginia G. Jelatis

Discussion Questions

1. Why did the expansion of slavery in South Carolina seem unlikely at the end of the 17th century?

2. How did rice production change the nature of the Carolina population and the occupations of African slaves?

3. How did rice set in motion all the variables necessary for the creation of a cotton South, an American Civil War, and the legacy of slavery?

4. How else might American culture be different today had slavery not spread through the South?

5. Without the legacy of slavery, how would the protests of the 1960s have been different? What would have been the issues involved?

Bibiography and Further Reading

Berlin, Ira. *Many Thousands Gone: The First Two Centuries of Slavery in North America*. Cambridge: Harvard University Press, 1998.

Dusinberre, William. *Them Dark Days: Slavery in the American Rice Swamps*. Oxford: Oxford University Press, 1996.

Edgar, Walter. *South Carolina: A History*. Columbia: University of South Carolina Press, 1998.

Jordan, Winthrop. *White over Black: American Attitudes toward the Negro, 1550–1812*. Chapel Hill: University of North Carolina Press, 1986.

Klein, Rachel. *Unification of a Slave State: The Rise of the Planter Class in the South Carolina Backcountry, 1760–1808*. Chapel Hill: University of North Carolina Press, 1990.

McCusker, John J. and Russell R. Menard. *The Economy of British America, 1607–1789*. Chapel Hill: University of North Carolina Press, 1985.

U.S. Bureau of the Census. *Historical Statistics of the United States: Colonial Times to 1957*. Washington, D.C.: General Printing Office, 1960.

Weir, Robert. *Colonial South Carolina: A History*. Columbia: University of South Carolina Press, 1983.

Wood, Peter. *Black Majority: Negroes in Colonial South Carolina, 1670 through the Stono Rebellion*. New York: W.W. Norton, 1974.

TURNING POINT

Georgia was officially founded by the British in 1733, in close proximity to Spanish forces. What if the Spanish repelled the British and the area became part of the Spanish Empire?

INTRODUCTION

During the 16th and 17th centuries, Spain possessed the largest and wealthiest empire in the New World. Spanish possessions were found across the Americas and the Caribbean. Spanish soldiers and missionaries conquered the native populations who were often enslaved or converted to Catholicism. Entrepreneurs ran mines or started plantations in an effort to acquire wealth for themselves and the Spanish Crown. After 1517, the majority of the labor was performed by enslaved Africans. Although Spain controlled a large and wealthy empire, the population of actual Spaniards would always remain small and overwhelmingly male. This meant that the Spanish often had to go to extraordinary lengths to defend their holdings, and their interrelations with blacks and Indians were markedly different than those in England's New World empire.

In 1513, Juan Ponce de León led a Spanish exploratory mission that landed in present-day Florida. This voyage is regarded as representing the first time that Europeans officially set foot on the North American continent. Spain would claim this continent and would refer to the entire Southeast, including Georgia, as La Florida.

Juan Ponce de León soon had to return to Spain, but over the next decade Spanish exploratory and slaving missions would regularly visit the coasts of modern-day South Carolina, Georgia, and Florida. Often the Spanish found themselves at violent odds with the local natives. In 1526, Lucas Vázquez de Ayllón received a charter to settle a great deal of land in modern South Carolina. Upon arriving at the allotted territory, Ayllón and his detachment found the area to be fairly inhospitable and they promptly sailed south. The Spanish sailed into Georgia's Sapelo Sound and established the town of San Miguel de Guadalupe on September 29. Although the town would only last a couple of months, it was the first named settlement in North America.

Despite this important date in North American history, Spain's primary interest in its New World holdings lay in the wealth-producing colonies of

KEY CONCEPT   Hernando de Soto

On May 28, 1539, the Spanish conquistador Hernando de Soto landed with an army of 620 men and 223 horses in Florida, probably not far

Hernando de Soto was one of the first European explorers seeking riches in Georgia and in the American South. (Library of Congress)

from Tampa Bay. When de Soto landed, he was still uncertain as to whether Florida was just another swampy island like the Spanish had found so many of in the Caribbean, or whether it might not be, as rumor suggested, a land of wealthy native cultures ripe for taking prodigious quantities of gold, silver, and jewels. More than anything, de Soto wanted to be like his fellow Spanish conquistador Hernán Cortés, who had enriched himself ravishing the Aztec capital at Mexico City in 1521, and Francisco Pizarro, who through treachery and barbarism had robbed the riches of the Peruvian Incas just 7 years earlier in 1532.

However, the main riches de Soto and his army would find as they marched north through Florida, and then for the next 3 years wandered through present-day Georgia, South Carolina, North Carolina, Tennessee, Alabama, Mississippi, Arkansas, Louisiana, and Texas, was a rich mosaic of native cultures. The de Soto party fought and blustered its way through a land of fairly prosperous native farmers and hunters, a land thickly populated with fair-sized native villages with impressive temples and traditions.

The natives reacted to the aggressive Spanish army in various ways. Sometimes they tried to be friendly, more often as not getting rid of their unwanted visitors by insisting that just a bit beyond their own land there were far richer natives. Some native nations resisted the Europeans before yielding to the Spaniards' superior technology; the natives' spears and arrows were arrayed against the soldiers' guns and horses.

the Caribbean and Central and South America. The Spanish presence in the Southeast would continue to be dominated by missions of exploration (Hernando de Soto's mission being the most famous) and slave raiding. However, in the early 1560s, the French became active in the Southeast, which caused a great degree of anxiety among the Spanish. In 1565, Pedro Menéndez de Avilés was given the responsibility of dislodging the French from the area and then more firmly staking the Spanish Crown's claim to the area by erecting settlements across the region. Menéndez encountered a number of difficulties but was ultimately successful in expelling the French and establishing the city of St. Augustine. Menéndez then ordered further explorations of the Georgia coast during which he met the Indian leader Guale, whose name would come to mean the entire coastal area of Georgia.

KEY CONCEPT *Hernando de Soto (Continued)*

In 1540, Hernando de Soto led his group of soldiers, businessmen, entrepreneurs, and priests through Georgia. At the area of present-day Carter's Lake, Georgia, he visited a capital city of the native Moundbuilders. The visit ended in a violent clash with the natives. In Cartersville, de Soto visited the former settlement along the Etowah River, the Etowah Indian Mounds. From there, the Spaniard traveled downriver to Ulibahali (some sources say Chiaha), a native village at the site of present-day Rome, Georgia. Here, de Soto arrested the town leaders, took hostages and slaves, and ransacked the granaries in August or September leaving nothing for the approaching winter. He left the state traveling west along the Coosa River.

De Soto and his band headed northwest where, on May 8, 1541, a few miles downriver from present-day Memphis, Tennessee, they "discovered" the Mississippi River, which the natives had lead them to. The army crossed the river and continued wandering; de Soto died farther downriver in 1542, and the remnants of de Soto's army never found gold.

Although pirate raids, native uprisings, and foreign incursions were an endemic threat to Spain's Guale colony, during the next 100 years the area would enjoy a fair degree of stability. As was the case across the Spanish Empire, the Spanish presence would be largely limited to missions and presidios that were most commonly located near the coast. Presidios were small forts that were manned by Spanish soldiers and their native allies. The soldiers' primary responsibility was to maintain order in a violent world and to make sure that Guale remained safe and in Spanish hands. After 1573, the missions were run by Jesuits who were charged with converting and "civilizing" the native population of Guale. The Jesuits worked tirelessly with the native population; often learning their languages, instructing them on Christianity, traveling among the natives, and teaching them European methods of farming and handiwork.

Regardless of the missionaries' intentions, in 1597 an Indian uprising nearly destroyed the Spanish presence in Guale. However, the Spanish forces were able to ferociously crush the uprising, and the decision was made to continue with the mission system. This decision would prove to be a good one because for the next 70 years the mission system flourished. As the 17th century wore on, the Spanish missionaries and soldiers extended their control further into the interior across a successful series of trading networks and agricultural settlements. Although the region's Spanish population was largely limited to soldiers and missionaries, this era would represent a time of stable prosperity in Guale.

Spain's virtual monopoly of control over North America was increasingly challenged over the course of the 17th century from a number of rivals. In 1607, the English founded the settlement of Jamestown in territory claimed by Spain. After an initial period of extreme hardship, the English colony of Virginia began to thrive, and its population spread further south.

A much more worrisome event occurred in 1670 when the English founded the colony of Carolina on territory that stretched all the way into Spanish Florida. The Spanish were furious at this development, and during the same year they signed the Treaty of Madrid with England. The Treaty of Madrid established the boundary between the English and Spanish claims at roughly the border between modern-day Georgia and South Carolina. The border was rarely respected, and the Southeast

IN CONTEXT Spanish Empire

The Spanish Empire was composed of territories that were conquered and ruled by Spain as a result of exploration and colonial expansion initiated in the 15th century. This expansion turned Spain into the first transcontinental superpower during the 16th and 17th centuries and helped shape much of the modern world. Built on military might and naval ingenuity, and maintained by trade and the mining of gold and silver, this period is appropriately known as "the Golden Age of Spain."

The Spanish imperial age had profound repercussions in Europe and especially in the conquered regions. The destruction of ancient civilizations, the decimation of indigenous populations, and the introduction of mass slavery rank among the worst consequences. However, the expansion also increased trade, spurred development, and allowed transplant of technologies and the adoption of new crops.

At its greatest extent, the empire included most of Central and South America, as well as important areas in North America, Africa, Asia, and Oceania. In the Americas, Spanish possessions stretched from present-day western United States, through Mexico and Central America, and along the western shores of South America to the edge of Patagonia; they included the state of Florida, the Caribbean islands, and what would become Venezuela, Colombia, Bolivia, Paraguay, Uruguay, and Argentina. In Africa, in different periods, Spain held possessions on the coast of present-day Equatorial Guinea, including the island of Fernando Póo (now Bioko), and occupied territories in the Western Sahara (part of modern Morocco). In Asia, Spain ruled the Philippine Islands. In Oceania, Spain held the Mariana Islands and later the Caroline Islands.

It is true that in some areas, especially in the Americas, Spanish sovereignty was more official than factual, with large tracts of wild and sparsely populated land remaining unexplored until the 1800s. But despite the difficulty to control such a vast domain, Spain maintained much of the empire until the 19th century. Today, only the North African exclaves of Ceuta and Melilla and the Canary Islands off the African coast remain under the Spanish flag.

quickly became the scene of nearly constant official and unofficial raids that pitted the Spanish against the English. Both sides used Native Americans against the other, but the Spanish sought to recruit African American slaves to serve against their former masters to the north.

As Carolina grew in population and wealth, the pressure on the Spanish in Georgia became overwhelming. This was compounded by the threat of a growing French presence along the Gulf Coast. By the 1680s the Spanish mission and presidio system in Georgia had ceased to exist, and Spain's presence in the Southeast was largely concentrated in and around St. Augustine. And this outpost was nearly destroyed by the end of Queen Anne's War in 1713. However, in 1715 the Yamasee natives led a native alliance against the English in Carolina in what would be known as the Yamasee War. The natives caught the English by surprise and, although ultimately defeated, they had a devastating effect on English Carolina. This, compounded by the fact that the remaining Yamasees and their allies flooded into Florida to join the Spanish, greatly strengthened Spain's position in the region at the expense of the English.

For the next 2 decades, the flashpoint for Anglo-Spanish hostilities in the Southeast would be in Georgia. Herbert Bolton has called Georgia during this period the "Debatable Land" because both England and Spain claimed the region, both made minor incursions into it, and both courted its native population. In 1732, the English took the impetus, and James Oglethorpe founded the colony officially known as Georgia.

James Oglethorpe, founder of Georgia, in council with Native Americans in the 1730s. (Library of Congress)

TURNING POINT

Oglethorpe and over 20 other trustees had a unique vision for the colony of Georgia that predated its official founding in 1733. Under the trustees' guidance, Georgia was to become an ambitious philanthropic experiment. The initial emigrants to Georgia were sought from the struggling ranks of the English working classes. It was believed that Georgia's nearly perfect climate would allow these people to easily make a living producing things such as silk and wine. Slavery and liquor were to be banned, and Georgia was to be the home of clean living and industrious moral farmers and laborers. The prospects of taking part in such an economic and moral experiment were so appealing that the trustees were overwhelmed by many more would-be colonists than they could possibly take to Georgia.

After a brief landing in Carolina, where vital supplies were acquired, Oglethorpe and the original Georgia settlers arrived at what would become Savannah in February 1733. The settlers quickly set about constructing a town, and a treaty was negotiated with the local Creek Indians. Georgia's lofty economic goals of becoming a land that produced exotic crops were quickly dashed as it became clear that the area's population lacked the necessary agricultural expertise and the climate was not as favorable as had been believed. However, Georgia's population continued to grow, and new settlements were founded in Frederica and Darrien while defensive outposts were built at Cumberland Island, Amelia Island, and the mouth of the St. John's River.

As Georgia's English population grew larger and more entrenched, so too did Spain's anger and frustration over these developments. Spain still claimed the majority of Georgia and felt imminently threatened by events to the north. In 1737, Oglethorpe and Francisco del Moral Sánchez, the governor of Spanish Florida, agreed that the English would withdraw from the St. John's River. Far from easing tensions in the Southeast, this agreement enraged Madrid and Sanchez was quickly relieved of his position. At the same time, St. Augustine was reinforced and a detachment of over 7,000 men was prepared in Havana for a Spanish invasion that would finally remove the English. Although the invasion was suddenly called off in March 1733, Oglethorpe was granted increased military power with the title of general and commander in chief of the Forces of South Carolina and Georgia, and more troops were sent to Georgia, resulting in an extremely precarious peace with the Spanish.

The tenuous peace between England and Spain in the Southeast ended in October 1739 with the outbreak of the War of Jenkins's Ear. This conflict, which grew out of tensions in the Caribbean, would prove to be a turning point in the history of Georgia. As South Carolina continued to reel from the Stono slave rebellion, Oglethorpe began to devise a plan to invade St. Augustine in the hopes of ending Spain's presence in the Southeast. In May 1740, Oglethorpe led a well-trained force of approximately 1,500 Georgia and Carolina militiamen who were meant to rendezvous with an English fleet from the Caribbean. As Oglethorpe approached, the entire Spanish population of St. Augustine retreated into the city's massive and well-supplied fort. Although a substantial fleet from the Caribbean would never materialize, Oglethorpe was successful in conquering a series of settlements outside of St. Augustine. The English began to bombard the fort, but the Spanish were well organized and confident under the leadership of Governor Manuel de Montiano. With the help of American refugee slaves and natives, the Spanish lifted the siege of St. Augustine by the summer of 1740, leaving the divided and embarrassed English to return to Georgia and Carolina.

It was now time for the Spanish to go on the offensive, and Montiano began to plan a massive invasion of Georgia. Ultimately, Montiano raised and trained a force of blacks, whites, and natives that numbered over 2,000 men, who would be transported north in a fleet of over 50 vessels that arrived off the Georgia coast at the end of June 1742. Montiano's goal was to capture Georgia's capital of Frederica on San Simons Island. Oglethorpe anticipated this move and evacuated his troops from Fort St. Simons in an effort to consolidate his forces and defend Frederica. Oglethorpe's decision would prove to be decisive, and in early July he encountered the numerically superior Spanish forces outside of Frederica. The Spanish were shocked when Oglethorpe led a charge into their ranks. The bold maneuver scattered the Spanish force, which was pursued and hounded by the English foe. For the next few days, the Spanish and English engaged in sporadic skirmishes, but the Battle of the Bloody Marsh would prove to be decisive as the humiliated and beleaguered Spanish were left to limp back to Florida. More importantly, England's claim to Georgia was now complete as both sides grudgingly accepted the others' presence in the Southeast and, in the future refrained from large scale military activities against the other. But what if the Spanish force had been successful?

ACTUAL HISTORY

With the Spanish menace now largely destroyed, Georgia appeared ready to thrive as the southernmost English colony in North America. However, Georgia quickly fell on hard times because its slave-free economy, based on the production of exotic staples and fair land distribution, began to falter. As Georgia's economic woes increased so too did criticism of the trustees. The majority of Georgia's population believed that the introduction of African slavery, along the lines practiced in South Carolina, was the solution to the colony's economic problems. In 1750, Georgia's proslavery advocates won the debate, and restrictions on slavery were lifted. Two years later, in 1752, the trustees returned their charter to the crown and Georgia's time as a noble experiment ended.

Georgia's shift from a trusteeship to a royal province was smooth, and being ruled by a series of royal governors and councils seemed to bother few of Georgia's inhabitants. The decision to allow slavery would have a much greater effect on the colony. Through the 1750s and 1760s enormous numbers of slaves were brought into Georgia, and by the eve of the American Revolution, Georgia would nearly have a black population majority. The introduction of slavery led to strong economic growth as land holdings were consolidated and rice and indigo production provided valuable cash crops that dominated the coast. The explosive growth of slavery in Georgia was not without its dangers. Initially, Georgia was founded as a buffer zone between slave-holding Carolina and Spanish Florida. It was correctly believed that the presence of the Spanish in

"Relics of Slavery Days": Slave quarters at the Hermitage Plantation outside Savannah, Georgia. (Library of Congress)

Florida held out a dangerous inducement to Carolina slaves to flee or violently resist their masters. From the 1750s onward, Georgians brought tens of thousands of slaves into close proximity to Spanish Florida.

With the profound shift in Georgia's economy, growing class and racial tensions emerged. Georgia's white population increased, but gone was the trusteeship's lofty commitment to social equality, and left in its place was an economy that favored increasingly large land and slave owners at the expense of small farmers and craftsmen. In many ways, Georgia became a colony divided between "crackers" and planters.

Georgia was largely untouched by the French and Indian War (1754–1763) and in the 12-year build up to the American Revolution, the colony's population and economy grew at a healthy rate. Georgia's path toward revolution was unique and far from unified. In 1766, Georgia became the only colony to pay the Stamp Tax, which nearly resulted in an invasion of angry Carolinians. Next, Georgia's response to the Townshend Acts was slow and half-hearted. It was not until the 1774 passage of the Intolerable Acts, which were primarily aimed at punishing Boston, that Georgia began to express a strong displeasure with Great Britain. However, Georgia failed to send a delegate to the First Continental Congress in Philadelphia in 1775. Despite a great degree of reluctance, Georgia began to move toward the revolutionary cause in the summer of 1775, in the months after Lexington and Concord. Increasingly organized radical elements successfully usurped the royal governor's power in the Georgia colony. By the summer of 1776, Georgia had installed a revolutionary government that recognized the Declaration of Independence.

The course of the Revolutionary War in Georgia was as strange as Georgia's march to war. The Revolutionary War in Georgia was marked by the stark divisions between Tories and Whigs, a restive slave population, the cunning Creek natives, and a great degree of savage frontier violence. During the first phase of the Revolutionary War, the Georgia Whigs devoted a great deal of time and effort to planning expeditions against British St. Augustine that never proved successful. In the meantime, the Red Coats recaptured Savannah at the end of 1778. This led to a situation where the British and their Tory allies controlled Savannah and the Whigs were distributed across the colony. As the Revolutionary War dragged on, both sides found it difficult to devote troops to Georgia and, as a result, the Whigs were able to liberate Savannah in the summer of 1782, essentially ending the American Revolution in Georgia.

With the peace treaty of 1783, Georgia, like the rest of the original 13 states, had its independence. Georgia now faced a difficult transitional period during which the old colonial social order would be challenged as the population grew steadily after independence. Georgia had suffered physical destruction during the Revolution from which the rice and indigo industries never fully recovered; many wealthy Tories had left the state, slaves fled, and a great deal of public land was redistributed to small farmers. The net result of these developments was to undermine the old privileged classes and provide a degree of upward mobility for the poorer classes.

Two more problems faced Georgia in the postwar years; the state's dealings with the Creek and Cherokee natives, and the return of Florida to the Spanish (between 1764 and 1783 East and West Florida had become British colonies). As land hunger grew, Georgia and its citizens sought to acquire Creek and Cherokee lands to the west through treaties, purchase, intimidation, and, often, coercion. Ultimately, Georgia was successful in displacing the natives, but not before the Creek War (1813–1814) and the 1830s' "Trail of Tears" that would serve as low points in relations with Native Americans. The Spanish in Florida were as weak as ever and, increasingly, the provinces were becoming home to anti-Spanish natives and fugitive American slaves. Georgia and the rest of the South wanted to see the Spanish presence in Florida ended, and in 1811, Georgia's governor George Mathews helped to organize the so-called Patriot Invasion of Florida. Not until 1819 would the United States acquire Florida, but the cost to Georgia in frontier violence had been immense.

All aspects of 19th-century Georgia's economy, society, and culture were profoundly shaped and influenced by the changing nature of slavery and race relations. Two interrelated events converged to reinvigorate slavery in Georgia after independence; the invention of the cotton gin, which made cotton production economically viable, and Georgia's expansion into western lands that were suited to the growth of cotton. Slavery spread across the state, and a new cotton aristocracy emerged as the dominant and conservative force in Georgia's economy and society. Although not all Georgians owned slaves nor was cotton the sole product, Georgia would become a society dominated by slavery, where slaves toiled in all tasks imaginable and whites sought to justify and defend the institution through a combination of religious, racial, and economic arguments.

Geographically, culturally, and economically, Georgia was the quintessential Southern state. Thus it was not surprising that Georgia was intimately involved with the South's march toward secession as regional differences over the regulation of slavery in the territories tore the Union apart. In January 1861, after Abraham Lincoln's election, Georgia held a convention that, surprisingly, voted narrowly to secede from the United States and join South Carolina, Alabama, Mississippi, and Florida in what would become the Confederacy.

Georgia had been swept along by a wave of secessionists' emotions and was far from alone in thinking that any hostilities would be quick and relatively bloodless. So when the first shots of the Civil War were fired in April at Fort Sumter, South Carolina, Georgians of all walks of life were quick to join the Confederate Army. The Civil War lasted for 4 long years, during which time thousands of Georgians were killed or disabled on the battlefield and on the home front. Georgia's economy was destroyed by the demands of the Civil War, by the Union blockade, and through the destruction and disruption of the Civil War. Many women were left at home with newly increased economic and familial responsibilities that they simply were not prepared for. Georgia's suffering was increased in 1864 when General William Tecumseh Sherman led the Union Army across Georgia in a mission of pure destruction that left Atlanta, Macon, Savannah, and much of the countryside reduced to smoldering ashes.

On April 9, 1865, the Civil War ended at Appomattox Courthouse in Virginia. Georgia lay in tatters with a broken economy and population. Slavery, which had formed the bedrock of Georgian society, was now abolished, and the Union Army occupied the state. After a failed effort to quickly rejoin the Union in 1866, Georgia would be subject to Radical Reconstruction, which saw an occupying Union army protect black rights and rebuild the state while assuring the rule of Republican politicians. Georgia Democrats violently interfered with Reconstruction and the state

KEY CONCEPT   Jim Crow Laws

From the 1880s into the 1960s, a majority of American states enforced segregation through Jim Crow laws (so-called after a white performer who performed in blackface in minstrel shows). From Delaware to California, and from North Dakota to Texas, many states (and cities too) could impose legal punishments on people for consorting with members of another race. The most common types of laws forbade intermarriage and ordered business owners and public institutions to keep their black and white clientele separated. Here is a sampling of laws from various states.

Nurses: No person or corporation shall require any white female nurse to nurse in wards or rooms in hospitals, either public or private, in which negro men are placed. *Alabama*

Buses: All passenger stations in this state operated by any motor transportation company shall have separate waiting rooms or space and separate ticket windows for the white and colored races. *Alabama*

Railroads: The conductor of each passenger train is authorized and required to assign each passenger to the car or the division of the car, when it is divided by a partition, designated for the race to which such passenger belongs. *Alabama*

Restaurants: It shall be unlawful to conduct a restaurant or other place for the serving of food in the city, at which white and colored people are served in the same room, unless such white and colored persons are effectually separated by a solid partition extending from the floor upward to a distance of seven feet or higher, and unless a separate entrance from the street is provided for each compartment. *Alabama*

Pool and Billiard Rooms: It shall be unlawful for a negro and white person to play together or in company with each other at any game of pool or billiards. *Alabama*

---

eventually returned to local control by the time the Compromise of 1877 officially ended Reconstruction.

Between 1877 and 1910, Georgia was dominated by Bourbon leaders (a small, fiscally conservative elite) who promoted the New South. The New South was built on a diversified economy consisting of industry and small farms that grew a range of crops. Some of the New South's economic reforms were realized, debt was reduced, and advances in education were made, but the vast majority of both white and black Georgians struggled to make ends meet in an overwhelmingly agricultural economy. A long period began where the state's majority worked as sharecroppers or tenant farmers trapped in a cycle of poverty, debt, and desperate subsistence.

The darkest legacy of post–Civil War Georgia occurred in the area of civil rights for blacks. The Thirteenth, Fourteenth, and Fifteenth Amendments had ended slavery, established black citizenship, and guaranteed fundamental civil rights. African Americans made advances in education, employment, and political participation, with many voting and even holding office across the South and Georgia. There was a great degree of hostility toward blacks during Reconstruction and the following years; however, not until the 1890s did the white South seek to systematically subjugate the black population. The increased racism that led to the introduction of "Jim Crow" Georgia was based on growing resentment toward a new generation of educated and empowered blacks. Blacks were disenfranchised, and a strict segregation of the races set in. Some whites perverted the law and used violence and intimidation to ensure that blacks were trapped as second-rate citizens. This state of affairs continued into the second half of the 20th century, and racial problems would poison many of Georgia's efforts at economic and social progress.

KEY CONCEPT   *Jim Crow Laws (Continued)*

Toilet Facilities, Male: Every employer of white or negro males shall provide for such white or negro males reasonably accessible and separate toilet facilities. *Alabama*

Intermarriage: It shall be unlawful for a white person to marry anyone except a white person. Any marriage in violation of this section shall be void. *Georgia*

Intermarriage: The marriage of a person of Caucasian blood with a Negro, Mongolian, Malay, or Hindu shall be null and void. *Arizona*

Intermarriage: All marriages between a white person and a negro, or between a white person and a person of negro descent to the fourth generation inclusive, are hereby forever prohibited. *Florida*

Cohabitation: Any negro man and white woman, or any white man and negro woman, who are not married to each other, who shall habitually live in and occupy in the nighttime the same room shall each be punished by imprisonment not exceeding twelve (12) months, or by fine not exceeding five hundred ($500.00) dollars. *Florida*

Education: The schools for white children and the schools for negro children shall be conducted separately. *Florida*

Juvenile Delinquents: There shall be separate buildings, not nearer than one-fourth mile to each other, one for white boys and one for negro boys. White boys and negro boys shall not, in any manner, be associated together or worked together. *Florida*

Mental Hospitals: The Board of Control shall see that proper and distinct apartments are arranged for said patients, so that in no case shall Negroes and white persons be together. *Georgia*

With the exception of the international Coca Cola empire based in Atlanta, Georgia remained a rural bastion of white supremacy where levels of education, income, industrialization, and urbanization paled in comparison to national averages until World War II, when things began to change. As a result of the war and the boom economy of the 1950s, Georgia began to develop a sizeable manufacturing sector, wages increased, the economy expanded, and cities grew, with Atlanta becoming the banking capital of the entire region. Rural life improved as advances in agriculture made farming much more profitable.

Although post–World War II Georgia quickly found itself on the path to prosperity and modernization, Jim Crow was still alive and well. In 1954, the Supreme Court handed down the landmark *Brown v. Board of Education* decision that challenged the legal basis of "separate but equal" in public schools and, by extension, every other aspect of segregated Southern society. Many whites in Georgia resisted desegregation, but the civil rights movement had been born, and the state would be a major battleground. In 1960, sit-ins began in Atlanta and spread across the state. In 1961, the Student Nonviolent Coordinating Committee began a voter registration drive. Across the state, blacks and whites joined protests designed to gain blacks their long overdue rights. Often, they were met with violence and intimidation from some whites who saw their entire way of life challenged. The culmination of the civil rights movement was the 1964 Civil Rights Act, and the greatest champion of the civil rights movement was Dr. Martin Luther King Jr., Georgia's most famous son.

Present-day Georgia is a prosperous and diverse state. Its citizens are conservative, frequent churchgoers, and tend to vote Republican while prizing family values. In 1976, Georgia's governor Jimmy Carter was elected president; in 1994 a Georgia Congressman Newt Gingrich became Speaker of the House; and in 1996, Atlanta hosted the Summer Olympics. All of these facts point to growing national and international respect and prestige for Georgia.

ALTERNATE HISTORY

In the alternate history, Montiano and the Spanish more firmly come to grasp the potential threat posed by a viable and sustained English colony in Georgia. The decision was made in St. Augustine and Havana to virtually ensure that the Spanish invasion force would be successful. Thus Montiano spent a great deal of time raising a force of blacks, natives, and Spanish that numbered well over 4,000. This represented the single largest army assembled in North America to that point, and these men were well trained and prepared over the course of a number of months. The naval force sent from Havana would number nearly 100 vessels.

As Montiano oversaw the training of his army during the spring of 1742, he envisioned that the greatest single threat to his mission to destroy Georgia was a military intervention by South Carolina. The decision was taken to divert South Carolina's attention by attempting to foment a slave uprising that would coincide with Spain's invasion of Georgia. South Carolina had yet to fully recover from the shock of the 1739 Stono Rebellion, and the Spanish were confident that another uprising would ensure that South Carolina would be too occupied at home to aid Georgia. A month before the Spanish invasion force left Florida in June 1742, a number of former American slaves who had been living under Spanish protection in St. Augustine were sent to the slave quarters of South Carolina to make promises of pending Spanish aid against their English masters and of freedom to be found in Spanish Florida.

Montiano's target was the same in both the alternate history and the actual history: Georgia's capital of Frederica. However, this time Oglethorpe failed to anticipate this fact and remained with the bulk of the English forces at Fort St. Simons, believing that it was essential to protect Georgia's southern perimeter. When the Spanish invasion force touched ground near Frederica in June, they found the capital virtually defenseless and were able to capture it with minimal hostilities. Before word had reached Oglethorpe of Frederica's fall, the Spanish force had successfully descended on Savannah and met with equally light resistance. With the fall of the two major settlements in Georgia, the colony's thin rural population were left to chaos, which served to exacerbate the situation.

Oglethorpe was overwhelmed at the news that an enormous multiracial Spanish force had captured both Frederica and Savannah. His despair was compounded when he received news that over 500 slaves had risen against their masters in the South Carolina low country, ending any chance of aid from their neighbors. Oglethorpe made the fateful decision to engage the numerically superior Spanish in a desperate effort that was a last ditch attempt to save his beloved experiment. In early July, less then 400 English soldiers met nearly 3,000 well-trained Spanish troops outside of Frederica. Again, Oglethorpe attempted to gain the advantage through a surprise assault into the Spanish ranks, but this time he was thoroughly defeated and he lost his life in the fighting. The remaining English soldiers disbanded into small guerrilla groups but were quickly and mercilessly defeated by the swarming Spanish, whose ranks had begun to swell with further native recruits.

By August, the remaining English settlers had been rounded up and were allowed to leave the colony. Spanish garrisons were established at Savannah and Frederica, and the English period of Georgia's history had ended. The decision was made to combine Spanish Florida and Georgia into one large colony that would stretch from the border of English South Carolina to the Caribbean. This colony would have regional capitals at St. Augustine, Pensacola, and Savannah. Each of the three cities would have a royal governor who controlled the area's military and economy.

Spain always found it difficult to attract substantial amounts of settlers to its southeastern colonies, which presented economic and military problems. A number of solutions were decided on. Large tracts of land would be offered to entice would-be farmers. Favorable conditions were offered to tradesmen and craftsmen in the hopes of stimulating an urban economy.

Regardless of these efforts to recruit Spanish settlers, numbers remained low. Spain decided to carefully cultivate positive relations with the Cherokee, Creek, and Seminole natives who frequently visited the Spanish settlements. At the same time, the Spanish continued to accept American refugee slaves as allies, and they were allowed to settle in close proximity to their settlements. Although Spanish soldiers were a frequent sight, the bulk of Georgia's defenses were provided by their black and native allies. Spanish Georgia quickly became a multiracial society where blacks and natives enjoyed enhanced status, much to the consternation of Anglo-America.

Spanish Georgia and Florida existed on the margins of Spain's increasingly weak New World empire. The region was largely passed over by the French and Indian War (1754–1763). However, the sheer size of the colony made Spain reluctant to exchange it with Britain for Cuba in 1763 as had been the case in the real history. The greatest problems created by the American Revolution (1775–1783) came from the heavy flow of American refugee slaves that swarmed into Spanish settlements across the colony. In the Southern colonies, many blacks followed Lord Dunmore's invitation to join the British in exchange for freedom. In the actual history, many of these "loyal blacks" who joined the "Ethiopian Regiment" and their families were transported to Canada after the Revolution, and then a portion of them went on to found Sierra Leone in West Africa. In this alternate version, the large influx of liberated blacks to Spanish Georgia–Florida would create an even greater refuge, and a southbound flow of escaped slaves, larger than the actual northbound Underground Railroad, would undermine slavery in the Carolinas.

In 1783, the Spanish faced a young and confident United States to the north that was no longer bound by British imperial restraints. Southern slave owners were deeply fearful of the bad example set by Spanish Georgia's large free black and native population, and the United States sought to officially and unofficially acquire Georgia and Florida. Between 1790 and 1810, the American forces frequently sent raiding parties across the South Carolina border while American diplomats tried to negotiate the purchase of Georgia and Florida.

However, a number of developments made Spain increasingly determined to retain possession of Georgia and Florida. In 1803, France's Napoleon and the United States agreed on the Louisiana Purchase; land was sold that was technically Spanish, and this greatly humiliated Spain. Cuba had recently become a valuable sugar-producing island, and the Spanish were fearful of the United States controlling land so close to Cuba. Much of Latin America had recently risen against Spain, but Georgia and Florida had remained loyal and represented two of the last bastions of Spain's New World empire. Most importantly, gold had been discovered on Cherokee land in Georgia. Due to these developments, the appeal and importance of Georgia and Florida were greatly enhanced.

Georgia's Spanish population grew as economic opportunists were joined by loyalist refugees from across Latin America. The increasing size and strength of Georgia and Florida's population made the Patriot Invasion (1812), Britain's Occupation of Pensacola and West Florida during the War of 1812, Andrew Jackson's invasion of West Florida (1814, 1816, and 1817) and the First Seminole War (1817) impossible because Britain and America had to respect Spain's neutrality. Spanish Georgia and Florida would not become part of the United States in 1819 and, along with Cuba and Puerto Rico, would fly the flag of Spain in the New World.

Spanish Georgia and Florida received ever greater attention from Spain. Savannah, Augusta, St. Augustine, Pensacola, and Miami became prosperous towns with diverse populations of Creoles, various Europeans, natives, and blacks. Gold was extracted from Georgia, and farmers tilled the fertile countryside. Trade was conducted with Europe and the rest of the Americas.

With a weary eye, the southeastern Spanish watched as the United States, behind the cry of "Manifest Destiny," expanded to the Pacific after the Mexican War (1846–1848). They also paid close attention to the increasingly fierce sectional debate over the extension of slavery in the territories that would lead to the Civil War. During the Civil War, Spanish Georgia and Florida would remain neutral but would profit from smuggling for the Confederate States and from the stimulus that was provided to their own small cotton sector.

After the Civil War, Spanish Georgia and Florida would face troubled times. In Europe, Spain was increasingly poor and weak, and this had an effect on the fortunes of its remaining colonial possessions. Financial and military aid to Georgia declined as did immigration. During the Spanish-American War of 1898 the territory was the scene of fighting and, at the war's conclusion, was turned over to the United States along with Cuba and Puerto Rico.

The United States debated whether to make Georgia and Florida a state, but the fear of giving citizenship to its Hispanic, black, and native inhabitants appealed to few American politicians. Few people in the Jim Crow South wanted to see the admission of a new "nonwhite" state. Instead Georgia and Florida, would be administered by an American-approved governor who oversaw the drafting of a constitution that would create a representative government. The American armed forces would remain in the territory.

American investors soon saw the potential for profit in Georgia and Florida. American money was poured into resorts, railroads, and farming (cane, rice, and cotton). American corporations had branches in Georgia and Florida, but they relied heavily on well-positioned locals to oversee their investments. The more America invested in Georgia and Florida, the wealthier this class grew and the poorer the vast majority of citizens became as they were left to toil on farms and in menial positions. As "neo-colonial" interests and corruption came to dominate Georgia, class tensions and resentment grew among the exploited masses. The Great Depression had an especially devastating effect on the masses, who were increasingly receptive to radical political ideas and blamed the American-backed government for their suffering. During the 1940s and 1950s a guerrilla movement began among the Georgians and Floridians. Their aim was independence from the United States, and they targeted American economic interests and those who worked with the Americans.

The United States was shocked by the successful communist revolution in Cuba and made the decision to avoid seeing Georgia and Florida follow a similar path. In 1960, President John F. Kennedy ordered 20,000 American troops to be sent to Georgia and Florida to crush the guerrilla movement. Within 2 years, the American mission had been deemed a success and Georgia and Florida would enter an extended period of stability.

In the alternate history, present-day Georgia is an American Commonwealth whose citizens carry American passports. The territory is dominated by agriculture and tourism from the United States. The people are Spanish speakers of European, African, and native ancestry who take great pride in the unique history of Georgia and Florida. Although Georgia enjoys many of the benefits of the United States, the average Georgian makes only $5,000 a year, and poverty and unemployment are chronic problems forcing many Georgians to move to the United States in search of economic opportunity. For nearly 500 years Georgia has been a unique Spanish outpost in North America.

Nathaniel Millett

Discussion Questions

1. How was Spanish settlement of its colonies different from British settlement? What factors made it so different—population, religion, culture, or political ideas of governance?

2. If Georgia had remained under Spanish control through the middle of the 19th century, in what ways would that have represented a threat to maintaining slavery in the other states of the South prior to the Civil War?

3. In actual history, the cotton frontier of the Old South moved from Georgia across Alabama and Mississippi, with labor supplied by slaves drawn from Virginia and the Carolinas. Do you think the presence of

a Spanish-controlled Florida and Georgia would have prevented this spread of cotton plantations and slavery?

4. In this alternate history, Florida and Georgia remain under Spanish control even after Mexico, Central America, and South America get their independence from Spain in the 1820s. What factors would have led to Spain retaining control of "Spanish North America" (in Florida and Georgia) through the 19th century rather than those territories becoming independent like the republics of Latin America?

5. In actual history, the Philippines, Cuba, and Puerto Rico were liberated from Spanish control in the Spanish-American War of 1898. The Philippines became a territory of the United States and then an independent nation after World War II; Cuba was immediately independent (although granting U.S. control over a military base at Guantanamo); Puerto Rico remained a territory and then a commonwealth of the United States. If Georgia and Florida remained in Spanish control until 1898, which aspects of these three models would have applied there in the 20th century? Which models did the author think applied, and why?

6. In this alternate history, Spanish North America, like Cuba in the 1960s, is drawn to radical Marxism. What factors would have made this likely or unlikely?

7. In actual history, President John Kennedy approved the invasion of Cuba in 1961 at the Bay of Pigs by an anti-Castro force of exiled Cubans with U.S. support, and that invasion was a spectacular failure. What factors would make sending U.S. troops into Georgia on a similar mission in this alternate history more likely to be successful?

Bibliography and Further Reading

Anderson, William, ed. *Cherokee Removal: Before and After.* Athens: University of Georgia Press, 1991.

Bartley, Numan. *The Creation of Modern Georgia.* Athens: University of Georgia Press, 1990.

Cobb, James. *Georgia Odyssey.* Athens: University of Georgia Press, 1997.

Coleman, Kenneth, ed. *A History of Georgia.* Athens: University of Georgia Press, 1991.

Coleman, Kenneth. *The American Revolution in Georgia: 1763–1789.* Athens: University of Georgia Press, 1958.

Davis, Harold Earl. *The Fledgling Province: Social and Cultural Life in Colonial Georgia, 1733–1776.* Chapel Hill: University of North Carolina Press, 1976.

Inscoe, John, ed. *Georgia in Black and White: Explorations in Race Relations of a Southern State, 1865–1950.* Athens: University of Georgia Press, 1994.

Lewis, Davis. *King: A Critical Biography.* Westport, CT: Praeger, 1970.

Mohr, Clarence. *On the Threshold of Freedom: Masters and Slaves in Civil War Georgia.* Athens: University of Georgia Press, 1986.

Reidy, Joseph. *From Slavery to Agrarian Capitalism in the Cotton South: Central Georgia, 1800–1880.* Chapel Hill: University of North Carolina Press, 1992.

Spalding, Phinizy. *Oglethorpe in America.* Athens: University of Georgia Press, 1984.

Tuck, Stephen. *Beyond Atlanta: The Struggle for Racial Equality in Georgia, 1940–1980.* Athens: University of Georgia Press, 2003.

Wood, Betty. *Slavery in Colonial Georgia, 1730–1775.* Athens: University of Georgia Press, 1984.

1492	Spanish Reconquista is completed. Spain is unified under rule of Ferdinand and Isabella.
1492, October 12	Searching for a route to the West Indies, Christopher Columbus claims the Bahamas for Spain. Ferdinand and Isabella of Spain sponsored his expedition. Believing that he had reached the West Indies, Columbus calls the native people Indians.
1493–1494	Pope Alexander VI convinces Spain and Portugal to divide any new overseas trading interests between them. He creates a line of demarcation, a north–south line drawn on a map, through the Atlantic Ocean. In the Treaty of Tordesillas, signed by Spain and Portugal in 1494, all the newly discovered land to the west of the demarcation line at about 48° is given to Spain, and that to the east was given to Portugal. The treaty establishes west longitude and extends it around the earth to secure Portuguese claims in Asia.
1496–1497	Henry VII of England authorizes John Cabot to sail west in search of lands yet undiscovered. Cabot makes two voyages to the New World. His voyages become the basis for English claims to North American territory.
1497–1499	Vasco da Gama of Portugal sets sail for India, following a route that circumvents Africa. He arrives at Calicut on the west coast of India in May 1498. He returns home safely in 1499. He is the first man to sail directly from Europe to India and back. Once opened, the sea route around Africa became a busy thoroughfare and established Portugal as the dominant spice-trading nation in Europe. Portugal's success aroused the envy of the rulers of Europe's other nations.
1504	Amerigo Vespucci publishes account of his voyage along the coast of South America. He is erroneously given credit for discovering the New World before Columbus. German mapmakers name the New World "America."
1506	Columbus dies unaware that he has reached new continents in the Western Hemisphere.
1513	Vasco Núñez de Balboa of Spain explores the Pacific Ocean. He mistakenly believes the ocean to be the Indian Ocean.
1513	Ponce de León of Spain explores Florida in search of the "fountain of youth." Though he does not find the fountain, he adds to Spanish claims in the New World.

1517–1521   Martin Luther launches the Protestant Reformation. Luther's call for reforms in the Catholic Church led to the creation of many different Christian denominations and created religious turmoil over the next century. If not for the turmoil created by the Reformation, religious dissenters would not have sought refuge in the New World.

1519–1522   Spain sends Portuguese sailor Ferdinand Magellan to accomplish what Christopher Columbus had not. While sailing along the South American coast Magellan discovered a strait at the tip of South America that allowed access to the Pacific Ocean. Magellan found an ocean route to the Far East by sailing west. Though Magellan did not survive the trip, and the route was far too long to be used for trade, the fact that his men had circumnavigated the globe was a milestone for humankind.

1519–1600   Native American populations are greatly diminished. The Indian population in Mexico is reduced from 25 million in 1519 to less than 2.5 million in 1600. Violence was not the only reason for this decrease. European diseases such as measles, smallpox, tuberculosis, and cholera hit native populations hard. The lack of immunity to such diseases at times devastated whole tribes.

1521   Hernán Cortés takes Aztec capital Tenochtitlán in modern day Mexico.

1524   French king, Francis I, sends Giovanni da Verrazano in search of a northwest passage to Asia. Verrazano explored the Atlantic coast from Newfoundland south to North Carolina.

1527–1539   Henry VIII of England takes a stand against the pope and declares himself head of a new Church of England. He created the first state supported Protestant church in England. Though his intentions were questionable (he created the church so he could divorce one wife and marry another), the Church of England would prove to be historically significant. Henry authorized an English translation of the Bible so that it could be read by all literate people. For the next century, England became a battleground between Catholics and Protestants.

1534   Jacques Cartier makes the first of three voyages to the Americas looking for a northwest passage. He explores the St. Lawrence River as far as Montreal but fails to find the passage.

1539   Hernando de Soto of Spain lands in Florida. De Soto explores the southeastern United States as far as the Mississippi River in search of treasure.

1540   Spaniard Francisco Vásquez de Coronado sets out from Mexico in 1540 in search of the mythical Seven Cities of Cibola. His journey took him to the Grand Canyon and Kansas, but he failed to find the cities or any treasure. Coronado unintentionally introduced horses to the Plains Indians. Enough horses escaped from his expedition to change the lives of Plains Indians. Within a few decades Plains Indians became masters of horsemanship.

1556   *Ordinary of the Mass* is first book printed in the Americas.

1565   French Huguenots attempt to settle the northern coast of Florida. Fearing that French colonists would prove a threat to Spanish trade routes, Spain has the Huguenot colony destroyed. Not far from the destroyed colony, Spain establishes the first permanent European settlement at St. Augustine.

1570   In an effort to curb further European encroachment, five Native American tribes form the most democratic nation of its time. The "Ho-De-No-Sau-Nee," or League of the Iroquois tribes, was run by a council of 50 representatives from each of the five member tribes. The League was a strong power in the 1600s and 1700s, siding with the British during the French and Indian War. It remained strong until the Revolutionary War when its members became indecisive about which side to support. As a result, everyone fought the Iroquois, and the League never recovered.

1577   Queen Elizabeth I of England privately begins to promote exploration and colonization in America. Elizabeth financed the world expedition of Sir Francis Drake, which established England's claim to present-day California and British Columbia. His expedition was not only exploratory. Drake also pirated a Spanish treasure galleon, making both himself and the queen very wealthy.

1578   Sir Francis Drake explores the California coast.

1580   Sir Francis Drake becomes the first Englishman to circumnavigate the globe.

1585–1588   Sir Walter Raleigh sends two expeditions to Roanoke Island off the coast of present-day North Carolina. The first expedition failed and in 1586 a small band returned home. The second expedition was launched in 1587. Virginia Dare was born soon after the second expedition arrived. Within a year of the second expedition's landing at Roanoke Island, the settlement had disappeared. The only clue to the whereabouts of the colonists was a word carved on a tree—CROATOAN, the name of a Native American group and of a nearby island. Mystery remains as to the fate of the settlers.

1588   The defeat of the Spanish Armada by Great Britain clears the way for English colonization in the Americas.

1590   Richard Hakluyt publishes an anthology of notable voyages to the New World that includes accounts by English explorers and settlers. Francis Drake, Humphrey Gilbert, and Walter Raleigh were highlighted in Hakluyt's work.

1593   John White publishes detailed drawings of Native Americans.

1607   The Virginia Company of London forms the first permanent English settlement at Jamestown. Between 1607 and 1624 approximately 14,000 people migrated to the colony, yet only about 1,300 were living there in 1624. High mortality rates were caused by starvation, disease, and Indian attacks.

1607   Captain John Smith is captured by Native American chief Powhatan. He was marked for death, but Powhatan's daughter, Pocahontas pleaded for his life. Smith was instrumental in saving the starving colony of Jamestown by trading with Native Americans.

1608   An additional 110 colonists arrive at Jamestown. In December, the first items of export trade are sent from Jamestown back to England.

1608   Samuel de Champlain, a French mapmaker, founds Quebec. Quebec was the first permanent French settlement in the Americas.

1609   Hired by the Dutch East India Company, Henry Hudson explores the area around what are now New York City and the river that bears his name. He laid the basis for Dutch claims and early settlements in the area.

1609–1610	During the winter of 1609–1610 the majority of Jamestown colonists succumb to disease. Only 60 of the original 300 settlers were still alive by May 1610.
1612	John Rolfe begins cross-breeding imported tobacco seed from the West Indies with native plants. He produced a new variety of tobacco that was pleasing to European tastes. Within 2 years the first shipment of this tobacco reached London and within a decade it had become Virginia's chief source of revenue.
1613	A Dutch trading post is established on Manhattan Island.
1614	Thomas Hunt, an English sea captain, kidnaps Native Americans off the Massachusetts coast. He took the kidnapped men to Spain, where they were sold as slaves.
1614	Pocahontas, daughter of Powhatan, marries English tobacco farmer, John Rolfe. The union helped establish temporary peace between the Powhatans and the English.
1616	Smallpox decimates Native American populations in New England.
1619	Slavery is introduced to America. Dutch warship brought 20 enslaved Africans to Jamestown. At first Africans were treated like indentured servants, with many earning their freedom after several years of work. Soon the enticement of free labor changed the status of the enslaved Africans to a permanent condition.
1619	In order to increase the number of immigrants to Jamestown, the London Company establishes the House of Burgesses as Virginia's legislature. It was the first representative political body in the New World.
1619	John Haney, a merchant, befriends Squanto and arranges for him to return to America.
1620, November	A group of Puritan Separatists, the Pilgrims arrive off the coast of Massachusetts. Recognizing the need for a strong government the group establishes the Mayflower Compact. Named after the ship on which they had traveled, the Mayflower Compact is often described as America's first constitution.
1621	One year after arriving in Plymouth, Pilgrims celebrate the first Thanksgiving. In the spring, Native Americans from the Wampanoag tribe taught the Pilgrims agricultural techniques to ensure the survival of the colonists. In November, the Pilgrims celebrated a successful harvest with a harvest festival.
1621	One of the first treaties between colonists and Native Americans is signed between the Pilgrims and the Wampanoag tribe. An English-speaking Native American, Squanto helped establish terms of the peace.
1622	In response to expanding white populations into Indian lands, Opechancanough, Powhatan's successor, leads a group of warriors against unsuspecting Virginia settlers. Opechancanough's warriors killed 357 men, women, and children. The English struck back with a vengeance. Whole communities of Native Americans were wiped out by the colonists. By the end of the campaign, the English had almost destroyed the coastal tribes of Virginia.

1624   Dutch investors in the Dutch West India Company establish several settlements along the Hudson River. The settlers called the area New Netherland, but the Dutch never considered the colony a success.

1624   On recommendation of a royal commission, King James I dissolved the Virginia Company and made it a royal colony that year.

1624   Captain John Smith publishes *The General Historie of Virginia, New England, and the Summer Isles.*

1629   King Charles I dissolves Parliament and attempts to rule as absolute monarch. His attempt at absolute monarchy prompted many to leave England for the American colonies.

1629   Several prominent Puritans purchase a trading company and rename it Massachusetts Bay Company and secure a charter directly from King Charles I. Twelve members signed an agreement at Cambridge igniting the beginning of the great Puritan migrations to New England. Organizers convinced graduate of Cambridge John Winthrop to serve as governor of the colony. Winthrop played a major role in the development of Massachusetts.

1629   Peter Minuit, a Dutch colonist, purchases Manhattan Island from Native Americans and names the island New Amsterdam

1630   Seventeen ships with about 1,000 Puritans sail for Massachusetts. During the next 10 years 20,000 settlers followed.

1631   *Blessing of the Bay*, the first colonially built ship, is launched.

1632   George Calvert, Lord Baltimore, obtains a charter for land north of the Potomac River from King Charles I in what becomes known as Maryland. Since the charter did not expressly prohibit the establishment of non-Protestant churches, Maryland became a haven for Catholics disillusioned with the Church of England and Puritan philosophy.

1633   The first town government in the colonies is organized in Dorchester, Massachusetts.

1635   Boston Latin School is established as the first public school in America.

1635   Maryland's first elected assembly meets at St. Mary's province.

1636   Roger Williams purchases land from the Narragansett Indians in what is now Providence, Rhode Island. Williams, pastor of a church in Salem, was banished from Massachusetts for advocating the separation of church and state and for decrying Puritan policies of mandatory participation in religious activities. The new colony welcomed Jews as well as people of any religion and guaranteed their religious freedom. Church and state were completely separate in Rhode Island.

1636   Harvard College is founded in Cambridge, Massachusetts.

1636   Thomas Hooker leads a small group of men and women seeking religious liberty to the banks of the Connecticut River. His group established Hartford and adopted the Fundamental Orders. The Fundamental Orders was a form of government that gave magistrates less power than they had in Massachusetts, and imposed a more lenient religious test for citizenship. Following Thomas Hooker's example, other settlements soon appeared in New Haven and all along the banks of the Connecticut River.

1637–1638 Native Americans try to prevent settlement of the Connecticut River region. The Pequot Indian tribes and European settlers by 1637 had engaged in several struggles over lands around the Connecticut River. Pequot warriors raided the unsuspecting settlement of Wethersfield on April 23 in response to a European-led attack on the Pequot. Thirty settlers were killed and two girls were kidnapped during the raid. In May an expeditionary force led by Captain John Underhill and Captain John Mason struck the Pequot settlement in Mystic. The settlement, made up of mainly women and children, was destroyed. Those who were not killed were sold into slavery. The Pequot War was not officially ended until September 1638, when a small group of remaining Pequot Indians were forced to sign the Treaty of Hartford, acknowledging the dissolution of the Pequot nation. The Connecticut River valley would not experience any significant Indian uprisings until the beginning of King Philip's War.

1637 Reverend John Wheelwright is expelled from the Massachusetts Bay Colony. He along with his followers settled in New Hampshire. Following the example of the Mayflower Compact, they created and signed the Exeter Compact and set up a civil government.

1638 Anne Hutchinson faces trial for openly challenging Puritan ministers and their interpretations of the Bible. Hutchinson was banished from the Massachusetts Bay Colony. She went to Rhode Island and began a new settlement later called Portsmouth.

1638 The first printing press in the colonies is set up in Cambridge, Massachusetts.

1638 Sweden founds a colony called New Sweden in what is now Delaware. The colony consists of Dutch and Swedish colonists.

1642–1659 The English Civil War and subsequently Oliver Cromwell's Puritan Commonwealth and Protectorate limits immigration to Colonial America while distracting England from its colonies.

1643 Massachusetts Bay, Plymouth, Connecticut, and New Haven colonies form the New England Confederation to provide for defense measures that England was neglecting. It was the first attempt by colonists for regional unity.

1643 Anne Hutchinson and her family are murdered by Native Americans near Eastchester, Long Island.

1646 Massachusetts Bay Colony's general court approves a law making the crime of religious heresy punishable by death.

1647 Massachusetts Bay Colony requires every town having more than 50 families to establish a grammar school.

1648 Connecticut's Blue Laws are enacted by the people of the "Dominion of New Haven." The laws became known as blue laws because they were printed on blue paper. Connecticut's Blue Laws mixed secular law with religious teaching. For example, the laws forbade the crossing of a river on the Sabbath except by authorized clergymen.

1649 The Maryland Assembly, composed of Puritans, members of the Church of England, and Roman Catholics, passed the Toleration Act. Under the Toleration Act every believer in Jesus Christ and the Trinity was allowed free exercise of religious opinion, but Jews, Unitarians, Muslims, Buddhists, Hindus, and Pagans were not given the same freedom.

1649   John Winthrop, first governor of Massachusetts dies. He left the colony in good standing.

1649   King Charles I is beheaded. England became a temporary commonwealth under the control of Puritan Oliver Cromwell.

1652   Rhode Island enacts a law making slavery illegal.

1653   John Eliot publishes first book in an Indian language, *Catechism in the Indian Language.*

1654   The first Jewish colonists arrive in New Amsterdam from Brazil.

1656   In Maryland, an all-woman jury, the first of its kind, acquits Judith Catchpole on charges that she murdered her unborn child.

1659–1661   Quaker missionaries travel to New England to deliver their religious message. Except for Rhode Island, New England officials had Quaker missionaries whipped and imprisoned. Massachusetts had four missionaries hanged for refusing to quit preaching. In December, Parliament intervened and ordered the suspension of corporal punishment for Quakers and other religious dissenters.

1659–1660   Quakers William Robinson and Marmaduke Stephenson are hanged for refusing to leave the Massachusetts Bay Colony. Mary Dyer, a follower of Anne Hutchinson, is scheduled to hang, but at the last minute she is reprieved. Dyer was instead banished from the Massachusetts Bay Colony but was hanged for disobeying an expulsion order after returning to Boston in May 1660.

1660   King Charles II is restored and the British once again turn their attentions to North America.

1660   Parliament approves a Navigation Act requiring the exclusive use of English ships for trade in the English colonies and limits exports of tobacco and sugar and other commodities to England or its colonies.

1661   Slavery is first recognized in Virginia law.

1661   John Eliot translates the Bible into Algonquian language.

1662   Virginia law declares that the status of a newborn child depends on the status of the mother, making slavery a permanent, inherited circumstance.

1662   Communities along the Connecticut River merge to form the self-governing colony of Connecticut.

1663   Eight nobles receive a grant to settle Carolina. Northern Carolina was an area for subsistence farming, whereas southern Carolina prospered with larger plantations.

1663   England follows up the Navigation Act of 1660 with the Navigation Act of 1663. This act required that most imports to the English colonies be shipped on English vessels.

1664   New Netherland, a Dutch colony, falls into the hands of the British. Charles II granted his brother James, Duke of York, lands controlled by the Dutch. James sent a fleet of four English warships to capture New Netherland. Without support of the colonists, Peter Stuyvesant, governor of New Netherland, was forced to surrender the colony without a fight. The Duke of York changed the colony's name to New York. New Jersey and Delaware were also acquired from the Dutch. William Penn purchased Delaware from the Duke of York and allowed those living there to elect an assembly. New Jersey was given to Lord Berkeley and Sir George Carteret. Dutch settlers were allowed to retain their property and worship as they pleased.

1664   The first proprietary governor arrives in North Carolina.

1664   Maryland Colony passes a law mandating lifetime servitude for African slaves. Prior to the new law, slaves who converted to Christianity and established legal residences in Maryland had been granted freedom.

1665   Maryland, New York, New Jersey, North Carolina, South Carolina, and Virginia legislatures pass laws allowing conversion and residence without freeing the slaves. English law provided that slaves could be freed if they converted and established residency in the colonies. The actions of the legislators served to cement slavery in the colonies.

1670   The first settlers, drawn from New England and the Caribbean island of Barbados, arrive in South Carolina.

1673   Dutch forces retake New York from the British.

1673   Jacques Marquette, a Jesuit priest and Louis Joliet, an American-born fur trader, explore the upper Mississippi for France.

1673   Parliament passes the Navigation Act of 1673. The act sets up the office of customs commissioner in the colonies to collect duties on goods traded between plantations.

1674   Dutch and British officials sign the Treaty of Westminster. Under the treaty Dutch colonies in America are returned to the British.

1675–1678   Philip, the son of the Indian chief who made the original peace with the Pilgrims in 1621, attempts to unite the tribes of New England against further European encroachment onto Indian territories. Called King Philip's War, the struggle that ensued took Philip's life and resulted in many Indians being sold into servitude. The war formally ended when Sir Edmund Andros agreed to peace in April 1678.

1675–1676   Nathaniel Bacon leads former indentured servants and landless men in a rebellion against the government of Virginia. The rebellion was sparked by a clash between Virginia frontiersmen and the Susquehannock Indians, but it soon turned into a fight between the privileged classes with the Virginia governor, William Berkeley, and the common farmer. Falling tobacco prices in the 1660s produced bands of homeless people. Only large plantations managed to sustain profitable enterprises. Berkeley refused to grant Bacon a commission to conduct Indian raids, but he did agree to call new elections to the House of Burgesses, which had remained unchanged since 1661. Bacon organized those angry with the government and in September 1676, this force burned Jamestown. Most of the state was under Bacon's control. His victory was short lived. Bacon died in October of dysentery. Leaderless, the rebellion soon lost momentum.

1677   North Carolinians rebel against taxation. The conflict was known as Culpeper's Rebellion.

1679   New Hampshire obtains a royal charter from King Charles II.

1681   William Penn, a wealthy Quaker, receives a large tract of land west of the Delaware River, which becomes known as Pennsylvania. To help populate the colony, Penn invites religious dissenters from Europe. Quakers, Mennonites, Amish, Moravians, and Baptists were all invited to Pennsylvania. Penn, motivated by a sense of equality not generally found among early colonists, granted rights to Pennsylvania women, long before women in other parts of America were granted rights. He also paid considerable attention to the colony's relations with the Delaware Indians, ensuring they were paid for any land that Europeans settled on.

1682   Robert de La Salle follows the Mississippi River to its delta, claiming the vast lands drained by it for France. He named the territory Louisiana.

1683   The first school in Pennsylvania is founded. It taught reading, writing, and accounting.

1683   William Penn and Native Americans negotiate a peace treaty at Shackamaxon under the Treaty Elm.

1684   The charter for Massachusetts Bay Colony is revoked. Church membership as a requirement to vote is overturned.

1685   The Duke of York ascends to the British throne as James II.

1685   King Louis XIV of France revokes the Edict of Nantes. The revocation of the Edict of Nantes eliminated religious freedom for Protestants in France. Many Protestants migrated to the American colonies in search of religious freedom.

1686   After being named governor of all of New England, Edmund Andros begins issuing a series of unpopular orders aimed at the consolidation of colonies into one large settlement. He dissolved the assemblies of New York and Connecticut, limited the number of town meetings in New England to one per year, placed the militia under his direct control, and forced Puritans and Anglicans to worship together in the Old South Church.

1688   King James II begins consolidating the colonies of New England into a single Dominion. His act deprived colonists of their local political rights and independence. Legislatures are dissolved, and the king's representatives assume all of the judicial and legislative power.

1688   James II is overthrown in the Glorious Revolution. The revolution was considered glorious because a tyrannical king was replaced without civil war.

1688   Governor Andros imposes a limit of one annual town meeting for New England towns. The governor then orders all militias to be placed under his control.

1688   Jacob Leisler, a German trader, leads a rebellion in New York. He established a government with an elected assembly that lasted until 1690, when a new British royal governor arrived. The new governor had Leisler captured, tried, and hanged. The governor, however, allowed the colony to continue to elect an assembly.

1688   The first formal protest against slavery is developed. Mennonite Quakers sign an antislavery resolution in Germantown, Pennsylvania.

1689   After the Glorious Revolution, England gets new royalty. William of Orange and Mary became king and queen of England in February.

1689   Colonists rebel against Governor Andros, forcing him to hide in a fort. In July Andros was ordered back to England to stand trial. Colonists disregarded his reforms and reestablished previous governments.

1690   American population rises to a quarter of a million. The population doubled every 25 years until 1775.

1690   John Locke publishes *Second Treatise on Government*. He sets forth a theory based on a contract between government and the governed. Locke asserted that people are endowed with the right to life, liberty, and property, and the right to rebel when governments violate the natural rights of the people. His theory had great influence during the Revolutionary period.

1690   King William's War begins. The first in a series of wars over European dominance in the colonies, King William's War pitted the French with Indian allies against England and the British colonies. Hostilities between the French and English spilled over to the colonies. In February, Schenectady, New York, was burned by the French with the aid of their Native American allies. The Treaty of Ryswick signed in 1697 was supposed to end the war but brought only temporary peace to the colonies.

1691   The newly appointed governor of New England, Henry Sloughter, arrives from England and institutes royally sanctioned representative government. In October, Massachusetts gets a new royal charter that includes government by a royal governor and a governor's council.

1691   Plymouth Colony is absorbed into Massachusetts Bay Colony and the newly formed colony becomes a royal charter.

1692   A group of adolescent girls in Salem Village, Massachusetts, set off the Salem witch trials. After the group of girls had listened to tales told by a West Indian slave, they accused several women of being witches. The people of the town were appalled, but certainly not surprised, because belief in witchcraft was widespread throughout the Americas and Europe. Panic and hysteria grew in Salem. By the fall of 1692, 20 men and women had been executed for the crime of witchcraft, and more than 100 were imprisoned. When the hysteria seemed to be destined to spread beyond Salem, ministers throughout the colony called for an end to the trials. The governor agreed and dismissed the court. Those still jailed were later acquitted or given reprieves.

1693   The College of William and Mary, the second school founded in the colonies, is founded at Middle Plantation, Virginia.

1696   The Navigation Act of 1696 is passed by the English parliament requiring colonial trade to be done exclusively via English-built ships. It expanded the powers of colonial customs commissioners, giving commissioners the right to forcibly enter private property, and required the posting of bonds on certain goods.

1696   The Royal African Trade Company loses its slave trade monopoly, spurring colonists in New England to engage in slave trading for profit.

1697   Massachusetts general court officially apologizes for the Salem witchcraft trials.

1697   The Treaty of Ryswick is signed, ending King William's War.

1699   Middle Plantation's name is changed to Williamsburg, when Virginia Colony moves its capital city from Jamestown to Middle Plantation.

1699   Massachusetts Bay Colony and Abenaki Indians sign peace treaty, bringing hostilities between them to an end.

1699   The English parliament passes the Wool Act. The act protected England's wool industry by limiting wool production in Ireland and forbidding the export of wool from the American colonies.

1700   Massachusetts and New York's representative assemblies order that all Roman Catholic priests leave the colonies.

1700   The Anglo population in the English colonies in America reaches 250,000.

1701   Delaware is officially organized as a colony.

1701   Yale College is founded in Connecticut.

1702   Queen Anne's War begins. The second in a series of wars fought between France and Britain for control of the colonies. In May, England declared war on France after the death of the King of Spain, Charles II, to stop the union of France and Spain. This War of the Spanish Succession was called Queen Anne's War in the colonies, where the English and American colonists battled the French, their Native American allies, and the Spanish for the next 11 years. The war ended with the signing of the Treaty of Utrecht. The peace proved to be only temporary.

1702   In Maryland, the Anglican Church is established as the official church. To finance the church, taxes are imposed on all free men, male servants, and slaves.

1702   Cotton Mather publishes *Magnalia Christi Americana*. The book explores New England's early history.

1704   Harvard launches the colonies' first successful newspaper. By 1745 there were 22 newspapers being published throughout the colonies.

1704   The first enduring newspaper in America, *The Boston News-Letter*, is published.

1705   Laws restricting the travel of slaves and banning interracial cohabitation are enacted in Massachusetts, New York, and Virginia. In New York, a law against runaway slaves assigned the death penalty for those caught over 40 miles north of Albany, and in Massachusetts marriage between African Americans and whites is explicitly banned.

1706   Benjamin Franklin is born.

1706   South Carolina establishes the Anglican Church as its official church.

1707   England, Scotland, and Wales are combined into the United Kingdom of Great Britain by the Act of the Union. The act is officially endorsed by Queen Anne.

1710   The English parliament enacts the Post Office Act, which creates a postal system in the American colonies. The colonial post office is controlled by the postmaster general of London and his deputy in New York City.

1711–1718   Hostilities break out between Native Americans and settlers in North Carolina after the massacre of settlers there. The conflict, known as the

Tuscarora Indian War, was a direct result of colonial encroachment by European settlers into Tuscaroran lands. Ultimately, Chief Hancock, leader of the Tuscarora tribes, felt there was no alternative but to attack the settlers. After several successful raids by Native Americans, the militia was sent in to settle the conflict. In a show of force, settlers routed the Tuscarora tribes and either captured or killed over 900. To escape the wrath of the colonists, many members of rhe Tuscarora tribe were forced to migrate north to New York. A peace treaty was signed with the remaining Tuscarora tribesmen, officially ending the conflict in 1718.

1712   Slaves rebel in New York City. Twenty-five armed slaves set fire to a white man's outhouse. When whites rushed to save the burning building, the slaves attacked. In the struggle nine white men were killed. The militia quickly dispensed with the insurrectionists. Twenty-one of the twenty-five rebels were executed.

1712   The Carolina colony is officially divided into North Carolina and South Carolina in May.

1712   The Pennsylvania assembly bans the import of slaves into that colony.

1713   The Treaty of Utrecht is signed, ending Queen Anne's War.

1714   Cotton Mather preaches a sermon in support of Copernicus's theory of the universe. Copernicus asserted (contrary to popular sentiment of the time) that the sun was in the center of the universe. Mather's support of Copernicus had wide-ranging affects.

1714   Tea is introduced for the first time into the American Colonies.

1715   Members of the Yamasee tribes attack and kill over 300 Carolina settlers.

1716   South Carolina colonists and their Cherokee allies attack and defeat the Yamasee tribes.

1716   The first group of black slaves is brought to the Louisiana territory.

1717   The first Scots-Irish immigrants settle in western Pennsylvania.

1718   French colonists found the city of New Orleans.

1718   Spanish colonists found the city of San Antonio.

1720   France solidifies its power in the colonies by building forts on the Mississippi, St. Lawrence, and Niagara rivers.

1727   Due to an influx of German immigrants, the Pennsylvania legislature requires the newcomers to take special oaths of fidelity to the king, the colonial proprietor, and the colony charter. Even after such great lengths, English-speaking colonists remained suspicious of German colonists.

1727   Benjamin Franklin forms the Junto Club with 12 of his closest friends. The club was dedicated to mutual improvement and eventually became the American Philosophical Society. One of the functions of the group was to discuss beneficial public works.

1728   The first prospective brides for French settlers arrive in New Orleans. They are known as "casket girls" because of the dresses packaged in caskets or trunks that each bride received as an incentive for migrating to the colony.

1728   William Byrd explores Virginia and North Carolina to determine the boundary between the two colonies.

1728   Jewish settlers build the first synagogue in the colonies in New York.

1729   Proprietors relinquish control of North and South Carolina to the king, making both colonies royal colonies.

1729   Baltimore is founded in the Maryland Colony.

1730   The *Pennsylvania Gazette* is first published. The paper is published by Benjamin Franklin. His paper eventually becomes the most popular colonial newspaper.

1731   Benjamin Franklin's Junto Club establishes the Library Company of Philadelphia. It is the first circulating library in America.

1732   Georgia, named after King George II, was the last of the 13 English colonies founded. James Oglethorpe founds the colony as a refuge for English debtors.

1732   The first mass is celebrated in the only Catholic church in colonial America, in Philadelphia.

1732   George Washington is born.

1732   Britain's parliament passes the Hat Act of 1732. The Hat Act prohibited the export of American hats from one colony to another and limited the number of workers in any hat-making industry.

1732   Benjamin Franklin begins publishing *Poor Richard's Almanac*. The popular almanac contained weather predictions, humor, and proverbs.

1733   Parliament enacts the Molasses Act of 1733. Under the act molasses, rum, and sugar incurred high taxes when brought into the colonies from the Dutch, French, and Spanish West Indies. The Molasses Act's intent was to protect the British Caribbean sugar planters from lower-priced competition. New England colonists were outraged because the act threatened profitable trade with the West Indies. New England merchants responded to the act by smuggling foreign sugar and molasses into the colonies.

1734–1754   The Great Awakening, a religious revival, sweeps throughout New England and the middle colonies. George Whitefield and Jonathan Edwards were the most influential ministers in the movement. George Whitefield began a religious revival in Philadelphia and then moved on to New England. He enchanted audiences of up to 20,000 people at any given time. The Great Awakening reached its culmination in 1741 with the sermon "Sinners in the Hands of an Angry God" by Jonathan Edwards. The Great Awakening gave rise to evangelical denominations, which continue to play significant roles in American religious, political, and cultural life.

1735   John Peter Zenger of the *New York Weekly Journal* unwittingly sets a precedent for freedom of the press in the Americas. Zenger accused the royal governor of corruption. As a result Zenger was brought to trial on the charge of libel. Andrew Hamilton argued that the charges printed by Zenger were true and therefore were not libelous. The jury returned a verdict of not guilty. Though the case did not receive much attention at the time, it would have great importance in the development of a free press in America.

1737   Connecticut mints the first copper coins in the colonies.

1738   In response to disputed claims over South Carolina and Georgia, the Spanish governor of Florida offered freedom to British colonial slaves who escaped to St. Augustine. Though Spain had long been part of the international slave trade and had used slaves throughout its colonies, Spain wanted to keep the British colonies as disrupted as possible.

1739   The Stono Rebellion ignites in South Carolina. A group of slaves broke into a storehouse and seized arms and supplies near Charleston in 1739. They planned to escape to Spanish-controlled Florida. As the group moved south it gained new members and attacked any white who got in the way. After a few days, the militia found the rebels and killed them. During the rebellion, 30 whites and 44 blacks were killed.

1739–1742   Aroused by Spanish treatment of British seamen, Great Britain declares war on Spain on October 9. Robert Jenkins, captain of the British ship *Rebecca* incited British feelings when he claimed that Spanish coast guards had cut off his ear. The struggle that ensued, known as the War of Jenkins's Ear, cost both sides many casualties without any territorial gains for either side. In one battle fought in the colonies, governor Oglethorpe of Georgia attacked Spanish forts in Florida but was soon routed by the Spanish. In what was to be a bloody end to the war, Spanish forces attacked Georgia but were repulsed. Meanwhile, England became embroiled in another war against both Spain and France in 1743. The War of Austrian Succession, or King William's War, pitted France and Spain against Austria's protector Great Britain. It was not until the Treaty of Aix-la-Chapelle was signed in 1748 that both the smaller War of Jenkins's Ear and the larger War of Austrian Succession were formally ended.

1740   Fifty black slaves are hanged in Charleston, South Carolina. The slaves were accused of planning a revolt.

1741   Exploring Russia's prospects for empire, Czar Peter the Great, enlists Danish navigator Vitus Bering to explore the coast of Alaska.

1743   The American Philosophical Society is founded in Philadelphia by Benjamin Franklin and his Junto Club.

1743–1748   King George's War begins when the French join the side of Spain. In the course of the war, British colonial forces captured the French strongholds, but the gains were returned to France under the Treaty of Aix-la-Chapelle. King George's War did nothing to stop the showdown between Britain and France; Austria shifted its allegiance from Britain to France as Britain became allies with Prussia, and the conflict continued. This would lead to the Seven Years' War, called the French and Indian War in North America.

1747   The New York Bar Association is founded in New York City.

1748   The Treaty of Aix-la-Chapelle is signed, ending the War of Austrian Succession or, as it was called in the colonies, King William's War.

1749   Georgia revokes the colony's prohibition on slavery, recognizing slavery as a legal institution.

1754–1763   The French and Indian War, known in Europe as the Seven Years' War, was fought between France and Great Britain over control of the upper Mississippi Valley and Great Lakes region of North America. France had established a strong relationship with Native American tribes in Canada and throughout the region in dispute. A series of trading posts and forts marked out a large empire stretching from Quebec to New Orleans, confining the British to the area east of the Appalachian Mountains. The

French not only threatened the British Empire but also limited the colonists themselves. Under the current boundaries France could limit westward expansion. In 1754 French soldiers drove English fur traders from the point where the Monongahela and Allegheny rivers meet to form the Ohio River in order to build a fort. Fort Duquesne was built in territory claimed by both Virginia and Pennsylvania. A French fort in this location threatened the safety of both colonies. The first armed conflict occurred in 1754 at Fort Duquesne between a band of French regulars and Virginia militiamen under the command of 22-year-old George Washington. War had begun without a formal declaration. During the war, Native Americans fought for both sides, often shifting allegiance as the tides of war shifted. In the end, England's superior strategic position and competent leadership ultimately led to the defeat of French forces.

1750   In order to protect the English iron industry, the English parliament passes the Iron Act, which limited the growth of the iron industry in the American colonies.

1751   The Currency Act is passed by the English parliament. The act banned the issuing of paper money by the New England colonies.

1754   Albany Congress is held. At an intercolonial meeting, Benjamin Franklin presented the Albany Plan. The plan advocated unifying the English colonies in America. The plan is later rejected by individual colonial assemblies and by the British government.

1758   Slaves on the plantation of William Byrd III create the first African American Christian church in Virginia in Lunenburg County.

1759   George Washington marries Martha Dandridge Custis, reputedly the richest widow in the Virginia Colony. The marriage was a lucrative venture for Washington, changing his status from a regular planter to a wealthy landowner.

1760   George III becomes king of England.

1760   The population of the 13 colonies rises to approximately 1.6 million.

1763   France and Great Britain sign the Treaty of Paris ending the French and Indian War. Under the treaty France relinquished all of Canada, the Great Lakes, and the upper Mississippi Valley to the British.

1763   King George issues Proclamation of 1763 forbidding colonization west of the Appalachian Mountains.

Mark Aaron Bond

A

African American slavery Slavery in the Americas based solely on race and ethnicity. Though slavery has existed throughout history, prior to African American slavery, slaves were attained through war and were not enslaved based on race. Slaves were captured in Africa in local wars and raids, bought there at slave "factories" on the coast by slave traders, transported by ship to the New World, and sold throughout the Americas. The first African American slaves were brought to America in 1619 by a Dutch slave ship. Slaves were introduced to the Americas at Jamestown, Virginia. Though slavery was legal in the northern colonies, the majority of African American slaves were to be found on the large plantations of the South.

Anabaptist sects Name meaning rebaptism, applied to Protestant Christian sects who believed that infant baptism was not authorized in scripture and that only adult believers should be baptized. Because many of the Anabaptists had been baptized as infants, their adult baptism was scornfully identified as a rebaptism. Anabaptists were persecuted by both Catholics and other Protestant groups. Many Anabaptists relocated to the Americas in hopes of escaping persecution. Anabaptists, or Baptists as they came to be called, influenced many Protestant faiths, including many of the Evangelical sects.

Anglican Church The official Church of England. It was originally formed during the Reformation by King Henry VIII and reorganized under his daughter Queen Elizabeth. As a Protestant religion the Anglican Church was weak within the colonies. The Anglican Church persecuted Catholics and those Protestants who called for reform within the Anglican Church. Many of the northern colonies were populated by Anglican dissenters seeking escape from the Anglican Church, with the most well known being the Puritans. Early southern colonies paid taxes to the Anglican Church even though administration of the church fell to laypeople, sparsely populated regions led to minimum church attendance, there were no official bishops in the colonies, and priests were forced to travel to England for ordination.

antinomianism The belief that Christians are not bound by moral law. As an extension of the Protestant Reformation, antinomianism asserted that, since good works did not promote salvation, then neither did evil works hinder it. Some Anabaptist sects accepted this logic.

B

Barbadian slave code The first code of law concerning slavery in the Americas. It influenced similar codes throughout the English colonies, since England had no slavery code for the colonies to mimic. The code required slaves to be provided clothes by their masters, but denied slaves basic rights, giving complete control to the slaveholder.

Bacon's Rebellion Former indentured servants and landless men rebel against the government of Virginia. Led by Nathaniel Bacon, the rebellion was sparked by a clash between Virginia frontiersmen and the Susquehannock Indians, but it soon turned into a fight between the privileged classes with Virginia governor, William Berkeley, and the common farmer. Bacon organized those angry with the government and in September 1676, this force burned Jamestown.

blue laws Laws that mixed secular law with religious teaching. Most such regulations referred to the prohibition of work or other activities on Sundays. For example, the laws forbade the crossing of a river on the Sabbath except by authorized clergymen. They were called blue laws because the laws were printed on blue paper.

British East India Company A joint-stock company of investors, which was granted a royal charter by Elizabeth I on December 31, 1600, with the intent to offer trade privileges in India. The royal charter effectively gave the newly created company a monopoly on all trade in the East Indies.

C

Calvinism Protestant religion founded by John Calvin during the Reformation that promoted the theory of predestination. Many Puritan sects were forms of Calvinism. Puritanism under Calvinistic influence called for reform of the Anglican Church, calling the elaborate rituals of the Anglican Church just another form of Catholicism. According to Calvinist teachings, God does not accept acts of goodwill in return for salvation. Instead he has predetermined those who can be redeemed.

Colonial Assembly One house of a two-house legislature that met within each colony to discuss taxes, budgets, and laws. The Assembly had a variety of titles such as the House of Delegates, the Burgesses, or the Assembly of Freemen. Members of the Assembly were elected annually by citizens of a town or county. Voters and members of the Assembly were male landowners, and in some colonies, property-holding single women.

colonial charter A formal document that gave colonies the legal right to exist. Colonial charters were granted to proprietors by the king with or without Parliament. The 13 original colonies were granted three different kinds of charters. Proprietary charters, royal charters, or corporate charters were granted to aristocratic gentlemen. These gentlemen were often England's second sons. According to English law, the firstborn son was granted all titles and inheritances from the father. Other sons were expected to make a life of their own. Many of these men saw the Americas as their path to fortune.

commonwealth Self-governing political unit governed as a republic.

Commonwealth of England Period between 1649 and 1653 in which England was a republic. Parliament ruled England without a king after Oliver Cromwell and his Parliamentary followers executed King Charles I. During this period the colonies gained relative self-rule because England was occupied with its own disputes. Oliver Cromwell ruled England as "Protector," but his dissenters likened the rule to a military dictatorship. He was soon deposed, and the royal family was reinstated.

congregation Body of church members meeting for worship and religious education.

Congregationalism The belief that each congregation of believers is independent and makes its decisions concerning church discipline and membership. In a Congregationalist church ministers have limited authority. Ministers are elected by the members and are expected to teach, preach, and pray, but the final authority lies within the congregation itself. In the colonies, the Puritans became known as Congregationalists.

Corn Laws Laws passed as part of the series of Navigation Acts by Parliament to protect the British citizens at home. The Corn Laws, passed in the interest of the British farmer, limited the importation of wheat and corn into England from the colonies.

corporate colony Colonies created when large land parcels were issued with authority to govern the colony, granted by both the king and Parliament.

cottage industry Industry in which creation of products is home based rather than on a mass scale. Home-based industry was the basis of colonial industry. During the period in which agriculture was the main source of income, many farmers found cottage industries a lucrative source of additional income.

cotton gin A machine invented by American inventor Eli Whitney in 1793. The machine mechanized the production of cotton fiber. It quickly and easily separated the cotton fibers from the seedpods and the sometimes sticky seeds. It used a combination of a wire screen and small wire hooks to pull the cotton through the screen, while brushes continuously remove the loose cotton lint to prevent jams. The invention was granted a patent on March 14, 1794. The cotton gin was a large asset to the American economy and helped solidify slavery in the South.

crown timber The reservation of all trees within many of the New England colonies with a diameter of 24 inches and upward for the Royal Navy masts. Anyone who cut trees meeting those measurements without express permission could be fined 100 pounds. Since much of the industry in New England involved the use of timber, when the colonists found enforcement of the law lax, they ignored the law.

D

Dutch East India Company Was established on March 20, 1602, when the government of the Netherlands granted it a monopoly to carry out colonial activities in Asia. It was the first multinational corporation in the world, and it was the first company to issue stocks.

duty Tax on imported goods. Parliament placed taxes on imported goods from the colonies to the benefit of merchants and farmers in the British Isles.

E

Enlightenment Movement during the 18th century that advocated a strong belief in science, logic, and reason. The movement gave rise to capitalism and set the stage for the American Revolution. Enlightenment thought concerning government and rights of the governed was developed by writers such as John Locke, Thomas Hobbes, and Jean-Jacques Rousseau. These writers influenced the Founding Fathers of the United States by advocating inalienable rights and the pursuit of happiness for all citizens.

established religion Religious body or creed officially endorsed by a state. Many of the colonies had established religions. Virginia, North Carolina, South Carolina, and Georgia accepted the Anglican Church as their official religion. Connecticut, Massachusetts, and New Hampshire endorsed Congregationalism as the state religion.

F

fall line Marks the area where upland regions and coastal plains meet. Fall lines crossed by a river are especially important for the development of towns and cities. Waterfalls or rapids deter boats from traveling any further inland along a fall line making port cities necessary. Waterpower mills provide power needed to grind grain into flour and are usually situated at a fall line. Many of the first colonial settlements are found along a fall line. For example, Richmond, Virginia, is located along the James River fall line, and Trenton, New Jersey, is located on the Delaware River fall line.

firearms Many of the firearms available during the colonial period were made in Europe. The most practical firearm was the long rifle. Its use was widespread in the colonies because of its easy operation. Each rifle consisted of a firelock or flint, stock, and a barrel. The firelock or flint is the firing mechanism, the stock is the wooden part of the weapon, and the barrel is the wrought iron tube in which the bullet is projected. All rifles during this period required shot and gunpowder, which was added directly to the barrel, one shot at a time. The accuracy of the firearms during the colonial period left much to be desired.

flax and linen Flax is a plant used to produce thread that, in turn, is made into linen. Though flax cultivation never reached commercial cash crop status in the colonies because of the intensive labor required, it was cultivated by colonists for their own use to make linen.

freedom of religion Religious freedom was rare in the colonies. Only a couple of the original colonies such as Pennsylvania and Rhode Island specifically allowed freedom of worship in their charters. Puritans that had sought to escape religious persecution in Europe were eager to persecute those who did not adhere to the Puritan belief system. Some colonies advocated state-endorsed religion. It was not until the inclusion of the Bill of Rights in the Constitution that freedom of religion was universal throughout the former colonies.

French and Indian War Known in Europe as the Seven Years' War, was fought between France and Great Britain over control of the upper Mississippi Valley and Great Lakes region of North America. France had established a strong relationship with Native American tribes in Canada and throughout the region in dispute. A series of trading posts and forts marked out a large empire stretching from Quebec to New Orleans, confining the British to the area east of the Appalachian Mountains. The French not only threatened the British Empire but also limited the colonists themselves. Under the current boundaries France could limit westward expansion. In 1754 French soldiers drove English fur traders from the point where the Monongahela and Allegheny rivers meet to form the Ohio River in order to build a fort. Fort Duquesne was built in territory claimed by both Virginia and Pennsylvania. A French fort in this location threatened the safety of both colonies. The first armed conflict occurred in 1754 at Fort Duquesne between a band of French regulars and Virginia militiamen under the command of 22-year-old George Washington. War had begun without a formal declaration. During the war, Native Americans fought for both sides, often shifting allegiance as the tides of war shifted. In the end, England's superior strategic position and competent leadership ultimately led to the defeat of French forces.

Fundamental Orders of Connecticut The first written constitution in the Americas. It provided for a representative government similar to the one in Massachusetts, except that voting for representatives and government was not limited to church members.

fur trade Trade between Europeans and Native Americans for animal fur. The fur trade flourished in New York and throughout New England. Wherever the trade flourished, there were drawbacks. Native Americans were exploited and whole populations of beaver and other animals were decimated. Eventually a fight for control of the fur trade became part of the fight that erupted between France and England, the French and Indian War.

G

Glorious Revolution Refers to the so-called bloodless overthrow of the Catholic English King James II in 1688. James II a devout Catholic found little support in the overwhelming Protestant kingdom of England.

His daughter Mary II, a Protestant, was anxiously awaited as James II's successor. The birth of a male heir, however, was too much for Protestant-controlled Parliament to bear. Parliament conspired with Mary and her husband William III to replace James as king. James fled and was replaced by William and Mary. Though no blood was shed in the immediate aftermath, much blood was shed in Ireland and Scotland before William's authority was accepted.

governor Head of colonial governments. Governors were appointed by the king or by Parliament. The powers of the governor were broad and sweeping. No action of the legislature became law without his approval. He appointed judges at all levels, commanded the militia, and could order the legislature disbanded. He had some direct authority and could order actions by the British Navy or regular army forces in his colony.

Governor's Council One part of a two-house legislature in colonial government. The Council performed judicial, legislative, and administrative duties. Members of the Council were generally appointed by the governor and served at the governor's pleasure. The Council approved laws passed by the Assembly and served as a supreme court for the colonies.

Great Awakening A religious revival that swept throughout New England and the middle colonies. George Whitefield and Jonathan Edwards were the most influential ministers in the movement. George Whitefield began a religious revival in Philadelphia and then moved on to New England. He enchanted audiences of up to 20,000 people at any given time. The Great Awakening reached its culmination in 1741 with the sermon "Sinners in the Hands of an Angry God" by Jonathan Edwards.

H

Hat Act An act passed by Parliament in 1732 that prohibited the export of American hats from one colony to another and limited the number of workers in any hat-making industry.

Huguenots Term referring to French Calvinists. Huguenots became known for their fiery criticisms of worship as performed in the Roman Catholic Church. They saw the Christian faith as something to be expressed in a strict and godly life, in obedience to biblical laws, out of gratitude for God's mercy. Like other Protestants of the time, they felt that the Roman church needed radical cleansing of its impurities. In reaction to the growing Huguenot influence, Catholic violence against them grew. Barred from settling in New France, many Huguenots moved instead to the 13 colonies of Great Britain in North America.

I

indentured servants A laborer under contract to work as a servant for a given amount of time to pay off debts or in return for a reward. Many indentured servants sold themselves in return for passage to the New World. Slaves were enslaved for life, but indentured servants were free upon completion of the contracted time. Once the contracted time had expired indentured servants were free to go their own way or remain employed by the planter or contractor for pay.

indigo A plant that is cultivated to produce a blue dye. Cultivation of indigo was very precise and intensive work requiring a great deal of skill. Indigo cultivation was introduced to the colonies by Eliza Lucas, a South Carolina woman who was seeking to add cash crops to her plantation. Once she had developed a system for indigo cultivation that worked, she shared her process and seeds with other plantation owners. Indigo plants like dry soil rather than the wetlands that were being used by rice growers. Processing indigo requires timing and precision. The indigo plants were placed in three successive fermentation vats, for the dye did not exist in the plant. Indigo was allowed to ferment or rot. The fermented indigo was then agitated by slaves with paddles. Limewater was added, and the clear solution changed to blue. After the liquid was drained, the residue was strained, bagged, and left to dry. The resulting fine, stiff paste was cut into cubes and placed into barrels for shipment to England. An average harvest for a planter usually resulted in 30 to 80 processed pounds of indigo per acre. Indigo cultivation thrived in the lower Southern colonies.

Intolerable Acts Called by the British the Coercive Acts, were a series of laws passed by the British parliament in 1774 in response to the growing unrest in the 13 American colonies, particularly in Boston, Massachusetts, after incidents such as the Boston Tea Party. Enforcement of the acts played a major role in the outbreak of the American Revolutionary War and the establishment of the First Continental Congress.

J

Jacobitism Was the political movement dedicated to the restoration of King James II to the thrones of England and Scotland. Jacobitism was a response to the deposition of James II in 1688 when he was replaced by his daughter Mary II jointly with her husband William of Orange.

joint-stock company Form of business organization in which pooled funds of many investors or stockholders are used to manage risks. Jamestown was founded through a joint-stock company.

L

Lutheranism Protestant religion based on the teachings of Martin Luther, a German religious scholar who sought to reform the Roman Catholic Church. Luther is regarded as the founder of the Protestant Reformation. The symbolic beginning of the Reformation occurred on October 31, 1517, when Doctor Luther posted an open invitation to debate his 95 theses concerning the teaching and practice of indulgences within the Church. Between 1517 and 1520, Luther preached and published his criticisms of the Catholic Church in books and pamphlets. Luther and his followers began a large exodus from the Catholic Church known as the Protestant Reformation. In the years and decades following Luther's posting of the 95 theses on the door of the Wittenberg church, large numbers of Europeans left the Roman Church. Luther's followers had great impact on the settlement of the Americas.

line of demarcation A north–south line drawn on a map through the Atlantic Ocean. The line, created by Pope Alexander VI, gave all the non-Christian lands to the west of the line to Spain, and all those to the east were given to Portugal.

M

manor system A large estate with hereditary rights granted by a royal charter or a form of tenure restricted to certain proprietary colonies. William Penn set up a manor system in the Pennsylvania colony.

Massachusetts Bay Company A trading company purchased by Puritans in 1629 for colonization purposes of the New World. The company was renamed Massachusetts Bay Company. A charter was secured directly from King Charles I. Twelve members signed an agreement at Cambridge describing the development of lands in America. The agreement sparked by the purchase of the company ignited the beginning of the great Puritan migrations to New England.

mercantilism The theory that a state's power is dependent on its wealth. The belief in mercantilism sparked exploration and eventually led to the colonization of the Americas. Colonies played an important role in the mercantilist system because they were the source of raw materials and provided a market for manufactured goods.

merchant class People who rely on trade or the sale of goods for income. The merchant classes were especially prominent in New England colonies. Most of the representatives in government and prominent positions in the New England colonies cited being a merchant as their profession. The opposite was true for Southern colonies, with many of the positions of power held by the planting classes.

militia Group of civilians declared by law to be called to military service and trained as soldiers to fight in emergencies. Members of the militia were from varied professions, with the majority recruited from small farms and businesses. Colonial governments relied on the militia to squash rebellions, to provide law and order within the colonies, and to help with disputes with Native Americans.

modus vivendi A compromise between adversaries that allows them to get along temporarily.

Molasses Act The act placed high taxes on molasses, rum, and sugar when brought into the colonies from the Dutch, French, and Spanish West Indies. The Molasses Act's intent was to protect the British Caribbean sugar planters from lower-priced competition. New England colonists were outraged because the act threatened profitable trade with the West Indies. New England merchants responded to the act by smuggling foreign sugar and molasses into the colonies.

N

Navigation Acts Were a series of laws that, beginning in 1651, restricted foreign shipping. The acts imposed severe restrictions on the colonial trade. All foreign shipping was banned from this trade, and the colonies themselves were forbidden from directly exporting certain goods, including tobacco, sugar, and cotton, to non-English consumers. The colonists were only allowed to trade with England and were only allowed to sell English goods. The colonists got around the law by extensive smuggling and bribery of officials.

naval stores Products of pine forests that are used in ship building such as tar, pitch, and turpentine. North Carolina's main export was naval stores.

northwest passage Water route to Asia through North America. Many European explorers sought this route unsuccessfully. In the 20th century, exploring ships have made a passage through the waterways of northern Canada from the Atlantic Ocean to the Arctic Ocean and the Pacific, but the route is too difficult for regular travel.

nonimportation agreement An agreement between colonial merchants and planters not to import certain goods as a protest against English policies.

P

Parliament Supreme legislative body in Britain made up of nobility, clergy, and commons.

patroon A proprietor of a tract of land in the 17th-century Dutch colony of New Netherland in North America. The Dutch West India Company granted patroons powerful rights and privileges. A patroon could create civil and criminal courts, appoint local officials, and provide land grants. Patroons received rent, taxes, and labor from tenant farmers.

Piedmont A region to the west of the fall line. The Piedmont region in the South is generally located on a plateau. Much of the land of the Piedmont has beautiful rolling hills and valleys. Rivers and streams that cut across the Piedmont Plateau have helped to form those hills and valleys. It includes grassy meadows that are good for grazing. Many farmers raise crops in this region. The Piedmont region of the South was ideal for many plantations.

Pietism A movement within Lutheranism, lasting from the late 17th century to the mid-18th century. The Pietist movement combined the Lutheran emphasis on biblical doctrine with the Puritan emphasis on individual piety and a vigorous Christian life. Many Pietists migrated to Pennsylvania during the 17th and 18th centuries.

planter and plantation system Large farms, employing 20 or more slaves, produced staple crops of cotton, rice, and tobacco for domestic and foreign markets. Planters owned both the means of production and the labor force. The plantation system originated in the tobacco economy of the 17th century and soon spread throughout the South. Plantation owners gained power as they gained wealth. By the end of the 18th century most of the prominent positions in government were held by the planter class.

presidios Spanish fort in the Americas built to protect mission settlements.

primogeniture The common tradition of inheritance by the firstborn of the entirety of a parent's wealth, estate, or office. Primogeniture led to colonization of the New World by Europe's gentlemen not included in the tradition.

Proclamation of 1763 Proclamation issued by King George III that forbade colonization west of the Appalachian Mountains. The British government issued the proclamation in hopes of avoiding the expense of frontier warfare. The proclamation was viewed by colonists as yet another instance of British power subordinating colonial interests to that of others.

proprietary colony One of the three types of colonies in the New World. Proprietary colonies were created when large grants of land and authority were granted by the king to one or a small group of men, known as the proprietors.

proprietor Individual who received legal and exclusive right to American colonial land from the King of England and who was expected to administer the land according to English laws.

Puritans Members of a group of English Protestants seeking further reforms or even separation from the established church. The Puritans objected to ornaments and ritual in the churches as idolatrous. Puritans argued for a restructuring and "purifying" of church practice through biblical supremacy. Puritans also advocated the belief in the priesthood of all believers. This belief held that individual believers could interpret scripture and atone for their sins through a personal relationship with God. Because Puritans were outspoken against the established Church of England, they faced persecution. To escape this persecution, many Puritans migrated to the New World. Puritan colonies mixed their religious beliefs with secular laws to create governments that were intolerant of other religions.

Q

Quebec Act Passed by the British parliament to institute a permanent administration in Canada replacing the temporary government created at the time of the Proclamation of 1763. It gave the French Canadians complete religious freedom and restored the French form of civil law. The 13 colonies considered this law one of the Intolerable Acts, because it nullified many of the western claims of the colonists by extending the boundaries of the province of Quebec to the Ohio River on the south and to the Mississippi River on the west.

R

Reformation A movement that emerged in the 16th century as a series of attempts to reform the Roman Catholic Church in western Europe. The reformation was started by Martin Luther and his 95 theses. The reformation ended in division and the establishment of new institutions such as Lutheranism, Calvinism, Anglicanism, and, later, Puritanism. The Reformation had great impact on the development of the American colonies.

Restoration Refers to the restoration of the English monarchy. Charles II regained the English throne after the parliamentarian rule in the wake of the English Civil War. The name "Restoration" may apply both to the actual event by which the English monarchy was restored and to the period immediately following the accession of Charles II.

rice A staple cash crop cultivated on large plantations in the low wetlands of the South. The cultivation process for rice in the Low Country was very labor intensive. Draft animals such as mules and oxen were rarely used in the fields because their weight would cause them to sink into the boggy soil. The land was cleared and a system of dikes and ditches was constructed using slave labor and hand tools.

royal colony One of the three types of colonies in the New World. Royal colonies were created by a grant of authority under the king's patent to a group.

rum, sugar, and molasses Major products of the triangular trade. Rum is made from molasses, a by-product of sugar production. Sugar grown in the French Caribbean on large plantations was processed into molasses and sent to the New England colonies to be made into rum. Rum production in New England was very efficient as well as profitable. During the 1700s and 1800s, New England rum was considered to be the best. Rhode Island and Massachusetts used the profits from rum to industrialize New England with ventures into textile manufacturing. Without slave labor, the industrialization of New England would not have been possible.

S

Salem witch trials Trials of men and women accused of witchcraft in Salem, Massachusetts, during 1692. After a group of girls had listened to tales told by a West Indian slave, they accused several women of being witches. The people of the town were appalled but certainly not surprised because belief in witchcraft was widespread throughout the Americas and Europe. Panic and hysteria grew in Salem. By the fall of 1692, 20 men and women had been executed for the crime of witchcraft, and more than 100 were imprisoned. When the hysteria seemed to be destined to spread beyond Salem, ministers throughout the colony called for an end to the trials. The governor agreed and dismissed the court. Those still jailed were later acquitted or given reprieves.

Society of Friends Commonly called Quakers or Friends, is a religious community founded in England in the 17th century. Quakers were considered religious radicals because they believed that paid clergy were unnecessary and that all individuals could know God's will through their own "inner light." As the movement expanded, it faced opposition and persecution. Quakers were imprisoned and beaten in both the British Isles and the British colonies. In the Massachusetts Bay Colony, some Quakers, such as Mary Dyer, were put to death for upholding their beliefs. The state of Pennsylvania was founded by William Penn as a safe place for Quakers to live and practice their faith. Despite persecution, the movement grew steadily into a strong and united society.

Stamp Act of 1765 The fourth Stamp Act to be passed by the British parliament and required all legal documents, permits, commercial contracts, newspapers, pamphlets, and playing cards in the American colonies to carry a tax stamp. The act was passed to defray the cost of maintaining the military presence protecting the colonies. Colonists were outraged by the tax and struck against tax collectors with violence, including the painful use of tarring and feathering.

Stono slave rebellion Slave rebellion in South Carolina. A group of slaves broke into a storehouse and seized arms and supplies near Charleston in 1739. They planned to escape to Spanish-controlled Florida. As the group moved south it gained new members and attacked any white who got in the way. After a few days, the militia found the rebels and killed them. During the rebellion, 30 whites and 44 blacks were killed.

subsistence farming Level of farming at which farmers produce only enough to feed and maintain their families. In direct contrast to much larger plantations, small farms that engaged in subsistence farming dotted the colonial landscape.

Sugar Act Modified version of the Sugar and Molasses Act of 1733. The Sugar Act reduced the rate of tax on molasses from six pence to three pence per gallon, and the duty was strictly enforced. The act also listed more foreign goods to be taxed, including sugar, certain wines, coffee, pimiento, cambric, and printed calico, and, further, regulated the export of lumber and iron. New enforcement of the tax on molasses caused the almost immediate decline in the rum industry in the colonies. Passage of the act led to outrage from the colonists.

T

tobacco A labor-intensive cash crop, produced first in Virginia then throughout the South. The hard labor required to cultivate tobacco and the lack of a labor force made the creation of large plantations with slave labor economically beneficial to the planter class in the South. In 1619 the first Africans were brought to the shores of Virginia on a Dutch ship and were probably sold as indentured servants. By 1700, Virginia was importing huge numbers of slaves to provide the labor required to plant, top, and harvest the tobacco leaves. Other Southern states followed Virginia's lead.

Toleration Act An act passed by the Maryland Assembly, composed of Puritans, members of the Church of England, and Roman Catholics. Under the Toleration Act every believer in Jesus Christ and the Trinity was allowed free exercise of religious opinion, but Jews, Unitarians, Muslims, Buddhists, Hindus, and Pagans were not given the same freedom.

town Indians Term used to describe Native Americans who cohabited with colonists in urban centers or who lived in settled towns of their own, rather than following a traditional and more nomadic pattern. Some even intermarried with the colonists.

Townshend Acts Acts passed in 1767 by the British parliament. The laws placed a tax on common products, such as lead, paper, paint, glass, and tea imports. Colonists were outraged over the acts and showed their dissent with the slogan "no taxation without representation."

Triangular Trade Involved three principal commodities sugar, rum, and slaves. European distillers made rum from Caribbean sugar. European slave ships took vats of the rum to Africa and bought African slaves from their African owners with the rum or with other manufactured goods, such as iron, glass, textiles, or weapons. The bulk of the human cargo was sold in the Caribbean in trade for cane sugar or molasses. The sugar was then taken back to Europe, and the cycle continued. At each stop along the way, an excellent profit was made.

V

Virginia Company of London Also called the London Company, the Virginia Company of London was an English joint-stock company established by royal charter by James I on April 10, 1606, with the purpose of establishing colonial settlements in North America. The London Company was responsible for establishing the Jamestown Settlement, the first permanent English settlement in the United States, in 1607.

W

War of Jenkins's Ear A war fought between Spain and England in the 18th century. Aroused by Spanish treatment of British seamen, Great Britain declared war on Spain on October 9, 1739. Robert Jenkins, captain of the British ship *Rebecca,* incited British feelings when he claimed that Spanish coast guards had cut off his ear. The struggle that ensued, known as the War of Jenkins's Ear, cost both sides many casualties without any territorial gains for either side. In one battle fought in the colonies, Governor Oglethorpe of Georgia attacked Spanish forts in Florida but was soon routed by the Spanish. In what was to be a bloody end to the war, Spanish forces attacked Georgia but were repulsed.

War of Spanish Succession Conflict that arose out of the disputed succession to the throne of Spain following the death of the childless Charles II, the last of the Spanish Habsburgs. All of Europe fought for control of the Spanish throne, with fighting spilling over into the Americas. The war in the colonies is known as Queen Anne's War.

Wool Act Passed by the English parliament in 1699. The act protected its own wool industry by limiting wool production in Ireland and forbidding the export of wool from the American colonies.

Y

yeoman farmer Term used to distinguish farmers, who labored along with servants or slaves, from gentlemen, who did not labor with their hands. Some yeomen had more wealth than the minor gentry but remained classed as yeomen by choice rather than by limits.

Mark Aaron Bond

Resources

Books

Altman, Ida. *Emigrants and Society: Extremadura and America in the Sixteenth Century.* Berkeley: University of California Press, 1989.

Andrews, Charles M. *The Colonial Background of the American Revolution.* Rev. ed. New Haven: Yale University Press, 1931.

Bailyn, Bernard. *The New England Merchants in the Seventeenth Century.* Cambridge: Harvard University Press, 1955.

Bedini, Silvio A., ed. *The Christopher Columbus Encyclopedia.* 2 vols. New York: Simon & Schuster, 1992.

Berkin, Carol. *First Generations: Women in Colonial America.* New York: Hill and Wang, 1996.

Billington, R.A., ed. *The Reinterpretation of Early American History.* San Marino, CA: Huntington Library, 1966.

Bitterli, Urs. *Cultures in Conflict: Encounters between European and Non-European Cultures, 1492–1800.* Stanford: Stanford University Press, 1989.

Boorstin, Daniel. *The Americans: The Colonial Experience.* New York: Alfred A. Knopf, 1958.

Bragdon, Kathleen J. *Native People of Southern New England, 1500–1650.* Norman: University of Oklahoma Press, 1996.

Breslaw, Elaine. *Tituba, Reluctant Witch of Salem: Devilish Indians and Puritan Fantasies.* New York: New York University Press, 1996.

Bridenbaugh, Carl. *Cities in the Wilderness: Urban Life in America 1625–1742.* New York: Ronald Press, 1938.

Caldwell, Patricia. *The Puritan Conversion Narrative: The Beginnings of American Expansion.* New York: Cambridge University Press, 1983.

Calloway, Colin G. *New Worlds for All: Indians, Europeans, and the Remaking of Early America.* Baltimore, MD: Johns Hopkins University Press, 1997.

Canny, Nicholas and Anthony Pagden, eds. *Colonial Identity in the Atlantic World, 1500–1800.* Princeton, NJ: Princeton University Press, 1987.

Cheyfitz, Eric. *The Poetics of Imperialism: Translation and Colonization from the Tempest to Tarzan.* New York: Oxford University Press, 1991.

Clinton, Catherine and Michele Gillespie. *The Devil's Lane: Sex and Race in the Early South.* New York: Oxford University Press, 1997.

Collier, George A., ed. *The Inca and Aztec States, 1400–1800.* New York: Academic Press, 1982.

Crane, Verner W. *The Southern Frontier, 1679–1732.* Durham: Duke University Press, 1928.

Cronon, William. *Changes in the Land: Indians, Colonists, and the Ecology of New England.* New York: Hill and Wang, 1983.

De Vorsey, Louis. *Keys to the Encounter: A Library of Congress Resource Guide for the Study of the Age of Discovery.* Washington, D.C.: Library of Congress, 1992.

Delbanco, Andrew. *The Puritan Ordeal.* Cambridge: Harvard University Press, 1989.

Demos, John. *A Little Commonwealth: Family Life in Plymouth Colony.* New York: Oxford University Press, 1970.

Dickason, Olive Patricia. *The Myth of the Savage and the Beginnings of French Colonialism in the Americas.* Calgary: University of Alberta Press, 1984.

Earle, Alice M. *The Sabbath in Puritan New England.* London: Hodder & Stoughton, 1982.

Egloff, Keith and Deborah Woodward. *First People: The Early Indians of Virginia*. Charlottesville: University Press of Virginia, 1994.

Elliott, J.H. *The Old World and the New, 1492–1650*. Cambridge: Cambridge University Press, 1970.

Farriss, Nancy M. *Maya Society under Colonial Rule: The Collective Enterprise of Survival*. Princeton, NJ: Princeton University Press, 1984.

Ferling, John E. *A Wilderness of Miseries: War and Warriors in Early America*. Westport, CT: Greenwood Press, 1980.

Fischer, David Hackett. *Paul Revere's Ride*. New York: Oxford University Press, 1994.

Gallivan, Martin D. *James River Chiefdoms: The Rise of Social Inequality in the Chesapeake*. Lincoln: University of Nebraska Press, 2003.

Hall, David D. *The Faithful Shepherd: A History of the New England Ministry in the Seventeenth Century*. Chapel Hill: University of North Carolina Press, 1972.

Hambrick-Stowe, Charles E. *The Practice of Piety: Puritan Devotional Disciplines in Seventeenth-Century New England*. Chapel Hill: University of North Carolina Press, 1982.

Harlan, David. *The Clergy and the Great Awakening in New England*. Ann Arbor: UMI Research Press, 1980.

Haskins, James and Kathleen Benson Building. *A New Land: African Americans in Colonial America*. New York: HarperCollins, 2001.

Hebert, John R., ed. *1492: An Ongoing Voyage*. Washington, D.C.: Library of Congress, 1992.

Hoxie, Frederick E., ed. *Indians in American History: An Introduction*. Arlington Heights, IL: Harlan Davidson, 1988.

Hulme, Peter. *Colonial Encounters: Europe and the Native Caribbean, 1492–1797*. New York: Routledge, 1992.

Hume, Ivor Noël. *A Guide to Artifacts of Colonial America*. New York: Alfred A. Knopf, 1985.

Hunt, George T. *The Wars of the Iroquois*. Madison: University of Wisconsin Press, 1940.

Jaenen, Cornelius J. *Friend and Foe: Aspects of French-Amerindian Cultural Encounter in the Sixteenth and Seventeenth Centuries*. New York: Columbia University Press, 1976.

Jennings, Francis. *The Invasion of America: Indians, Colonialism, and the Cant of Conquest*. Chapel Hill: University of North Carolina Press, 1975.

Jordan, Winthrop. *White over Black: American Attitudes toward the Negro, 1550–1812*.

Chapel Hill: University of North Carolina Press, 1968.

Karlsen, Carol. *The Devil in the Shape of a Woman: Witchcraft in Colonial New England*. New York: W. W. Norton, 1987.

Kenney, William H., ed. *Laughter in the Wilderness: Early American Humor to 1783*. Kent, OH : Kent State University Press, 1976.

Kupperman, Karen Ordahl, ed. *America in European Consciousness, 1493–1750*. Chapel Hill: University of North Carolina Press, 1995.

Leach, Douglas E. *Arms for Empire: A Military History of the British Colonies in North America*. New York: Macmillan, 1973.

Leach, Douglas E. *The Northern Colonial Frontier, 1607–1763*. New York: Holt, Rinehart, and Winston, 1966.

Lestringant, Frank. *Mapping the Renaissance World: The Geographical Imagination in the Age of Discovery*. Trans. David Fausett. Los Angeles: University of California Press, 1994.

Lunenfeld, Marvin, ed. *1492: Discovery, Invasion, Encounter; Sources and Interpretations*. Lexington, MA: D. C. Heath, 1991.

Mapp, Alfred. *The Virginia Experiment: The Old Dominion's Role in the Making of America*. Lanham, MD: Madison Books, 1985.

McCrady, Edward. *The History of South Carolina under the Proprietary Government, 1670–1719*. New York: Macmillan, 1897.

McManus, Edgar J. *Law and Liberty in Early New England: Criminal Justice and Due Process, 1620–1692*. Amherst: University of Massachusetts Press, 1993.

Merrell, James Hart. *The Indians' New World: Catawbas and Their Neighbors from European Contact through the Era of Removal*. Chapel Hill: Institute of Early American History and Culture, 1989.

Middleton, Richard. *Colonial America: A History, 1565–1776*. Malden, MA: Blackwell Publishers 2002.

Miller, Perry. *The New England Mind: From Colony to Province*. Boston: Beacon Press, 1953.

Moffitt, John F. and Santiago Sebastián. *O Brave New People: The European Invention of the American Indian*. Albuquerque: University of New Mexico Press, 1996.

Morgan, Edmund S. *American Slavery, American Freedom: The Ordeal of Colonial Virginia*. New York: W. W. Norton, 1975.

Morgan, Edmund S. *Puritan Political Ideas.* Indianapolis: Bobbs, Merrill, 1965.

Morgan, Edmund S. *The Puritan Family: Religion and Domestic Relations in Seventeenth-Century New England.* New York: Harper & Row, 1966.

Morison, Samuel Eliot. *The European Discovery of America: The Northern Voyages, 500–1600.* New York: Oxford University Press, 1971.

Morton, Richard. *Colonial Virginia.* Chapel Hill: University of North Carolina Press, 1960.

Murray, David. *Forked Tongues: Speech, Writing, and Representation in North American Indian Texts.* Bloomington: Indiana University Press, 1991.

Namias, June. *White Captives: Gender and Ethnicity on the American Frontier.* Chapel Hill: University of North Carolina Press, 1993.

Nash, Gary B. *Red, White, and Black: The Peoples of Early America.* Englewood Cliffs, NJ: Prentice-Hall, 1982.

O'Gorman, Edmundo. *The Invention of America: An Inquiry into the Historical Nature of the New World and the Meaning of Its History.* Bloomington: Indiana University Press, 1961.

Olmstead, Clifton E. *History of Religion in the United States.* Englewood Cliffs, NJ: Prentice-Hall, 1960.

Ong, Walter. *Orality and Literacy: The Technologizing of the Word.* London: Routledge, 1991.

Pagden, Anthony. *European Encounters with the New World from Renaissance to Romanticism.* New Haven: Yale University Press, 1993.

Pearce, Roy Harvey. *Savagism and Civilization: A Study of the Indian and the American Mind.* Berkeley: University of California Press, 1988.

Peckham, Howard H. *The Colonial Wars, 1689–1763.* Chicago: University of Chicago Press, 1964.

Phillips, William D., Jr. and Carla Rahn Phillips. *The Worlds of Christopher Columbus.* Cambridge: Cambridge University Press, 1992.

Porterfield, Amanda. *Female Piety in Puritan New England: The Emergence of Religious Humanism.* New York: Oxford University Press, 1992.

Potter, Stephen R. *Commoners, Tribute, and Chiefs: The Development of Algonquian Culture in the Potomac Valley.* Charlottesville: University of Virginia Press, 1993.

Richter, Daniel. *The Ordeal of the Longhouse: The Peoples of the Iroquois League in the Era of European Colonization.* Chapel Hill: University of North Carolina Press, 1992.

Rogers, Alan. *Empire and Liberty: American Resistance to British Authority 1755–1763.* Berkeley: University of California Press, 1974.

Rountree, Helen C. and E. Randolph Turner III. *Before and after Jamestown: Virginia's Powhatans and Their Predecessors.* Gainesville: University Press of Florida, 2002.

Rountree, Helen C. and Thomas E. Davidson. *Eastern Shore Indians of Virginia and Maryland.* Charlottesville: University Press of Virginia, 1997.

Rountree, Helen C., ed. *Powhatan Foreign Relations, 1500–1722.* Charlottesville: University Press of Virginia, 1993.

Rutman, Darrett and Anita Rutman. *A Place in Time: Middlesex County, Virginia, 1650–1750.* New York: W. W. Norton, 1984.

Salisbury, Neal. *Manitou and Providence: Indians, Europeans, and the Making of New England, 1500–1643.* New York: Oxford University Press, 1982.

Schneider, Herbert W. *The Puritan Mind.* Ann Arbor: University of Michigan Press, 1958.

Seed, Patricia. *Ceremonies of Possession in Europe's Conquest of the New World, 1492–1640.* New York: Cambridge University Press, 1995.

Shea, William Lee. *The Virginia Militia in the Seventeenth Century.* Baton Rouge: Louisiana State University Press, 1983.

Shy, John W. *Toward Lexington: The Role of the British Army in the Coming of the Revolution.* Princeton, NJ: Princeton University Press, 1965.

Slotkin, Richard. *Regeneration through Violence: The Mythology of the American Frontier, 1600–1860.* Middletown, CT: Wesleyan University Press, 1973.

Solberg, Winton U. *Redeem the Time: The Puritan Sabbath in Early New England.* Cambridge: Harvard University Press, 1977.

Stannard, David E. *The Puritan Way of Death.* New York: Oxford University Press, 1977.

Stout, Harry S. *The New England Soul: Preaching and Religious Culture in Colonial New England.* New York: Oxford University Press, 1986.

Ulrich, Laurel. *Good Wives: Image and Reality in the Lives of Women in Northern New England, 1650–1750.* New York: Knopf, 1982.

Vaughn, Alden T. *New England Frontier: Puritans and Indians, 1600–1675.* Boston: Little, Brown, 1965.

Warhus, Mark. *Another America: Native American Maps and the History of Our Land.* New York: St. Martin's Press, 1997.

Williamson, Margaret Holmes. *Powhatan Lords of Life and Death: Command and Consent in Seventeenth-Century Virginia.* Lincoln: University of Nebraska Press, 2003.

Wright, Edward. *Jamestown Narratives: Eyewitness Accounts of the Virginia Colony: The First Decade, 1607–1617.* Champlain, VA: Round House, 1998.

Wright, J. Leitch, Jr. *Anglo-American Rivalry in North America.* Athens: University of Georgia Press, 1971.

Journals

American Anthropologist
American Anthropological Association

American Antiquity
Society for American Archaeology

American Historical Review
American Historical Association

American Quarterly
Johns Hopkins University Press

Eighteenth Century Studies
Johns Hopkins University Press

English Historical Review
Oxford University Press

Journal of American History
Organization of American Historians

Journal of Colonialism and Colonial History
Johns Hopkins University Press

Journal of Southern History
Southern Historical Association

Mississippi Valley Historical Review
Organization of American Historians

New England Quarterly
New England Quarterly, Inc.

Reviews in American History
Johns Hopkins University Press

William and Mary Quarterly
Omohundro Institute of Early American History and Culture

Internet

American Journeys; Eyewitness Accounts of Early American Exploration and Settlement
www.americanjourneys.org

Archiving Early America
www.earlyamerica.com

Colonial Salem
www.salemweb.com

Colonial Williamsburg
www.history.org

The History Net
www.historynet.com

Old Deerfield
www.old-deerfield.org

The 13 Original Colonies
www.timepage.org/spl/13colony.html

Virtual Jamestown
www.virtualjamestown.org

Colonial Tourism Sites

Colonial Salem
Salem, Massachusetts,
www.salemweb.com

Colonial Williamsburg
Williamsburg, Virginia,
www.history.org

Historic Alexandria
Alexandria, Virginia,
www.oha.ci.alexandria.va.us/

Historic Edenton
Edenton, North Carolina,
www.visitedenton.com

Historic Jamestown
Jamestown, Virginia,
www.virtualjamestown.org

Historic Sleepy Hollow
Sleepy Hollow, New York,
www.sleepyhollowny.com

Old Deerfield Village
Deerfield, Massachusetts,
www.old-deerfield.org

Old Sturbridge Village
Sturbridge Village, Massachusetts,
www.osv.org

Historic Districts

Alexandria Historic District
Alexandria Virginia

Chestertown Historic District
Chestertown, Maryland

College Hill Historic District
Providence, Rhode Island

Colonial Annapolis Historic District
Annapolis, Maryland

Colonial Germantown Historic District
Germantown, Pennsylvania

Colonial Niagara Historic District
Niagara, New York

Elfreth's Alley Historic District
Philadelphia, Pennsylvania

Green Springs Historic District
Green Springs, Virginia

Hudson River Historic District
Staatsburg, New York

Litchfield Historic District
Litchfield, Connecticut

Nantucket Historic District
Nantucket, Massachusetts

New Castle Historic District
New Castle, Delaware

Old Deerfield Village
Deerfield, Massachusetts

Old Salem Historic District
Salem, Massachusetts

Rittenhousetown Historic District
Philadelphia, Pennsylvania

Saint Mary's City Historic District
Saint Mary's City, Maryland

Williamsburg Historic District
Williamsburg, Virginia

Museums

Memorial Hall Museum
8 Memorial Street, Deerfield, MA 01342;
413-774-3768;
www.old-deerfield.org/museum.htm

National Museum of American History
14th Street and Constitution Avenue, N.W.,
Washington, D.C.; 202-633-3129;
www.americanhistory.si.edu

The Salem Witch Museum
Washington Square, Salem, Massachusetts 01970;
978-744-1692;
www.salemwitchmuseum.com

Index